A GALAXY OF IMMORTAL WOMEN

- Brian Griffith
May 14, 2012

A GALAXY OF IMMORTAL WOMEN
The Yin Side of Chinese Civilization

BRIAN GRIFFITH

EXTERMINATING ANGEL
PRESS

Portions of this book first appeared, some in different form,
on the Exterminating Angel Press online magazine at
www.exterminatingangel.com

EXTERMINATING ANGEL PRESS
"Creative Solutions for Practical Idealists"
Visit **www.exterminatingangel.com** to join the conversation
info@exterminatingangel.com

Exterminating Angel Press book design by Mike Madrid
Cover art by Paul Mavrides
Layout, typesetting, and maps by John Sutherland

305. women

ISBN: 978-1-935259-14-5
ebook ISBN: 978-1-935259-15-2
Library of Congress Control Number: 2011940574

Distributed by Consortium Book Sales & Distribution
(800) 283-3572
www.cbsd.com

Printed in The United States of America

Contents

Acknowledgements

This book builds on the efforts of a group of Chinese scholars called the "Chinese Partnership Studies Group." In 1995 this group, headed by chief editor Min Jiayin, produced a book called *The Chalice and the Blade in Chinese History*. This is a major account of the relations between men and women through all of China's history, from the earliest Neolithic villages before 5000 BCE to the 1990s. As the book's name implies, it was inspired by Riane Eisler's book *The Chalice & the Blade: Our History, Our Future*. As Eisler does for Western society, the Chinese Partnership Studies Group presents a fresh and balanced vision of social evolution, which restores proper emphasis to women's values and creativity in shaping the world. Both books do this using a fascinating combination of new evidence from archaeology, history, sociology, plus great reviews on literature and popular religion. I want to thank Min Jiayin, all the members of the Chinese Partnership Studies Group, and Riane Eisler for their inspiring work, which has led me to explore the worlds of Chinese goddesses. I also want to thank my visionary publisher, Tod Davies, and the artists who shaped the project, Paul Mavrides, Mike Madrid, and John Sutherland, plus my extremely helpful wife.

Neolithic China, ca. 10,000 BCE to 2,000 CE

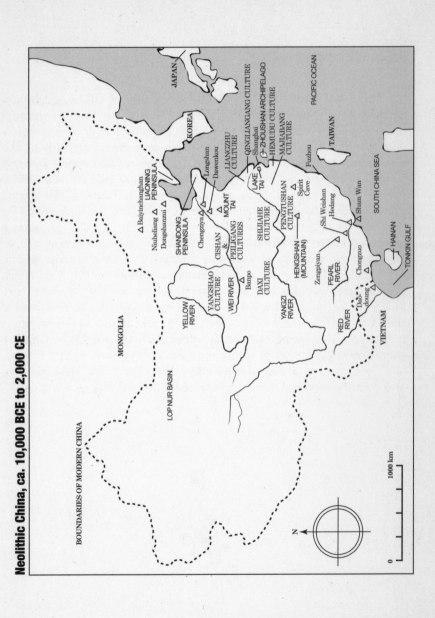

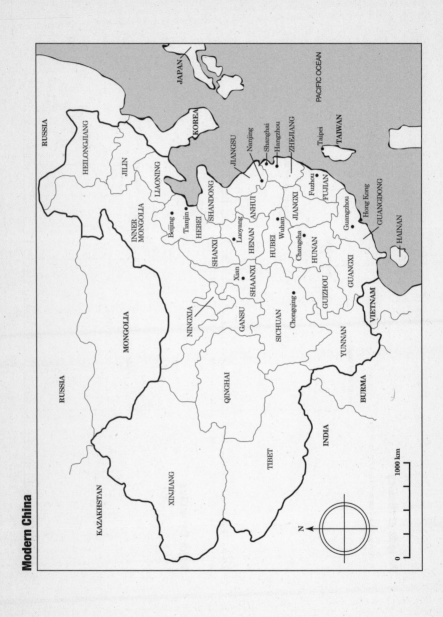

Modern China

RUSSIA

HEILONGJIANG

JILIN

JAPAN

KOREA

INNER MONGOLIA

LIAONING

MONGOLIA

RUSSIA

SHANDONG

Beijing • Tianjin •
HEBEI

JIANGSU

Nanjing •
Shanghai
Hangzhou •
ZHEJIANG

PACIFIC OCEAN

Taipei •
TAIWAN

KAZAKHSTAN

XINJIANG

NINGXIA

SHANXI

Laoyang •
HENAN

ANHUI

JIANGXI

Fuzhou •
FUJIAN

GANSU

Xian •
SHAANXI

Wuhan •
HUBEI

Changsha •
HUNAN

Guangzhou •
GUANGDONG

Hong Kong

TIBET

QINGHAI

Chongqing •
SICHUAN

GUIZHOU

GUANGXI

HAINAN

INDIA

BURMA

YUNNAN

VIETNAM

N

0 ────── 1000 km

v

Periods of History

Prehistoric Village Cultures (the Mythical Golden Age)
(7000s–2100 BCE)

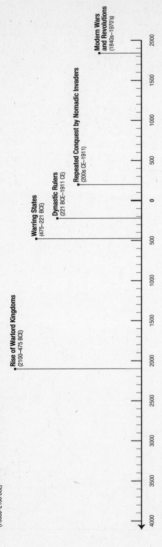

Rise of Warlord Kingdoms
(2100–475 BCE)

Warring States
(475–221 BCE)

Dynastic Rulers
(221 BCE–1911 CE)

Repeated Conquest by Nomadic Invaders
(200s CE–1911)

Modern Wars and Revolutions
(1840s–1970's)

4000 3500 3000 2500 2000 1500 1000 500 0 500 1000 1500 2000

Major Dynasties

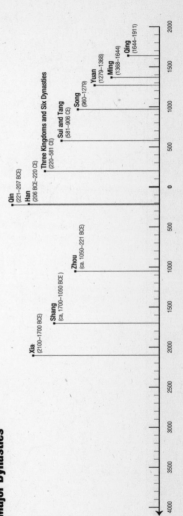

Xia
(2100–1700 BCE)

Shang
(ca. 1700–1050 BCE)

Zhou
(ca. 1050–221 BCE)

Qin
(221–207 BCE)

Han
(206 BCE–220 CE)

Three Kingdoms and Six Dynasties
(220–581 CE)

Sui and Tang
(581–906 CE)

Song
(960–1279)

Yuan
(1279–1368)

Ming
(1368–1644)

Qing
(1644–1911)

4000 3500 3000 2500 2000 1500 1000 500 0 500 1000 1500 2000

A Few of the Women Who Became Goddesses, or at Least Legends

Numerous Goddess Figures Found in Prehistoric Villages.	Goddesses Whose Legends Relate to Semi-historical Events, such as:	Heroes and Resistance Figures, such as:	Enlightened Saviors and Immortals, like:	Daoist or Buddhist Masters:	More Spiritual Guides or Heroes:	Heroes of the People, Religious or not:
Mythic creator goddesses, including: Nü Wa, Jun Di, Hu Tu Yao Chi Jinmu The Jade Maiden of Profound Wonder Sao Cing Niang Bixia Yuanjun Feng Bo Bo Lo Shen Green Jade Mother	Xi Wang Mu (the Queen Mother of the West) Jiang Yuan Sien Zang Chang'e Luozu Wusheng Laomu Yao Chi Momu Cangu Nainai (The Silkworm Mother)	Ti Ying Meng Jiang Nu Qi Gu (an outhouse goddess) Yu Jiang (the "hairy lady" of the forest") Yaoji	Guanyin (the goddess of universal compassion) Wei Huacun Zheng Wei He Xiangu (?) (one of the Eight Immortals of the Bamboo Grove)	Mazu Chen Jinggu The Holy Mother of Dongling (?) Yeshe Tsogyal Xie Xiran Zu Shu	Sun Buer Cao Wenyi Mulan (?) Miaoshan Dagmema Machig Lapdrön Chokyidronme	Qiu Jin Deng Yingchao Ruan Lingyu Zhengyan The Compassion Society millions of *nu qiang ren* (or superwomen)

4000 3500 3000 2500 2000 1500 1000 500 0 500 1000 1500 2000

Other Important People

Village elders and wise women The Yellow Emperor (supposedly)	Lord Dang of the Shang	The Duke of Zhou	Confucius Laozi (Lao Tzu)	Bodhidharma	Empress Wu Zetian	Genghis Khan	Mao Zedong

4000 3500 3000 2500 2000 1500 1000 500 0 500 1000 1500 2000

Note: For times before 500 BCE, the periods when goddesses first appeared in popular myth are just estimates. After that, most deified women have recorded dates of birth and death, though these records are basically written folklore. Where the folklore gives widely varying dates, a (?) appears beside the name.

1. How a Texan Man Became an Admirer of Chinese Goddesses

Maybe I'm not qualified to write this book. I'm not Chinese and don't speak any Chinese languages. I'm just a curious independent historian, who hopes to praise good people. I think lies have been told about who's important in this world. And the greatness of China's women is underappreciated, both in China and the West. These women have their own traditions, religions, and visions of the future. I think they're a gigantic force for good in the world, and they always have been. Maybe this view of women's culture is simplistic. But I'd like to tell some stories about their wisdom, their history, their heroes, and their goddesses. First though, my publisher wanted me to give a brief explanation of how a Texan man got so interested, so here it is.

In the city of Corpus Christi, Texas, where I grew up, my dad was the only person I knew with a short-wave radio. He made it himself, because the stores didn't have short-wave radios. He'd listen to the news from other countries, like radio Moscow, Beijing, or Havana. It seemed like everybody else heard only local American AM or FM radio stations, or American TV. Back then, short-wave radio was the only sort of internet. Near as I could tell, other families I knew never heard about the world from anyone except a fellow American.

I got an urge to learn what was outside the bubble of my society, which to me seemed a kind football society. There was lots of cheerleading for the home team—our school, our lifestyle, our nation, our religion. And a lot of this cheerleading concerned the legend of how the West was won. We saw a lot of heroic movies about the Wild West, or WWII. I heard we were a nation that had never been defeated. We were the best and most advanced people the world had ever seen. Maybe we didn't even need to go to church, because we were already so close to God.

Supposedly, we Americans gained our position in the world by dint of cultural superiority. But a lot of the heroic movies we saw were about victory in battle. Later, I learned it was an ancient Roman belief—victory goes to those favored by the gods. It was an ego-boosting belief, depending on who you identified with. In my city, the Whites, Hispanics, or Blacks seemed to be clustered in separate sections of town. My high school was almost entirely White, though most people in the city were Hispanic.

When I took history in school, I wasn't that interested in the West. I already heard how it was won. I wanted to know about Chinese, African, Russian, or Latin American history. And of course it was plain to see in the histories of all these places—those who managed to dominate others were not the best people.

I did a few things to see the world. One was to join a village development organization and work for seven years in India and Kenya.

In India, our village was running out of water. The villagers climbed down their wells to dig them deeper. But across the Deccan Plateau, the water table was falling at maybe a foot per year. Near the end of the dry season, the wells in our neighborhood reached rock bottom. And this brought me the deepest, most basic fear I had ever known. I had assumed that these villagers of huge Asian nations were struggling with problems of the past. But they were dealing with problems of the future.

In Kenya the villages were mainly female. The young men were mostly gone to the cities, leaving the women to work the farms and raise the kids. And these people were marvelous. Among other things, they were covering the hillsides in young trees. Looking out from their hilltops, I realized that these women were the main force holding back the great African desert. That's when I started to see the power and importance of women's wisdom. The person who helped me the most with this was Riane Eisler, with her book *The Chalice & the Blade* (1988). This book exposed a whole world of women's values and cultures and how they have shaped society in every age. After that, and cultures and how they have shaped society in every age. After that, I got more interested in learning about women's values and dreams. After going back to North America, I wanted to tell stories about that. That's why I wrote *The Gardens of Their Dreams*, about the culture wars behind environmental decline or renewal.

It slowly dawned on me that women commonly have their own alternative versions of culture and religion, even in officially patriarchal religions like Islam and Christianity. This struck me strongly when a Muslim friend had trouble at her mosque. She said that some men had watched her from the doorway as she prayed in the women's section. This wasn't surprising, because she's a beautiful woman. But then some of these men complained. They said that she was inspiring sinful thoughts in their house of prayer. On hearing this, I asked her why she stayed in a community where such prejudice passed for morality. And she answered that those men knew nothing of the real Islam. The first Muslim women were business managers, religious leaders, or generals in the army. Those men at the mosque were not the real Muslims—she was.

I realized that I had believed the claims of dominators. When bigoted Christians or Muslims claimed that their prejudices were fundamental to their religion, I had believed them. I had said, "If you're the real Christians (or Muslims), then I want none of it." What if I responded like my Muslim friend?

Later I spent several years writing about alternative versions of Christianity. And to a large extent, the alternatives were women's versions of the religion. Instead of trying to enforce holy laws and chains of command, they were mostly trying to explore how good our relations can get. I wrote two books about the long-running culture wars between these visions. The first one was *Different Visions of Love: Partnership and Dominator Values in Christian History,* and the second was *Correcting Jesus: 2000 Years of Changing the Story.*

After that, I wanted to do something similar about China. I'd always loved Chinese culture, religion, and history. And here again were the same issues: an "official" tradition of dominators, warlords, and patriarchs—with a huge counterculture of women's values. China even has numerous religious sects, made by women, for women, with a host of popular goddesses. I realized that the rise of women's values and religions in the world's biggest society may be something that transforms the world. I want to write about that, and tell stories about people I can really admire.

2: The Yin Side of Chinese Civilization

This is a story about an alternative civilization. It's a beautiful, powerful culture made by China's women. This civilization is older than any empire, and has evolved throughout history. It's a heritage of founding mothers, shamanesses, goddesses, and ordinary heroines. China's women have always made their own values, their own goals, and their own versions of religion. I believe this vast tradition is the greatest counterculture in the world. It's a culture with its own visions concerning partnership of the sexes, relations with nature, leadership, community, health, and spirituality. In recent decades this counterculture has grown stronger. It is rising within China, and is shaping the planetary society. I want to tell about it, partly because it's important. But also because it's a treasure trove of good stories.

Of course all this may sound totally out of touch with reality. Because everybody knows that "official" Chinese culture has denigrated women for thousands of years. The novelist Maxine Hong Kingston heard traditional sayings about it when she was a girl: "It is more profitable to raise geese than daughters"; "Feeding girls is feeding cowbirds"; "Girls are maggots in the rice" (Snyder, 1980, xv). In the past, nomadic warlords from Inner Asia repeatedly conquered the country. They brought sayings like "The wife I marry is like the horse I buy. They are mine to ride and mine to beat" (Chen, 2004, 163). Even modern women commonly suffer abuses so great, that Jan Wong suggested correcting the slogan "women hold up half of heaven" to say they hold up half of hell.

But China's women have always been far more than victims. They have chased their own dreams and built their own social worlds. They've commonly believed in themselves. As a caller to a Chinese radio talk show said, "Women are the creative force in the universe. They give the world beauty, feeling and sensitivity. Women are the best of all creatures" (Xinran, 2002, 103).

We've probably all heard that traditional Chinese women were basically powerless, and only started to claim their rights with the dawn of Westernization. But there's another side of Chinese tradition, where the folklore is rich in goddesses, immortal women, and female heroes. For example, in the Daozang collection of Daoist works, we find this tribute to the Holy Mother of Lao Jun (Lao Chün):

She controls the heavens and the earth
She controls the yin and the yang
Employs wind and rain as her servants
She makes the five planets advance and retreat
And rules over the immortals of the three realms
The life and death of men
The rise and decline of generations
All proceed from her
It is from the Holy Mother of Lao Chün
That heaven, earth, and all beings received life. (Rainey, 1991, 95)

As a Western man, I always thought religion was a mainly male thing. The Gods, priests, rabbis, or mullahs I knew of all seemed to be male. I heard there used to be women's religions, like the cults of witches. But those were stamped out as superstitious nonsense long ago, by whatever means necessary. Reportedly, those women's powers did not come from God, and besides, they were evil. Naturally, as a young boy, the notion of evil, powerful females stimulated me. I read about ancient civilizations with female deities and priests. Later I heard of new discoveries and theories about an "age of the goddess" at the dawn of history. I wondered why something like that passed away in the march of progress.

In university, at first I wanted to study the history of revolutions. But the courses I loved most were about China. Maybe it was the titanic clash of philosophies, the heroic idealism, the murderous cruelty, or the enchanting art. Probably it was the hard-working, hard-headed, gloriously beautiful women. And then, obviously, this was the biggest society in world history. In the future, it would have proportional influence on the whole planet.

And the most popular deity in China was a woman.

The greatest deity in China is, of course, Guanyin (or Kuan Yin), the goddess of universal compassion. Unlike most other goddesses of world mythology, she isn't portrayed as a mother, wife, or image of ideal sexuality. Instead, she is pictured as a fully enlightened world savior. Also, where most deities belong to only one religion, Guanyin is revered by followers of Daoism, Confucianism, Shinto, Cao Dai, and Buddhism (Palmer, Ramsay, Kwok, 1995, xii). A large statue of her stands in a temple courtyard down the street from my home in Toronto. Of course many worshipers see her as a superior being, probably made of spiritual matter, who lives in heaven and responds to prayers. But I like to think of her as a figure of popular literature. As Joseph Campbell might say, a deity is an image of whatever people feel is the highest and best in life. An image like that shapes people's dreams and goals. In a future planetary culture, it's possible that Guanyin will be the most widely respected image of female spirituality on earth.

But besides Guanyin there are thousands of other Chinese goddesses. Some are mythical spirits of nature like Lo Shen, a ruler of water magic. Others are masters of yoga-like spiritual disciplines, like Daoist master Sun Buer. Some are heroic fighting shamanesses, like Chen Jinggu and her band of sworn sisters. Many goddesses are scarcely remembered outside their own villages. But a fair number have nationwide or global appeal. For example, there are around 100 million devotees of the goddess Mazu. If the cults of deified women like Guanyin, Sun Buer, Chen Jinggu, or Mazu were lumped together, they would count as one of the world's largest religions. And these cults commonly have female leaders. In general, these are religions created by women, for women. Naturally, I'm interested in what they say about life, death, and the ultimate happiness.

Shouldn't the whole world know about that?

The Shadow Religions

China's goddess cults are not normally classed as independent religions. They seem to be sub-sects of Daoism, Buddhism, or Confucianism. We could say that the goddess cults are women's versions of these traditions. Some people call them "shadow religions." Even today, the cults of women and goddesses are not classified as organized religions. They fall under the supposedly less important category of "popular religion." Where men have usually dominated official religious institutions and professional priesthoods, the cults of women have spread informally among common people.

Official religion was almost all male, but popular religion was probably more influential.

Throughout China's history, the legends, lives, and teachings of local wise women formed a counterculture to the values of warlords or patriarchs. And as in many countries, the traditional values of women and villagers bore little resemblance to those of their rulers. In a view from the rulers' throne, the cults of peasants and women usually seemed unimportant. That's one reason for the seemingly low profile of goddess religions. But there are additional reasons. Thomas Cleary lists a series of old sayings about the invisibility of real virtue in his *Immortal Sisters: Secrets of Daoist Women*:

"A skilled artisan leaves no traces."
"She enters the water without making a ripple."
"The skilled appear to have no abilities; the wise appear to be ignorant." (1989, 6)

So when a mother teaches her children, it is best done when the children believe they did everything themselves. And the virtues celebrated in local goddess cults were often invisible to little emperors, or to sycophants who glorified tyrants.

At various times in the past, the rulers and state-backed priests treated goddess cults as subversive. The authorities occasionally tried to discredit female shamans or teachers as "stupid superstitious women." They did it for roughly the same reasons that medieval churchmen tried to silence Europe's wise women. But fortunately, the wise women of China never faced a seriously murderous extermination campaign. I suspect they were too popular, or the officials had too much respect their mothers' values.

Over the centuries, a female-friendly counterculture evolved within Daoism, Confucianism, Buddhism, and village folklore. There are "yin" versions of all these traditions. For anyone interested in a culture of balance between male and female powers, the women's religions offer a world of experience and insight. Their visions of life are strikingly different from what we find in most any official religion of the East, the West, or the Middle East.

In the West, of course, female deities are few and mostly long forgotten. Christianity has its thin line of sainted women from the Virgin Mary to Mother Teresa. But any goddess is an artifact from classical paganism. Islam has its cluster of holy women, especially from the faith's early days. But a goddess would be a relic from the pre-Islamic "time of ignorance." Judaism has its half-recalled mother of Israel, the spouse of Yahweh, the Matronit, the Shekhina, the Sophia, "the Discarded Cornerstone" (Patai, 1990, 128). But the goddesses of China are legion, and their cults have been popular from prehistoric times forward.

The Galaxy of Immortal Women

As in India, China's countryside is haunted by thousands of local deities. Some of them seem to date from the Stone Age. Xi Wang Mu (the Queen Mother of the West) was originally a shamanic tiger woman in charge of death and immortality. Feng Bo Bo represents the primordial forces of winds and storms. There are goddesses of mountains, rivers, lightning, drought, or smallpox. Naturally, we have Shin Mu, the holy mother of perfect intelligence, and Pan Jinlian, the goddess of prostitutes. Some deities have a farcical side, because in popular Chinese religion, holiness and comedy tend to mix. We have the outhouse goddesses, Qi Gu and Zi Gu. They bring spirit writing from the great beyond, and bestow deep thoughts in the lavatory. Chuang Mu is the goddess of the bedchamber, who is honored in the Lantern Festival. Her husband, Chuang Kong, is in charge of changing linens and folding sheets. An extraordinarily ugly woman, Momu, has a hunched back and club-feet. She oversees administration of the Yellow Emperor's heavenly palace. Her governance is ever proficient, partly because her ugliness drives evil spirits away. To this day villagers keep pictures of Momu to ward off evil. The goddess of light, Jun Di, has three heads, one of which is a pig head. Her chariot is also pulled by pigs, which are the seven stars of the Great Bear constellation. As for the great goddesses of creation, here is how the *Huainanzi* described the snake-woman Nü Wa:

> *When one considers her achievement, it knows only the bounds of Ninth Heaven above and the limits of the Yellow clod below. She is acclaimed by later generations, and her brilliant glory sweetly suffuses the whole world. She rides in a thunder-carriage driving shaft-steeds of winged dragons and an outer pair of green hornless dragons. She bears the emblem of the Fortune of Life and Death. Her seat is the Visionary Chart. (Birrell, 1993, 71)*

But the vast majority of deities in China are just deified people. In Chinese religions, there is usually little difference between a deity and a spiritually realized person. Henri Maspero argued that in China, "every god, great and small, is a man who, after death, was promoted for various reasons to the dignity of a god" (1981, 86). Maspero's use of "god" and "man" was generic, since many thousands of the deified people were women. Concerning their immortal status, Zhu Xi (Chu Hsi, d. 1200 CE) explained, "They distinguished themselves a hundred generations ago, and after a hundred generations, all those who hear of them are inspired" (Neskar, 1996, 300). Sometimes simple goodness was enough for a modest sort of deification. On the mountain Zijing Shan in Guangxi there is a typical "dead girl's temple." This one is devoted to "Grandaunt Lu," a girl who died young and childless, who did good deeds in her life, but has no descendants to remember her spirit.

It's true that China has more gods than goddesses. But still the countryside is teeming with legendary female immortals. I've mentioned Sun Buer, a Daoist master of the 1100s CE, and the powerful fighting shamaness Chen Jinggu (700s CE). And when Wang Jianghang compiled his *Stories of Immortals Through the Centuries* (around 215 BCE) he included tales of 145 deified women. Other Daoist books, such as the *Records of the Assembled Transcendents of the Fortified Walled City*, were devoted entirely to female saints and goddesses. As that book explained, "The ultimate position for men who attain the Way is realized lord, and the ultimate position for women who attain the Way is primal ruler" (Cahill, 1993, 214–215).

The stories of enlightened women have several recurring themes. Numerous tales tell of daughters whose "parents could not rob them of their will." They often left their families to embark on spiritual quests, like the immortals Cai Xun Zhen or Qi Xiao Yao (Chan, 1990, 49, 52). And the legends of such women are usually embellished with miracles. The Holy Mother of Dongling (300s CE) left only her shoes behind on being transformed into a goddess. A bird appeared at her consecrated place, and this bird answered all questions about stolen objects by flying to the thief. Soon all people in the region avoided stealing anything, even objects abandoned in the roads (Cleary, 1989, 11). One obviously historical person who became a goddess is Ti Ying, who dared challenge the Han emperor (in 167 BCE) with an appeal for mercy on prisoners. Her boldness won a legal ban on the worst kinds of torture. In recent times (1907) the fiery rebel Qiu Jin was beheaded for leading a revolt against Manchu tyranny, and won a goddess-like status in modern China. The process of "deification" resembles the canonization of saints in Christianity. Except that the Chinese usually deified people by popular demand, regardless of approval from any "higher" authority. Over time, the ranks of women recognized in this way grew, till they seem numerous as stars. Their stories form an ever-growing folklore of women's wisdom.

The Family of Patriarchs and Goddesses

People typically imagine their deities as family members of some kind. Some religions have one male father, but no mother, or one male ruler with no queen. But Chinese religion and society has had a mix of male lords with queens of heaven. It's true that male rulers commonly claimed to be the central objects of their peoples' devotion. The all-male Confucian bureaucrats posed as official spokesmen for their civilization. The eldest males of each family often claimed to be the family heads, and many people believed them. But each family has other important actors, with other views and values. The goddesses and queenly mothers are also there. And in many cases, the values of rulers or patriarchs are not the values closest to most people's hearts.

Though most Chinese families have been strongly patriarchal for over 2,000 years, popular family traditions often send a different message. During the 1930s, the famous male writer Lin Yutang questioned the assumption that traditional women had no power: "The Chinese woman is, on the whole, a constitutionally sounder animal than her male companion, and we still have plenty of matriarchs even in Confucian households" (1935, 137). Though Lin was known to disparage women as females, a matriarch had his respect. And this power of matriarchs appeared in ways most curious to Westerners. In the mid-1800s, British interpreter Thomas Meadows described a Chinese gentleman introducing a friend to his mother:

> The friend introduced [to the mother] ... then performs a kow-tow to the lady, i.e., he kneels before her and touches the ground repeatedly with his forehead. The son ... returns the salute by

kneeling and kow-towing toward his friend. Thus two men, and often, of course, gray bearded men of high stations, will in China be found knocking their heads against the floor in honor of a woman of their own class in society. (Yang, 1992, 19)

Though the power of men over women seemed obvious, Chinese mothers often retained a certain primordial majesty. In many cases their influence was vast, and the roles they played were arguably central. But the powers of women and goddesses were generally different from those of headmen or gods. The women commonly had different goals in life, and different paths to get there.

The Journey and Its Goal in Women's Religions

In the Middle East, ancient deities were usually portrayed as superhuman kings. Their instructions to mortals were like commands from rulers to subjects, given in books of holy law. The main practice of these religions was to fully obey the laws. That was one story of life's meaning. And China had its own versions of this tale, with a Jade Emperor in the sky, his appointed ruler on earth, Confucius as a prophet of heaven's will, and a priestly bureaucracy to enforce the holy law.

But most goddesses of China have been saint-like or guru-like figures. They were "masters" who attained some sort of enlightenment, taught groups of friends, and were reported returning in spirit after they died. To their devotees, these women were perfected beings. But since their followers could learn what the teachers taught, most goddesses were examples to be learned from, not eternally superior beings to be obeyed. The lives of most divine women were not just images of perfected womanhood, but biographies of goddesses in the making. The boundary lines between "mortal and immortal" or "human and divine" were permeable. People were all these things at once. In a sense, any person might become a deity. As Judith Simmer-Brown described the dakini goddesses of Tibet, "She may appear in humble or ordinary form as a shopkeeper, a wife or sister, or a decrepit or diseased hag. If she reveals herself, if she is recognized, she has tremendous ability to point out obstacles, reveal new dimensions, or awaken spiritual potential" (2002, 4). Such divine women appeared, or did not appear, seemingly at random over the course of Chinese history. The authorities tried to control their people's loyalties. They tried to tell the villagers which leaders to follow. But nobody managed to control who the people considered holy.

In woman-friendly traditions, people commonly picture their deities as ultimate parents, teachers, or friends—not as kings, governors, or lords. Accordingly, most goddess cults have flourished among common people, not the dominant classes. They have seldom sought or gained official status as cults of state. Their goddesses are seldom pictured as high officials in a heavenly government. Female religious leaders have often been popular, but rarely controlled big organizations. Their authority has come from their personal qualities, not from any position of rank or office. Their legends commonly underline this.

In general, goddess religions grow out of women's experience, including mothers' experience. But the results of spiritual creativity are impossible to predict. As David Kinsley said, "Some goddesses have nothing to do with motherhood, fertility, or the earth. Others play traditional male roles and often seem to take delight in violating roles that are associated with women in the cultures where they are revered. Some goddesses ... provide paradigms for female subordination to males" (1989, x). So it's true that China's goddesses are extremely diverse. But still their cults tend to share certain values. They usually assume a reverence for life, and for the power to conceive or nurture it. They commonly take this literally female power as the greatest power of all. As the *Dao De Jing (Tao Te Ching)* put it, "To beget, to nourish / To beget but not to claim / To achieve but not to cherish / To be leader but not master— / This is called the Mystic Virtue" (Stanza 10, De Bary and Chan, 1960, vol. I, 53).

Of course these values are not unique to Chinese goddess cults. They are common among aboriginal cultures around the world. Probably they are the values of China's own first cultures. According to traditional myths, there was a time in the distant past when such values prevailed. And the myths predict they will prevail again.

3: The Legendary Age of the Goddess

I used to buy the notion that equality for women was a foreign idea in China. I heard that traditional Chinese people, both the men and the women, accepted that male supremacy was heaven's eternal will. The women only thought of questioning this when Christian missionaries started teaching them in the 1800s. But of course there was always a women's counterculture. We find it recorded from the beginning, and it probably formed the foundation of Chinese civilization. For example we have the ever-popular legend of the Golden Age, about how things were in the beginning, and how they should be in the future. According to this legend of an original paradise, social equality and servant leadership are the natural standards of human life. The rise of force-backed ranking (of men over women and lords over subjects) was a temporary departure from the Way. It was a foolish error, which will soon be corrected. In one version of the story or another, this is what mothers told their children through the ages.

Until about a century ago, most professional historians thought this legend of a golden age had no basis in fact. It was a myth, and myths were imaginary. More recently came "the golden age of Chinese archaeology," which uncovered early civilizations all over China. And these earliest cultures were often called "goddess cultures." Partly it's because their artwork tended to emphasize female images. Also, the remains of their villages suggested a rough social equality. The houses were usually all about the same size. The graves were also basically equal, suggesting a similar status for all the dead. And it seems these people had few if any weapons of war. According to Marxist theory, the earliest Chinese villagers lived in an age of "primitive communism." Later came the rise of warlords and empires, which involved "the historic defeat of the female sex."

Europe also had its early "civilizations of the goddess," such as Old Europe or Minoan Crete. But these civilizations were destroyed and forgotten, till modern archaeologists uncovered their remains. In China it was slightly different. The early cultures were conquered, but not erased. Their folklore survived to be recorded in writing. In popular culture, the village people retained myths and values from an age before warlords, including numerous legends of female deities. We can say that in China, the age of the goddess never died.

The Time of Unspoiled Nature and Uncorrupted Human Virtue

In Chinese mythology, the legend of a lost "golden age" looms very large. The dawn of history is idealized as an original paradise, like a memory of childhood bliss. When early Daoists spoke of the Golden Age, they said it was a time of wonder, natural beauty, and real equality. With fond and likely exaggerated memory, they called it "the Great Peace," "the Great Equality," "the time of unspoiled nature and uncorrupted human virtue." As Zhuangzi (Chuang-tzu) explained its primitive beauties,

> In that age, there were no paths over the mountains, no boats and bridges to cross rivers. The ten thousand creatures grew abundantly, each in its own sphere. Birds and animals formed herds; plants and trees shot up as they pleased. Therefore birds and animals could be led by the hand (and they did not try to run away), and one could climb to the nests of ravens and look into them (without disturbing them). Indeed, in the age of highest virtue, man had the same habitation as birds and animals and constituted a single race with the ten thousand creatures. Nothing was known of a "superior" and a "common" man. (Bauer, 1976, 34)

The early Daoist sages like Laozi (Lao-tzu) or Zhuangzi meant to contrast such a past with their own age of rising warlords (in the 500s to 300s BCE). Looking back in nostalgic protest, they recalled an age of autonomous villages, boundless forests, peace, and freedom. If these legends have any historical background, they would best fit the period before 2100 BCE.

Confucius also spoke repeatedly of the Golden Age. He claimed that the people of that time followed natural virtues of compassion and mutual respect. As the *Classic of Rites* (section 9) said,

> *When the Great Way was practiced, the world was shared by all alike. The worthy and the able were promoted to office and men practiced good faith and lived in affection. Therefore they did not regard as parents only their own parents, or as sons only their own sons ... Therefore all evil plotting was prevented and thieves and rebels did not arise, so that people could leave their outer gates unbolted. This was the age of Grand Unity. (De Bary and Chan, 1960, vol. I, 176)*

Confucius reportedly learned of that time from the records of early Zhou (Chou) dynasty princes, who lived around 1000 BCE. But according to these records, the first Zhou princes claimed to be mere students of yet wiser and more ancient "sage emperors," who behaved as servants rather than masters of their people. The legends of these "emperors" place them prior to the Xia (Hsia) era, or sometime before 2100 BCE. It seems that both Confucian and Daoist legends of the Golden Age refer to the roughly same period.

China's Buddhists also had legends of a golden time, or a place where things remained as they were in the beginning. It's unclear if these stories are modifications of Chinese legends, or imported from India, or both. But according to one story,

> *When the people of Uttarakuru bathe in one of the four miraculous rivers flowing through the country ... they simply go to the banks, undress, leave their clothing on the beach, step into boats and move out onto the water. There they bathe and play in the waves for as long as they enjoy themselves. When they return to the beach, they all pick up the garments lying nearest them. ...*

They dress and wander off without looking for their own clothes.
Why? Because the people of Uttarakuru pay no attention to what
does and does not belong to them. (Bauer, 1976, 167)

Most Daoists, Confucianists, and Buddhists, all agreed that the
Golden Age had ended long ago. With the rise of military empires,
the Great Equality had been destroyed. Rulers had become armed
thieves rather than kindly elders. Official religion was now mainly
concerned with enforcing obedience to superiors. But idealists and
common people still dreamed of a return to the ancient ways. They
compared their external reality with mental images of the Golden
Age. These were their pictures of how life should be, which appeared
like collective memories, inherited by every generation.

In China's perennial vision of the Golden Age, the land is lush and
green, with hillside forests, languid ponds, and sparkling beaches. The
world is a numinous, living thing. The plants and animals are fellow
travelers on life's journey. Most people would rather cooperate than
compete with their neighbors. They make few distinctions of status,
and feel that ambition for superiority is foolish. The community
respects those who give the most—not those who possess the most, or
take the most. Men and women generally regard each other with
mutual admiration. They value their leisure with friends and family.
Their work is unhurried, because the quality of life is more important
than the scale of production. Technology either enables these values,
or else people don't want it. In this perennial dream, an almost tangible
memory of original bliss fills the background of personal and collective
history. Life's glimpses of peace and joy come surrounded with a scent
of *deja-vu*. People know what they love because they've tasted it before.

This sense of *deja-vu* has been unusually strong in China.
Probably most peasant rebellions or religious movements, including
the White Lotus societies, the Taiping or Boxer rebels, Sun Yat-sen's
Republicans, or Mao Zedong's Communists, have been fired by some
version of an ancient national dream called "the Great Equality."

This dream has appeared in thousands of popular legends, religious visions, festival dramas, novels, raucous peasant songs, or subversive political tracts. In the 1920s, Liu Renhang (Liu Jen-hang) wrote a book called *Preliminary Studies Concerning the Great Equality of the East*. In this, he classified various utopian visions animating the popular mind. There were "fantasy" paradises such as the Buddhist Pure Land, dreams of a return to Mother Nature, or mystical realizations of the great equality as a state of higher awareness. There were ideals of primitive socialism, revolutionary demands for economic justice, visions of equality for women, or notions of progress for all through sharing the fruits of technology. These dreams were variations on a theme that runs through Chinese history from the first to now. They reflect a moral common sense that seems characteristic of popular culture. Daniel Overmyer reports that from the earliest times, folk religions have shared "a common basic outlook, or 'theology'—a belief that the living, the dead, the spirits of nature, ghosts and gods, are all connected by bonds of mutual influence and obligation, and these mutual ties form a moral universe, where respect, greed, compassion, or destruction all bring their own rewards" (2008, 177).

Of course Mao's Red Guards seemed to totally reject such superstitious traditions. But perhaps these young radicals were more traditional than they knew. They basically denounced their elders for failing to live up to their own ancient ideals of "the Great Equality." In the past, those who defended similar dreams often claimed patronage from goddesses of antiquity, such as Lao Mu, the Old Mother; Xi Wang Mu, the Queen Mother; or Yao Chi Jinmu, the Keeper of Paradise. The values of the Golden Age were originally the values of prehistoric clan mothers. And throughout history, these were the counterculture values popular among women.

We could easily dismiss China's legends of the Golden Age as "trivial utopianism." But these legends have been widely believed throughout Chinese history. Mao Zedong explained it this way in 1939: "Developing along the same lines as many other nations of the world, the Chinese nation ... first went through some tens of thousands of years of life in classless primitive communes. Up to now, approximately 4,000 years have passed since the collapse of the primitive communes and the transition to class society, first slave society and then feudalism" (De Bary and Chan, 1960, vol. II, 216). More recently, Wang Qingshu, the Secretary for the All-China Women's Federation, said the problem was obvious: "After the decline of the matriarchal culture of ancient China, women's status gave them no rights in public affairs" (2004, 92). Both Mao and Wang believed in the legendary time of Great Equality.

Probably most people in Chinese history have recalled the age of "primitive communes" with a certain reverent nostalgia. And many believed that the legends showed an original equality between men and women. Even patriarchal authorities believed this, and criticized their ancestors for it. So, back in the 300s BCE, the philosopher Shang Yang ridiculed the ancients for giving too much respect to mothers: "During the time when heaven and earth were established and the people were produced, people knew their mothers but not their fathers" (Cai, 1995, 36). To his mind, nothing could be more barbaric. But most people, especially the women, took the age before patriarchy as a source of inspiration. In 1898, the feminist educator Qiu Yufang gave her own enthusiastic twist to the legend:

Prior to the period of the Three Dynasties [which started ca. 2100 BCE] ... there were many rational, educated women. Women had governesses, and these governesses were female teachers. I believe that in ancient times there were also schools for girls. Later, the custom of regarding men as superior to women grew stronger as time went on, and women were not allowed to know the principles and learning of the world. (Xia, 2004, 7)

In teaching her girls, Qiu aimed to restore traditions of the Golden Age.

The Relevance of Golden Ages and Paradise Myths

Clearly, China has been famous for nostalgia. And a lot of nostalgia involves wishful thinking. Naturally, many people have rejected reverence for the primitive past as an escapist, infantile fantasy. Back in the 300s CE, Bao Jingyan complained that in legends of the Golden Age, "men behave like children ... comparable to sucklings and babes, in whom cleverness and intelligence have not yet been awakened" (Bauer, 1976, 131–152). Wu Jingheng, the head of the Academia Sinica till 1953, discounted all myths of the Golden Age as gossip from foolish peasants. Countless modern nationalists have felt that China's fixation on a supposedly golden past was just a block in the road to the future. Modern young people commonly think that the past is a nightmare they are trying to escape. And many show a certain fatalism we can probably all relate to. A factory girl in the industry boom city of Shenzhen told her English teacher, "In original society, people lived in groups. Eventually, these groups broke down into families, and now they're breaking down again, into so many different people. Finally, it will be just one single person ... If you could have some kind of perfect socialism, that would be the best. But it's impossible. That was just a beautiful ideal" (Hessler, 2006, 167).

Clearly, dreams of paradise are controversial, and the dreams themselves often seem to be the problem. But, of course it depends on how people use them.

A glance at North American religion may give some perspective on myths of an idealized past. In modern North America, probably most people believe that their society is the best in history. By comparison, all past cultures and probably all foreign ones seem backward. Yet every Sunday morning, millions of these self-confident North Americans go to church, seeking to learn a better way to live. And their chosen teachers in this vital subject are an assortment of impoverished villagers from ancient West Asia. In this case, certain ancient people are deemed to have wisdom that the modern world both lacks and needs. And in church, we usually have a full reversal of normal workaday assumptions. Instead of believing that modern ways are superior to ancient ones, we have an assumption that certain revered ancients are to teach us, and we moderns should conform to their ways as best we can.

In both the Bible and the Quran, we have accounts of an original earthly paradise. And both these accounts of the Garden of Eden are widely believed to be historic fact. These "western" scriptures say that our first ancestors were cast out from a garden of paradise as a punishment for their sins. In China also, the Golden Age was reportedly lost due to human failings. But the western accounts say that the earthly paradise has been lost forever. It can never be recovered; paradise is now attainable only in another world beyond the grave. In China, however, most dreams of paradise have been set on earth. And probably most Chinese people through the centuries have believed it possible that the time of unspoiled nature and uncorrupted human virtue can be recovered in this world. This might be the ultimate pipe dream. Or maybe it's the greatest, bravest hope of all.

Concerning the whole notion of "golden ages," probably most nations and individuals have their own memories of "the golden times." In Greece, most people feel that the golden age was roughly the 400s BCE. This was not the period of greatest military glory under Alexander, but the peak of cultural creativity in Athens. In Italy, we might expect nostalgia for the Roman empire, but actually this is not the most popular sentiment. The hordes of tourists visiting Italy each year come mainly to see the arts and historic sites of the Renaissance. And this is probably the most valid verdict on which age or vision of Italy has been the best so far. The Dutch commonly refer to the 1500s and 1600s as their golden age. That was their time of political liberation, with an explosion of practical and artistic genius. In the USA, some feel that the great conquest of the western frontiers was America's finest hour. But this view is falling from favor. Probably most Americans think their greatest time was the founding revolution, when their country's guiding principles took form in a creative rush, and were enshrined in timeless prose.

In China, the golden age is traditionally assigned to the very dawn of history. The landscape was then rich and majestic. The villagers were creative inventors, forging new ways of living from each environment. Their leaders were independent elders and matrons, as yet unconquered by any "higher" lords.

We may suspect that all these memories of golden times are just illusions, and memory makes the past seem better than it was. We've also seen grand and dangerous delusions about the past. We've had proud nationalists who idealized their own roots. These people typically claimed descent from a select group of pure ancestors, with God-given traditions. We've seen ethnic purists treat all change from their founding traditions as heresy, and all influence from other cultures as social pollution. But people's recollections of their "golden times" can also be a positive inspiration. They can make people feel that they've been great in the past, and may be great again. I suspect these legends feed an unhealthy obsession with the past only if people grow convinced that their greatness is gone. We moderns may think that dreaming of paradise is a waste of time. But what future are we hoping for? In our minds we hold pictures of the world as it should be. And what are we striving toward if not those dreams?

The Legend Emerges as a Future Dream

After the first emperor conquered the whole Middle Kingdom in 221 BCE, China usually remained an empire under varying degrees of martial law. People were then ranked by their value to the rulers, and given privileges or restrictions accordingly. Women were generally regarded as existing to serve more powerful men. According to Pan Shaoping, "in the post-Qin centralized autocratic society [after 207 BCE], the partnership life of the male and the female ... was the stuff of myths and legends, and the memory of remote antiquity was no more than a spiritual consolation in the face of reality" (Sun and Pan, 1995, 238).

So the dominators of China tried to supplant and subordinate all ancient village cultures. The villagers, however, were resilient, comparing themselves to bamboo. Their memories of a pre-militarized world lived on, like dreams indelibly printed inside their eyelids. Both peasants and learned people commonly idealized their vanished past. Onto the slate of antiquity they projected their fondest dreams. Where memory and vision combined, the legendary Golden Age emerged. So in the chaotic period after the fall of the Han dynasty (ca. 300s CE), Bao Jingyan claimed to clearly recall,

> *In ancient times there were no Lords or officials. People (spontaneously) dug wells for water and plowed fields for food. In the morning they went forth to their labor (without being ordered to do so) and rested in the evening. People were free and uninhibited and at peace: they did not compete with one another, and knew neither shame nor honors. There were no paths through the mountains, and no bridges over waters, nor boats upon them . . . Thus invasions and annexations were not possible, nor did soldiers gather together in large companies in order to attack one another in organized war. (Needham and Wang, 1956, 435)*

Who could prove such memories false? Where did these legends come from if not inherited memory, passed on by grandparents in bedtime stories?

So the Golden Age became an historical memory, a living ideal, and a vision of the future. It was the goal of psychological unity with the source of life. It was the lost tenderness between mother and child, around which the world should turn. It was a real time in the not-so-distant past, with known traditions and moral standards, by which the present age would be judged.

According to popular legend, the Queen Mother of the West came to the court of Han Emperor Wu in 110 BCE to deliver her judgment against him. This emperor had launched victorious wars against the barbarians, building the might of China to rival that of Rome. He had adopted an official version of Confucianism as the state religion, in which the main moral obligation was for subjects to serve their superiors. In his political and spiritual roles, Emperor Wu would be roughly equivalent to the combined figures of Roman emperors Augustus and Constantine. And to this great figure, the goddess reportedly said, "You were born licentious, extravagant, and violent; and you live in the midst of blood and force—no matter how many Daoists you invite here in hopes of immortality, you will only wear yourself out" (Cleary, 1989, 3–4). Maybe that suggests something about the role of women's religions in Chinese history.

The Chinese age of the goddess probably began over 7,000 years ago, and it continues in the crowded streets today. It is not just an archaeological corpse to be disinterred and studied, the way we study ancient Crete. It's a living heritage of dreams and values which will shape the future. The Chinese perennial vision of a restored earthly paradise is unique in form and style. But it's also part of a dream unfolding across the planet.

4: The Original Partnership of Sexes

In many Chinese creation myths "the Creator" is a just a swirl of cosmic forces. The universe begins with a rising mist, which separates into the energies of Yin and Yang. These energies seem like positive-negative figures in a binary code, but they function like a divine couple to generate the universe. The symbols for Yin and Yang (– – and —) are probably shorthand images of female and male sex organs (Min, 1995, 26). So in the beginning, there was sexual love on a cosmic scale. As Laozi (Lao-tzu) explained, "All the myriad things carry Yin on their backs and hold Yang in their embrace, deriving their vital harmony from the proper blending of the two vital breaths" (*Dao De Jing*, stanza 42).

That's the philosophical version. But in popular folklore, the creative principles are pictured as gods and goddesses, like the snake deities Fu Xi and Nü Wa.

The Joint Creators

The goddess Nü Wa was a beautiful woman above her waist, and a serpent below. One admirer wrote, "Nü Wa was endowed with such a body; who could have conceived and wrought such a wonder?" She is first recorded in the *Songs of Chu* (ca. 300 BCE) which asked, "If she became empress, who appointed her? If Nü Wa had a form, who created her?" (Ching, 1993, 26).

Reportedly, she gave birth to all creatures in ten days. First she brought forth chickens, then dogs, pigs, sheep, horses, and cows. On the seventh day she gave birth to human beings. Then she crowned her creation with grains, fruits, and finally vegetables (Cai, 1995, 35, 38–39). The Yao people have a similar story, where mother Milotou populated the earth with grasses first, and insects last. In a rather sarcastic version of Nü Wa's tale, she created humans from mud. At first she made each person carefully, but then she got sloppy and started slinging clay. Glancing at her shoddy work, she shrugged and said the slipshod people could serve as peasants. If life was cruel, maybe the great mother made it that way. But however she made it, life appeared from a celestial mother, not by a heavenly king's command. As the *Dao De Jing* says,

> *Every living thing*
> *comes from the mother of us all:*
> *If we can understand the mother*
> *then we can understand her children;*
> *and if we know ourselves as children*
> *we can see the source as her. (stanza 52)*

Of course Nü Wa came with a partner—the snake-man, Fu Xi. He gave the newly created people skills in hunting, cooking, fishing, and making music. He also helped people to foretell the future by providing the hexagrams of the *Yi Jing* (*I Ching*). With their serpent bodies entwined, Fu Xi and Nü Wa presided as god and goddess of the world. And the various non-Han ethnic groups also had creator couples of their own. The Achang people had Zhepama and Zhemima, while the Dai had Busangga and Yasangga (Cai, 1995, 42). In general, the male deities played a supportive role, but their part in procreation seemed unclear.

Another famous creation story is etched in stone on the holy Tai Mountain in Shandong. As pilgrims wind their way up the mountain, they pass shrines and statues devoted to the mountain goddess. She is called "Old Mother," "Old Grandmother of Tai," "the Heavenly Immortal," "Green Jade Mother," or "Goddess of the Azure Clouds." On reaching the mountaintop, people arrive at the shrine of the goddess's brother, the Jade Emperor. This sister-brother pair reportedly descended to earth on Tai Mountain. After bringing all plants, fishes, and other creatures to life, they ruled the world from this mountain peak (Martin et al., 1995, 10).

Later, after the first dramas of creation, the various divine couples faced serious threats to their world. For example, a titanic struggle broke out between the powers of fire and water, personified by the gods Zhu Rong and Gong Gong. As usual with jealous gods, they battled for supremacy, heedless of wreaking havoc on the cosmos. When Gong Gong finally lost the match, he tried to bring down the universe by head-butting a column of heaven. One corner of the sky fell in, and a huge flood engulfed the earth. Only the goddess Nü Wa was able to save the planet. She quickly patched the sky with stones of five colors. Then she severed the legs of a giant sea turtle, to use as props for the four corners of heaven. Last, she piled up ashes from burned reeds to dam the surging floods. In one version of the tale, no humans survived the disaster, so Nü Wa and Fu Xi had to re-produce the race. Nü Wa then became "the mother of the Chinese nation." As the *Huainanzi* (ca. 139 CE) gratefully explained, "She contributed to the sky and earth and was well known to coming generations, and her achievements shed brilliance on all living things ... Yet she did not mention or speak of what she had done; she maintained the virtue of a sage and let all living things develop in their own way" (Cai, 1995, 39–40).

Like all creation stories, these myths present a series of messages. They suggest that the ultimate power of creation is the sexual energy of love. They also picture the world as a family, with mama, papa, and all creatures as brothers and sisters. Third, these myths portray the cosmic mother and father as roughly equal. The Chinese Partnership Studies Group claims that these divine couples symbolize the original equality of men and women in primitive clans (Cai, 1995, 47–48). In these folk memories, the earliest society was not a matriarchy, but a partnership. If we say these myths express "goddess religions," it basically means that goddesses are included. And if this book focuses mainly on female divinities, it's partly because Western religions came to exclude them—not because "the goddess" in China was ever a female equivalent of Yahweh.

The Founding Culture Heroes

After the rise of empires and dynasties, the prehistoric myths of creator couples were modified to fit the times. *The Classic of Mountains and Seas* (written between the 200s BCE and 100s CE) was the earliest text to mention Di Jun, a seemingly monotheistic Lord of Heaven and Earth. Next, in the 200s CE, the legend of an original first man (named Pan Gu) appeared in a book by Xu Zhang (Birrell, 1993, 124, 25). These accounts made humanity originate with male rulers. And this complemented older Confucian legends, which attributed the inventions of tools, hunting, farming, etc. to a series of primordial kings known as the "Three Sovereigns" and the "Five Primary Emperors." Supposedly, these great lords taught humanity all the basics of civilized life. The period of their mythic rule is placed sometime around 2900 to 2100 BCE. As portrayed in later art, these primal rulers evolved into true patriarchs, seated pompously on ornate dragon thrones. So the myths of China's origins grew almost as patriarchal as Bible stories. But in the folklore versions of these myths, the primal emperor's wives were also credited with major feats of creation.

For example, Empress Xi He, a wife of the Yellow Emperor, reportedly gave birth to the sun (or to ten suns). Xi He was also the original driver for the chariot of the sun, though later myths changed the driver's sex (Birrell, 1993, 124–125). The Confucian *Classic of History* changed Xi He into two brothers, Xi and He, who were commissioned by Emperor Yao "to compute and delineate the sun, moon and stars, and the celestial markers, and so deliver respectfully the seasons to be observed by the people" (Chan, 1990, 13–14). Another empress, Chang Xi, was the mother of the moon (or twelve moons). Later legends made her the second consort of Di Jun, the Lord of Heaven. (Wu, 1982, 60; Birrell, 1993, 38). Sien Zang, a wife of the divine farmer Shennong, wove the clouds that clothe the heavens. And Luozu, another wife of the Yellow Emperor, initiated silk production, though Can Nu was the actual goddess of silkworms.

Besides these empresses and consorts, a number of early culture heroes were portrayed without indication of gender. These include Youchao, who taught people to built tree houses, and Suiren, who invented fire-making with wooden drills. No doubt somebody invented these things, though it may have been fearless leaders of the *Homo erectus pekinensis* ("Peking Man") who lived about 500,000 years ago.

Min Jiayin feels that all these primal culture-heroes were probably prehistoric clans rather than individuals. Their inventions of hunting, farming, weaving, or cooking evolved slowly over many generations, by the efforts of many people. Min also believes that the early clan leaders were groups of male and female elders, not "emperors." (1995, 554). Cai Junsheng applies the same logic to the myths of great goddesses: "Nü Wa should not be regarded as a specific individual but rather as an archetype of the great feminine spirit of the matriarchal age that once prevailed across the Central Plain" (1995, 35).

Concerning the primordial "Three Sovereigns," some legends claim that two of these lords were the snake deities, Fu Xi and Nü Wa. Some accounts even pin the reign of this divine couple to certain dates, such as 2852 to 2738 BCE. Other legends say that one of the original three sovereigns was the Queen Mother of the West, who ruled while taking several husbands, including the Jade Emperor. In that case, it's fitting that the Queen Mother was also called "The Primordial Ruler" (Cahill, 1993, 68).

The Queen Mother

The Queen Mother of the West, Xi Wang Mu, is first recorded on Shang dynasty oracle bones from around 1300 BCE. One inscription reads, "on IX.9 day: If we make offerings to the Eastern Mother and the Western Mother, there will be approval." Shang bronze artwork also shows the Queen Mother riding a tiger. Later she appears in classical myth. As Zhuangzi (Chuang-tzu, 300s BCE) explained, "The Queen Mother of the West obtained it [the Way] and took up her seat on Shao Guang [mountain]. No one knows her beginning; no one knows her end." It seems she was simply there from the first, as if her role in creation was taken for granted (Cahill, 1993, 12, 3, 14). In the oldest images she is dressed in the furs and feathers of a stone-age shaman, or even a cat woman ancestress. In the *Classic of Mountains and Seas*, the Queen Mother's appearance "is like that of a human, with a leopard's tail and tiger's teeth. Moreover, she is skilled at whistling. In her disheveled hair she wears a sheng headdress. She is controller of the Grindstone and the Five Shards Constellations in the Heavens" (Cahill, 1993, 15–16).

The Queen Mother reportedly lived on Tortoise Mountain, which was the grindstone base for the world pillar, around which the earth turned. Up and down that pillar, prehistoric shamans flew as emissaries between worlds. And the Queen Mother was apparently chief of the shamans. Her pillar reached heaven at a point in the Five Shards Constellations. This was the unmoving spot around which the stars revolved, also called the "womb point" from which the universe was born.

The Queen Mother was also a directional deity. She ruled the west, which was the direction of death. There, the sun went down into the earth, as the dead went down to their original mother. The goddess of the west ruled the realm of the dead. Her tiger was the very symbol of death—like a Chinese-style grim reaper. Her garb of wild cat furs and disheveled hair made her resemble India's goddess Kali. As the *Classic of Mountains and Seas* said, the Queen Mother "is the official in charge of vile plagues sent from heaven, and of the five dread evils" (Birrell, 1993, 174). So, ancient shamans traveled in spirit to the Queen Mother's realm, appealing to her as the gatekeeper of death, birth, and immortality (Wong, 1997, 160).

In her most primitive guise as half cat and half human, the Queen Mother was a prehistoric shaman like those painted on cave walls in France. The *Songs of Chu* (300s BCE) report an encounter with a similar "Mountain Goddess":

In a coat of fig-leaves with a rabbit floss girdle ...
Driving tawny leopards, leading the stripped lynxes;
Her cloak of stone orchids, her belt of asarum:
She gathers sweet scents for the one she loves. (Snyder, 1980, xiv)

Later, in classical times, the Queen Mother evolved into a proud, beautiful woman, who ruled the animal powers as an empress. To her right stood the tiger of the west; to her left the dragon of the east. At her feet, two hares pounded the elixir of immortality. Still later she took on Buddhist-style robes, as befit her role as mistress of the wheel of rebirth. Under Buddhist influence she slowly changed from a cold, aloof, queen of death, into a figure of motherly compassion. Her titles included "Primal Pneuma of Grand Yin," "Ruling Thought," "Supine Jade," "Primordial Ruler," "The Perfected Marvel of the Western Florescence," and "Ultimate Worthy of the Grotto Yin" (Cahill, 1993, 35–36, 68).

In medieval times, Daoist clerics spun myths of a multi-layered cosmic administration, reflecting the imperial order on earth. But for many Daoists, the great cosmic bureaucracy was still headed by two divinities—the Jade Emperor and the Queen Mother. As in older myths, this divine pair presented an image of shared power. The Jade Emperor governed people's fates in this life, and the Queen Mother decided who should receive immortality (Wong, 1997, 160). She was commonly shown holding a basket of peaches, which were peaches of eternal life.

The emperors of dynastic times (after 221 BCE) sometimes sent expeditions searching for the Queen Mother's mountain. It was like when Columbus hoped to find Mount Purgatory. According to the *Bamboo Annals*, Emperor Shun (allegedly ca. 2300 BCE) and the later Emperor Mu both traveled to the Queen Mother's court to offer her gifts (Cai, 1995, 56–57). This would be like King Solomon traveling to pay homage at the Queen of Sheba's court, instead of her coming to him. Later, some Chinese emperors claimed they were honored by a visit from the Queen Mother. And this would be like Constantine or Charlemagne claiming the Virgin Mary had brought them tribute from heaven. Emperor Wu, the "Martial Emperor" of the Han dynasty, claimed a visitation from the Queen Mother in 110 BCE. According to an official history of Wu's reign, she came

> *riding on purple clouds and six-color dragons, accompanied by fifty goddesses. She was wearing a golden gown, colorful, yet solemn and respectful. She tied a silk belt about her waist from which a sword hung. She had a "Tai-hua" hair style and was wearing a crown and a pair of blue jade shoes patterned with a phoenix. She was about thirty years old, of medium height, slim and graceful, and was the most beautiful goddess. (Cai, 1995, 58)*

The emperors' scribes claimed that the Queen Mother was favorable to Wu, offering him her wisdom and even her love. But other sources say that the goddess issued harsh warnings. We have already heard her rebuke: "You were born licentious, extravagant, and violent; and you live in the midst of blood and force—no matter how many Daoists you invite here in hopes of immortality, you will only wear yourself out." She also made demands: "Cleanse yourself of this whole multitude of disorders; reject annihilation and change your intentions ... lock up the palace of debauchery and do not open it. Still your profligacy and extravagance in a quiet room. Cherish all living beings and do not endanger them" (Cleary, 1989, 3–4).

Though Emperor Wu may have been the most powerful man on earth, he allegedly promised to obey the goddess's orders. Perhaps he claimed that his future wars were endorsed by the Queen Mother. But according to popular accounts, "He could not make use of the Queen Mother's admonitions." To hold and expand his empire, Wu needed to make others fear him. Soon he conscripted new armies and invaded Korea: "From this time on he lost the Way" (Cahill, 1993, 152–153). So in this case and others, the emperors tried to claim sanction for their rule from the villagers' time-honored deities. But many of those deities represented values from the age before warlords. And these values were so different from the imperial court's ruling passions, that the very comparison seemed to invite rebuke for the rulers.

The Queen Mother, Xi Wang Mu, was the greatest female deity in Daoism at least through Tang dynasty times (618–906 CE). In Korea, a mountain is named for her. In Japan she is worshiped in the Tanabata festival. She is a guiding deity for the modern Compassion Society in Taiwan. She has been a patron of all women, but especially for outcastes—singing girls, nuns, shamans, widows, unmarried women, or those who died outside marriage. Basically, Xi Wang Mu has been a deity for women who determined their own lives and vocations (Cahill, 1986, 155).

The Female and Male Shamans

In Siberia, shamanhood was a male vocation. But from earliest times in China we hear of both male and female shamans (Hawkins, 2004, 268). Shamans, of course, were the villagers' ambassadors to the spirit realm. Probably each community had its shamanic "sensitives," who showed a capacity for conscious dreaming, visioning, or traveling in spirit. They bore responsibility for securing good relations between their people and the world's animating powers. In Zhou times (ca. 1050 to 221 BCE) we hear of shamans contacting spirits, mediating at funerals, or evoking rain. And down to the present time we still have local healers, rain-makers, exorcists, or mediums throughout China. In all probability, every ancient culture in the world started with shamanic-style leaders. And Julia Ching feels that popular religion in China has remained close to its roots. It has always been basically "ecstatic" or shamanistic (1993, 40–41).

The methods of shamanism can be described as "techniques of ecstasy," for altering consciousness at will. Our earliest written account of their methods is the *Songs of Chu* (ca. 300 BCE), which describes a shamaness dancing herself into a trance:

Strike the lutes, beat the drums
[Let] the bells in their jade-ornamented stands [resound] to the
notes of the trumpets,
let the flutes sing! Blow the hautboys!
The sorceress is clever and beautiful, like a kingfisher
In her whirling flight, she rises up
Her dance follows the rhythm of the verse,
Her steps respond to the notes. (Maspero, 1978, 118)

The songs depict shamanesses working in teams of drummers and dancers. First the women purify themselves in water perfumed with orchids and irises. Then they put on robes bearing symbols of the deity they wish to evoke. Taking up a flower appropriate to the season (orchid in spring, chrysanthemum in fall) each shamaness takes her turn dancing to the pounding drums. Her aim is to dance herself to a point of collapse, and send her soul into an out-of-body experience. As she feels herself close to losing consciousness, she passes her flower to the next dancer. If successful, she becomes spirit possessed (*lingbao*). The deities might speak through her words or body movements (Maspero, 1978, 116–119). Or her soul might fly, leaving her body behind "like dead wood" or "burned-out cinders." Hopefully, the human and spirit realms will communicate.

This kind of trance-born communication with another world, or a deeper world, is part of all folk religion in greater China. In Tibet, the modern Buddhist teacher Chagdud Tulku described his mother's role as a village shamaness: "As a child in Tibet, I sometimes found my mother, Delog Dawa Drolma, surrounded by an audience listening with utmost attention as she told of her journeys to other realms. Her face was radiant as she spoke of the deities." When she made journeys, she lay cold and devoid of vital signs for up to five days. All this time she was reportedly traveling between worlds, often escorted by White Tara, the goddess of wisdom (Ray, 2000, 31–32).

The traditional Chinese term for female shamans is *wu*, which Christian missionaries often translated as "witch." Male shamans are called *xi*. In Shang dynasty oracle bone inscriptions (ca. 1300 BCE), the term "wu" applied to both male and female shamans. Later, around 300 BCE, the *Songs of Chu* distinguished xi from wu, but described their powers as basically the same:

> *In ancient times ... there were people who possessed concentrated and undivided minds; who were at the same time reverent and upright; whose intelligence was such as to be invariably able to find out what was fitting and proper for things both above and below; whose wisdom was enough to light up and shine in the remote and dark places; who were as penetrating in seeing as they were thorough in hearing—when there were such people, then illustrious gods would descend on them. If this happened to men, these were called xi; if it happened to women, these women were called wu. (Wu, 1982, 12–13)*

But a division of roles slowly grew between male and female shamans. As the *Rites of Zhou* explained, "The xi [male shamans] officiated over sacrificial ceremonies and healing, while the wu [female shamans] conducted prayers for good fortune and for averting disasters, and danced for rainfall in times of drought" (Du Fangqin, 1995, 201). In general, the xi took more roles serving the rulers. Also, some arts like fengshui (or geomancy) were increasingly reserved for men. Ancient female shamans still played public roles, dealing with community issues like droughts or plagues. But by recent centuries, most people went to shamanesses for private, personal reasons, such as fortune telling, interpreting dreams, contacting dead relatives, or getting herbs for sick babies.

In general, the ancient female shamans of China became its village wise women. Over the centuries, probably most people at least occasionally consulted their local wise women for help with the problems of life. And some of these women were more than neighbors with specialized abilities. Some became famous as guru-like spiritual guides and "masters" in "the way." Daoism has its roots in such local "masters." Before the rise of organized Daoism (in the 100s CE) there were no Daoist "priests." There were only individuals, both men and women, who seemed to be spiritually transcendent (Ching, 1993, 39).

Some "realized masters" were reclusive, living like yogis in caves or mountain forests. Zhuangzi described such a sage-shaman in prose worthy of India's lord Shiva: "There is a holy man living on the distant Gushe mountain, with skin like ice or snow ... He does not eat the five grains, but sucks the wind, drinks the dew ... By concentrating his spirit he can protect creatures from sickness and plague and make the harvest plentiful" (Ching, 1993, 94). It seems people expected their sages to act as shamans, and bring blessings from the spirit world for the whole community.

The schools of female shamanic masters reportedly began with ten immortal sorceresses who collected herbs on Wushan (which means "Shamaness mountain"). These legendary figures founded various branches of women's sorcery, which passed down the generations through lineages of apprenticeship. Some masters of these arts were powerful village leaders. Others were reclusive sages. "Immortal damsels" like Chang Rong, Ziwei Furen, He Xiangu, or Lu Meining lived alone in the forests or mountains. Some of them grew identified with goddesses of nature. The legends of their adventures grew marvelous in the retelling. We hear fantastic tales of divine women retaining their youth far past a normal lifespan. Some are reported riding the clouds as "masters of wind and rain." They shape-shift into birds, or appear as fairy beings of luminous ectoplasmic mist (Shafer, 1980, 44). The Taimu goddess reportedly moved to a cave on Mount Lanshan, achieved immortality, and rose to heaven on a dragon horse of nine colors. In Tang times, the poet Li Bo paid tribute to such an immortal, who took her vows as a Daoist shamaness in 711 (CE):

The immortal lady Jade Perfection
often goes to the peaks of great Mount Hua.
At pure dawn she sounds the celestial drum;
a whirlwind arising, she soars upward on paired dragons.
She plays with lightning without resting her hands,
traverses the clouds without leaving a trace.
Whenever she enters the Minor Apartment Park,
the Queen Mother is there to meet her. (Despeux and Kohn, 2003, 40)

To their followers or students, such women of power were living goddesses. In popular folktales they appeared in spirit, played bewitching music, danced like elves, or talked with ghosts. The link between wu shamaness, enlightened master, and incarnate goddess is preserved in the Buddhist term "dakini," which means "sky dancer" (Simmer-Brown, 2002, 51).

Clearly, the wu and xi shamans were powerful people, able to lead or deceive whole communities. And as certain ambitious leaders became warlord kings, they began trying to control the powers of local shamans. These warlords gathered "official" priests and soothsayers around their courts. In the logic of rising kings, only loyal court priests should predict the future. Only messages that were auspicious for the rulers should come from the spirit world. So the warlords tried to monopolize the role of mediation between people and deities. Some rulers even appointed themselves as high priests. Then they claimed sole authority to represent the people, secure the seasons, and receive an exclusive "mandate of heaven." One legend has it that King Zhuanxu (supposedly of around 2500 BCE) conducted China's first campaign to ban the practices of local holy people. He forbade any humans (other than himself and his court priests) from speaking in the name of gods or spirits. This rule was called "Stopping communication between heaven and earth," which was a fairly honest term for religious censorship. But evidently, Zhuanxu's decree was one of the least effective ever. Because historian Du Fangqin reports that "Shamanism was so prevalent in the Shang dynasty [ca. 1700 to 1050 BCE] that statesmen ... regarded it as a social pollution" (1995, 201). Women still served as shamans in nearly every village. Within their homes, women were still responsible for good relations with the hearth deity. But the difference in power between ruler-sponsored priests and independent shamans grew ever wider with time (Ching, 1993, 21, 39–41, 46).

After the imperial rulers turned to Confucianism as their state religion, there was even less room for female leaders. The Confucian religious bureaucrats simply consulted oracle texts rather than sending shamans on spirit journeys (Palmer, Ramsay, Kwok, 2009, 125). Emperor Wu (141–87 BCE) still had many women playing ritual roles for him. But when he accused one of these women of using magic against him, he had her plus 300 of her friends and relatives executed. During the Tang dynasty (618–906 CE), Confucian officials demanded the removal of Daoist court priestesses such as Li Ye and Yu Xuanji, claiming they were "next to prostitutes" for mixing the roles of official clerics with those of shamanic women (Gou, 1995, 303). By that time, most female shamans were leaders only within local communities, or private gatherings of Daoists.

Outside the ruler's courts, the local female shamans were still numerous and often famous. In heroism, compassion, or magic, women like Chen Jinggu and her band of sworn sisters (on the coast of Fujian in the 700s CE) could shine like voodoo queens of China. Whatever their "official status," the female shamans produced an unending stream of popular cults and saints. The rulers tried to influence which values or leaders the local people followed, but were no more successful than the rajas of India. Most of China's emperors simply offered the lure of special patronage for cults that met their approval. When the cults of wise women grew popular, the rulers often tried to claim credit as patrons of the cult.

Spiritual Teachers of the Opposite Sex

In longstanding Daoist tradition it was necessary, or at least helpful, for spiritual teachers and students to be of the opposite sex. So we commonly find female immortals guiding men, and male immortals teaching women. Some legends say the Yellow Emperor sought wisdom from "the Dark Lady" on Tai Mountain. Then Emperor Yu took instruction on coping with floods from "The Lady of Flowers and Clouds" on Wushan.

In better recorded times, the Daoist master Yang Xi (300s CE) claimed to receive his Shangqing (Highest Clarity) teachings in visions from Lady Wei Huacun, who was the "Primordial Goddess of the Southern Ultimate" (Chan, 1990, 43). Wang Wenqing, founder of the Five Thunders sect of Daoism (1100s CE) was guided to his Thunder Texts by an old lady. She appeared to him in a mountainside hut, saying "I have no surname" (Hymes, 1996, 63). In Tang times, the Daoist seeker Li Quan found a scroll called *The Yellow Emperor's Classic of Using Yin Fire*. He copied and studied it, but couldn't understand it till an old woman appeared and gave him special grains of rice. In one of the more touching tales, a widower man named Hanzi followed his dog into a cave, and emerged into another world. There he found his deceased wife, cleaning fish in the immortals' kitchen. She gave him instructions over several visits, by which he gained the Way. In these and many other stories, a relation with a wise woman was essential for a man's spiritual success.

Such master-disciple relationships could be highly amorous. Yang Xi's visions of Wei Huacun were clearly erotic, despite Yang's emphasis on outward chastity. Besides, the whole shamanic tradition of contacting deities involved ecstatic communion of spirits. As Henri Maspero put it, "It was the beauty of the sorceress which attracted the god and made him choose her" (1978, 117). The term *lingbao*, for spirit possession, is a compound of words for "treasure" and "sacred spirit." *Ling* is a masculine term, and *bao* is feminine. It's a word of sexual connotation (Robinet, 1997, 149–150). Likewise in Tibet, deities are often pictured with consorts, as *yab yum* combinations symbolizing creative union of opposites.

The popular poetry of Tang times (618–906 CE) gives numerous accounts of love affairs between transcendent teachers and disciples. In one poem, a man named Dongfang Shuo follows a strange woman known as Refined Master Jiao to her hut on a mountainside. There, she reveals herself as an intoxicating beauty, glorious as Dante's Beatrice. Dong vows to inscribe her teachings on his bones if she will instruct him. The ancient Master Redpine (Chisongzi) was pursued by the Red Emperor's daughter. She joined him, learned his spiritual secrets, gained immortality with him, and the two flew away to heaven.

Contrary to patriarchal conventions, the holy women in these tales are often portrayed choosing male students, initiating relationships, and leading spiritual lineages. (Bokenkamp, 1996, 169). So a Tang dynasty Daoist master calling herself "a woman of Mount Sung," described a proposal of spiritual marriage:

> I was originally registered at the Realm of Supreme Clarity;
> Dwelling in exile, I wandered the five marchmounts.
> Taking you, milord, as not bound by the common,
> I come here to urge you to divine transcendents' studies.
> Even Ko Hung had a wife!
> The Queen Mother also had a husband!
> Divine transcendents all have numinous mates!
> What would you think of getting together, milord? (Cahill, 1993, 89)

In China, probably most people felt that spirituality and sexuality were quite compatible, and even mutually reinforcing. The spiritual quest was a kind of natural passion. As Suzanne Cahill explains, "Divine passion is the desire of deities and humans for mutual union and communication." Male devotees "united their two greatest longings in worship of the goddess: the wish to transcend death and the desire for perfect love" (1993, 3, 242). In the *Scripture of the Mysterious*

Perfected, Daoist students were instructed to practice visualizing the Jade Maiden of Highest Mystery. They pictured her wearing a purple cap with a cloak and skirt of vermillion brocade. Through practice in visualization her image grew stronger, till her physical presence could be felt. Next, the students pictured the Jade Maiden opening her mouth to emit a brilliant red spiritual light. They opened their mouths to absorb this energy. In the most advanced practice, they visualized the goddess pressing her mouth to theirs, letting her energy fill their hearts (Kohn, 2009, 144). As for female seekers, there's a whole literature on women's relations with gods, and on sex as a spiritual practice for women, which I'll describe in the chapter on Daoism.

Of course the quest for an ultimate union of sex and spirit could turn into ribald comedy, especially in the hands of fun-loving peasants. So the drunken Daoist immortal Lü Dongbin reportedly sought his ultimate union with prostitutes, seducing the courtesan Bai Mudan. Next he made a ludicrous pass at the goddess Guanyin (Katz, 1996, 96). Concerning religious women, He Longxiang rightly observed, "There are those who go on pilgrimages, enter temples, and throw themselves in a disorderly manner at Buddhist and Daoist monks; others again plant the seed of passion into male teachers of good schools. And, of course, there are those who merely use the Dao to collect riches" (Valussi, 2009, 149). But in most religious folklore, the male and female seekers showed more reverence than lust for their opposite-sex teachers. Male students commonly called their teachers "mother," or even "amah" (wet nurse), while female adepts might address male teachers as "milord." Such expressions conveyed both loving intimacy and highest respect for a guide (Cahill, 1993, 154, 208).

These teacher-student relationships were often quite intimate, like Indian guru-devotee relationships. It was not like joining an organization and following whatever leader the institution appointed. The masters often represented "teaching lineages," which transmitted specific bodies of knowledge to a handful of students in each generation. And for such "mind to mind" transmissions, the masters and pupils had to choose each other personally. Of course many, or even most, master-pupil relationships were strictly non-erotic, as the term "mother" suggests. And probably most disciples of goddesses or wise women have always been women, learning from other women. Probably the main point is that men and women commonly thought they had much to learn from each other. As the male Daoist teacher Cao Heng explained (in 1631),

> As for the practice of the "other," it is to borrow what the "other" possesses to refine what "I" does not have. It is the key to perfecting Dao, and the wondrous secret for the ultimate transformation. It is not to be confused with what the world calls the deviant ways of the bedchamber arts. All the immortals and buddhas who ascended to Heaven have done so without exception by these means. (Xun, 2009, 121)

Of course many "teachers" in shamanic religion are said to be disembodied spirits, channelled by "sensitive" souls. Probably most leaders of "popular religion" have believed themselves channels for spirit guides. Most Daoist scriptures have been "spirit writing," taken down as dictated from beyond. And the spirits so channeled commonly fit the pattern of opposite-sex teachers. So it was with Yang Xi's Shangqing scriptures. Qu Yuan (ca. 300 BCE) also claimed that his *Songs of Chu* came from a female shaman spirit. She told him of her journeys to the Princess of the East, the goddess of the sun, the directors of destiny, or the goddesses of the Xiang River (Maspero, 1978, 366–368). Spirit writing was always a big part of Chinese religion. We even have goddesses of spirit writing, whose tales are combinations of comedy and tragedy, such as Qi Gu and Zi Gu. These are "toilet goddesses." They were women killed in nasty love triangles, and their bodies dumped in outhouses. Thereafter they appeared to people in the toilet, giving them deep thoughts. Where else do people get all their good ideas?

The Ancient Ways of Family Life

Like in most countries, the wealthiest and most powerful families usually set "the standards" for family life. And after the rise of nobles and warlords, the top males in top families commonly became true patriarchs. In these standard-setting families, the supremacy of males over females seemed almost as fundamental as in top families of Arabia. But these kinds of families were actually abnormal in China. Most people were poorer, less powerful, and less concerned with anyone's status. The average family could never afford to confine women; everybody had to work. Most villagers lived far from the power-centers and followed their own local ways. In ordinary working families, it was mainly a matter of opinion as to who was important. The women could easily view themselves as the central actors.

Of course the oldest, most traditional family values were those of nomadic hunters and gatherers, who roamed the countryside for about 99% of human history. And concerning such primitive clans (as observed in many corners of the world), Robert O'Connell feels we can make a few generalizations. Their lives involved "a relatively low-key existence emphasizing personal independence, general equality among group members, including women, consensus-based decision making achieved through open and protracted discussion, and freedom of movement, particularly as a means of conflict resolution" (1995, 226). In this kind of community, there was basically no way for men or women to systematically control each other. If anyone got abusive or demanded primacy, other people could just go their own way. Men and women probably behaved as in the ancient Buddhist legend of Uttarakuru: "When the men and women of Uttarakuru want to unite in love, they only obey their hearts and show their desire by casting glances at each other. When a girl recognizes the feelings of a man in this way, she immediately accompanies him, and thus they walk together under the miracle trees" (Bauer, 1976, 168).

In prehistoric clans, people probably didn't understand the role of males in producing children. The old myths told of women getting pregnant from spirits of wind or water. In that world, men didn't own the women or children. They just knew that women bore children, and the clan members helped raise them.

During the "Golden Age," clans from this background formed settled bases of operations. But despite living in villages, their ways of life changed little for another several thousand years. Down to Zhou dynasty times (1000s to 200s BCE), the names of even noble families were recorded as "womb clans." Among the 24 recorded names of Zhou princely families, 16 contained the radical *nu*, for "woman," so that the clan names meant "born of woman X" (Ho, 1975, 277). For the Zhou warlords, these were just ancient names inherited from a previous age. But outside the domains of warlord rulers, many "barbarian tribes" kept their traditional matrilineal clans alive.

In a matrilineal clan, people traced their ancestry through their mothers, with land or houses inherited by the daughters. The men either married into the household, or visited the clan's women as "special friends." These were traditions the rising warlords and male autocrats presumed to correct. By Zhou times (ca. 1000 to the 200s BCE), the warlord states of the northern plains had strongly patriarchal ruling families. And their court scribes recorded tall tales of contrary customs among the "southern barbarians." There were reports of lands where women ruled, and only daughters were raised. In some accounts the women were ferocious warriors, and sexually rapacious on capturing men (Cai, 1995, 59). Such stories were fanciful inversions of the warlords' "family values," but they were not total fantasies. There really were non-patriarchal tribes across most of China. Their traditions survived into historic times, or even down to the present.

Especially in the deep South, or on islands like Hainan or Taiwan, many regional cultures still reflect old matrilineal customs (Min, 1995, 555). On Taiwan, the ethnic groups with a history of "matriarchal" clans include the Ahmei, the Pingpu, Yamei, and the Beinan (Cai, 1995, 76–77). In Tongtou village of Fujian, a famous matrilineal family, (named Zou) thrived until the nineteenth century. A hundred or more family members lived together under a grand matron. Only after their collective great-grandmother died did the family break into smaller units (Zhao Shiyu, 1995, 369). In Tibet or Yunnan, many local cultures allowed married women to stay in their mother's households, or even to marry more than one man. Cai Junsheng suggests that all these cases "should be regarded as prehistoric vestiges." In these cultures, women generally stayed in their mother's homes to carry on the female lineage, and they kept control of their sexual lives (1995, 89, 36). Shocking as it seemed to most later subjects of the empire, it appears that primitive women had sexual freedom. The exclusive, legally binding arranged marriages came later.

Some community rituals from pre-patriarchal culture remained popular over most of recorded history. Many communities worshiped the snake goddess Nü Wa in an annual spring festival, somewhat like the pagan European May Day. The ceremonies involved sacrificing animals for a communal feast, and holding folk dances with song fests, mostly of love songs. After viewing each-others' performances, young men and women were free to choose partners and go to the fields to make love. Such ceremonies continued as "spring festivals" for Yao communities down to recent times in Guangxi or Guangdong. In many areas, rites of spring involved communal bathing in a river or lake. Even married people who wished to ensure their fertility could join in. According to Cai Junsheng, "This was clearly a practice derived from the custom of group marriage handed down from the matriarchal age" (1995, 41, 84). From the memory of such traditions, Nü Wa became a divine match-maker in Chinese myths (Gernet, 1962, 124).

Naturally, such "pre-Confucian" traditions drew the interest of modern social scientists and artists. The Communist government produced an educational video called *Amazing Marriage Practices*, to explore the diversity of traditions throughout the country. The film made sense of variety by arranging different customs in an evolutionary order, from "matriarchal" to "patriarchal," and finally to socialist monogamy (Brownell and Wasserstrom, 2002, 382). A more sympathetic view appeared in the 1985 film *Sacrificed Youth*, by Zhang Nuanxin. This told the tale of a young Han Chinese woman who was sent to an ethnic Dai village in Guangxi during the 1960s Cultural Revolution. There, she learned from the "uninhibited" Dai girls to express her sexuality. Of course we also have the modern rumor mill of titillating tales about women in China's cultural minorities. The cruder rumors usually report that non-Han women are sexually available, go about with bare breasts, or have orgies.

We might get an impression that these ethnic minorities are like exotic aboriginals, whose ways are totally different from those of mainstream Han Chinese. But though recognized cultural minorities comprise only 8.1 % of China's population (1990 census), the land they occupy covers between 50 and 60% of the country (Schein, 2002, 392, 386). These vast regions were conquered by an expanding empire. Then the rulers worked to standardize social customs on the model of their imperial courts. The communities which conformed the slowest were labeled as less civilized, and less Chinese.

The Na, or Moso people of Yunnan are one minority group where many people still follow an ancient lifestyle of matrilineal extended families. In their villages, land and houses are commonly inherited by daughters, and people take their mothers' surnames. Each lineage traces itself back to a founding mother, and many villagers worship a supreme goddess. The nearby Naxi people also traditionally lived in matrilineal "daughter clans." Their buildings, lands, animals, and farm tools all belonged the matrilineal household, with earnings or crop yields pooled and distributed among relatives (Cai, 1995, 64–65).

In Na and Naxi tradition, men and women did not practice marriage as established in North China. Usually, lovers did not live together, but visited each other as "special friends" by night. Both men and women lived with their mother's clans, and helped provide for any children their sisters had. The men played a parenting role, but it was mainly to their sister's children, not to the children of their lovers. It was an arrangement with priority on the bonds of mothers, sisters, and brothers.

Since the Na men were not formal heads of their households, many outside observers described the culture negatively, claiming it was "a society without fathers or husbands" (Cai, 2001, 123). The men were often managers of the family business, but their mothers were the real family heads. Below the clan matriarchs, family chiefs oversaw day-to-day operations, and most families had both a male and a female chief.

The sexual life of the Naxi and Na has generated a lot of interest in recent decades. Especially for the Na, there is a tradition of fairly free sexual visitation between men and women of different lineages. Anthropologist Cai Hua calls it "polyandrogyny" (2001, 259). In this tradition, girls are initiated into womanhood at about age 13, and receive rooms of their own. Then they are free to receive night visits from any boys they like. The boys come to a girl's door, identify themselves, and ask to be admitted. The girl chooses whether or not to unlock her door. Of course many mothers remain protective of their girls for some time. One mother accosted boys hiding in her girl's courtyard after dark, saying "Come back later. She is still too young. She is only 13 years old." The boys answered, "That's okay! By fooling around with us now, she'll grow even faster and better!" (Cai, 2001, 219).

The Na term for lovers is *ah xiao,* or "special friends." Cai Hua translates this as an "açia" relationship. The most common convention is for lovers to visit each other in a "furtive visit," with an option to keep the affair totally secret. As Cai describes the rules of the game:

> *The furtive visit, as a modality of sexual life, is basically characterized by the following facts: the free will of each person*

*is both necessary and sufficient to establish and maintain the
açia relationship; the desire of one partner is enough to end
it; a multiplicity of partners; and the discontinuity of the açia
relationship. It includes four restrictions: a woman must not visit
a man; a visitor must avoid the male consanguineal relatives of
the woman he is visiting; daytime visits are forbidden; and the
individuals who want the same person must not argue or fight.
(2001, 232)*

It's taboo for persons of the same matrilineage to have sexual
relations, and it's even taboo for males and females of the same family
to mention sexual matters to each other. Sexual life is considered very
private, and therefore the family members most commonly practice
the furtive visit. By custom, a man visits his lover after midnight,
and disappears before dawn.

Cai Hua found the Na extremely vivacious, yet shy and secretive.
Of course secrets get around in a small village. For example, "Adga
was a beautiful and hospitable 23-year-old woman. According to the
villagers she had already had 102 açia, only one of which lasted for
more than a year" (2001, 197). The men are free to try their luck
with any woman within a few hours walking distance. In general, the
further away her visitor lives, the prouder a woman is. The length
of her lover's journey proves the strong attraction of her beauty. The
same thing is true for a man. The more success he has winning lovers
in far-off villages, the prouder he is. Being welcomed so far from his
home gives proof of his desirability (2001, 212).

If two or more men want the same woman, most Na regard it as
immaturity if one tries to get controlling. They have a saying: "Your
çia is also my çia and your çia is also my çia." Cai says, "an attempt to
monopolize one's partner is always considered shameful and stupid,
and the villagers will mock it for a long time" (2001, 214, 247). Where
this is the social reality, "special friends" do not "own" each other,
and have no exclusive rights over each other. Lovers can visit each

other freely, but don't set up economically separate households. They usually offer each other gifts, but don't depend on each other for essential needs. Any children born are raised in their mother's house, with all the brothers and sisters serving as extra parents.

In the Na's "family values," there is little or no sense that some "special friendships" are legitimate, while others are "sinful" (save between relatives of the same mother). There is no sense that some children are more "legitimate" than others. There have always been cases of mothers aborting unwanted babies. But the Na style of family life avoided some problems of patriarchal culture, such as abandoned orphans, "illegitimate bastards," unhappy arranged marriages, or cast off widows and divorcees.

The Na, Naxi, and other groups may seem "non-Chinese." But according to their own legends, the Naxi came south to Yunnan and Sichuan from northern China in ancient times, perhaps to escape domination by the rising empires there. In that case, the Naxi could represent something of early traditions from the northern plains, before those areas came under an increasingly patriarchal system.

Why did matrilineal families fade away over so much of China? In later chapters I'll describe in some detail how imperial rulers slowly imposed their values on the subject people. But in the case of the Naxi, this didn't start until the 1200s (CE), when the Mongol horde swept further south than most invading armies. The conquerors presumed to inflict their system on the southerners, who they regarded as unusually backward. For example, the Yuan (Mongol) dynasty official Zhou Zhihong contemptuously wrote (of the Loulou people in northern Yunnan), "Their leader was a woman, and mothers were in charge of everything. A noblewoman had as many as one hundred husbands" (Cai, 1995, 61).

Despite this judgmental tone, the Mongols were somewhat tolerant, or at least indifferent. They let locals like the Naxi live according to their own traditions—provided that (as the *History of the Yuan Dynasty* put it) "they accept the command of the central authorities, hand in tribute and taxes, and allow their headmen to be appointed by the higher authorities." If they did all that, then "the rest would remain unchanged" (Cai, 1995, 63). But of course the appointment of male headmen accountable to the central warlords changed the very nature of matrilineal clans. And a slow erosion of the matriarchs' powers continued down to recent decades. Still, to this day most Naxi people know which matrilineal clan their ancestors belong to (Cai, 1995, 61–62).

This story of the Naxi under Mongol rule is quite normal in Chinese history. Because a basically similar chain of events unfolded in every region of the country. In the empire's heartlands it happened earlier, but even there the Han Chinese villagers retained something of their oldest traditions. For example, the old Chinese word for "family name" (xing) is a compound of symbols for "woman" and "bear," which suggests a typical matrilineal totem-clan (Min, 1995, 553). A traditional term for the dead describes them as "in Amah's [the mother's] household." In modern China, one of the most common phrases for "home" means "my mother's house." The residential classification system of the People's Republic has categorized people by their mother's birthplace (Cahill, 1993, 240; Davis, 1989, 88–89; Jankowiak, 2008, 92–93). The Communist Party has typically addressed the people as "tongbao." Usually this is translated as "brothers," but it means "children of the same womb" (Brownell and Wasserstrom, 2002, 438). Especially in the southern half of the country, women's authority has remained famously strong. Mao Zedong said that in villages of his native Hunan province, the men had scarcely any authority over women. Women worked the fields along with men, had roughly equal say in all decisions, and had "considerable sexual freedom" (Spence, 1999, 376). As for the present day, Shaun Rein says "Shanghai women are very powerful creatures; they control the money in most households" (2009, 52).

So in China's founding myths, men and women were created equal. Later, ambitious warlords tried to "correct" that image, with limited success. But the dream of equal partnership still filled the folk tales, love songs, and religious visions of popular culture. It was like the nagging Western intuition that in the beginning there were no slaves. Dreams like that were persistent, and at times overwhelmingly powerful.

5: Deities of Living Lands and Seas

Like peasants in medieval Europe, the "superstitious" villagers of ancient China believed that everything was alive. To them, the streams, forests, mountains, or shorelines seemed enchanted, like the landscapes of ancient Japan. In the days of humanity's childhood, the world seemed vibrant with spirits of majestic power and beauty, be they storm dragons, fox women, or mountain immortals. That wonder-filled countryside was imprinted in popular memory as the earth's original face.

In classical landscape painting, South China was a tapestry of misty peaks and bamboo forests. The artists seemed to capture their vistas from above, like shamans in flight. Far below, tiny human figures appeared like ants, plodding on their journeys through a land of mystery. Each valley in that environment was largely self-enclosed, and its people self-reliant. Each village or cluster of villages had its local deity of the earth. Sometimes the domains of deities matched the borders of clan territories (Wu, 1982, 8). Or maybe the deities were animating spirits of each environment, regardless of who came there.

In the view of some cultures, the areas of natural wilderness were just godless wastelands. The cities and palaces of rulers seemed far closer to the divine. But most Chinese people felt that wild nature was closer to the sacred. In countless Daoist tales, travelers in the forests claimed to meet an old man with twinkling eyes, or a proud woman with disheveled hair (Hymes, 1996, 64). In popular myth, the gods or goddesses of each place could appear in human form. Maybe they were there from the beginning. Or maybe they were people transformed, like shamans who left on a journey and never came back. But however people imagined their local deities, most hard-headed villagers were believers. They felt it obvious that behind their surrounding environment, they were dealing with something alive, willful, and intelligent. People raised shrines to their local deities, praised their beauty in poems, or wooed them like dream lovers. Seldom in world mythology do we see nature treated with such tender admiration.

The Women Behind the World

Ancient people tended to project their own image on the universe, so that everything seemed to have gender. As gold was solid Yang essence of the sun, so pearls were Yin essence of the moon. Water especially seemed to be female. The rivers, rainclouds, mountain mists, or glittering seas were fountains of liquid life, flowing from the source of life. Behind their sparkling surfaces moved animating spirits, whose beauty the waters only reflected. As a modern businesswoman in Shanghai explained, "Everybody says women are like water. I think it's because water is the source of life, and it adapts itself to its environment. Like women, water also gives itself wherever it goes to nurture life" (Xinran, 2002, 223).

Of course people see the angels, demons, or deities they expect to see. And their divinities usually wear the fashions of local convention. So the goddesses behind China's environment slowly changed with the styles of the times. The earliest deities shifted between human and animal shape, taking the forms of all their creatures. So, around 220 CE, a carriage driver told the poet Cao Zhi of the goddess he saw in the Lo River waters:

> As to her form,
> she flutters like a startled swan,
> she twists and turns like a roving dragon.
> She wears head ornaments of gold and halcyon feathers,
> and strewn with shining pearls that make her torso radiant!
> (Shafer, 1980, 68–70)

Ancient people commonly pictured the animating power in water as a dragon, or a snake woman like Nü Wa. In hundreds of local cults they evoked the spirits of life's essence, much as they would a beloved woman. During the Tang dynasty, Cen Shen described such rites at the shrine of the Dragon Woman:

The Dragon Woman—from whence does she come?
But when she comes—she rides the wind and rain!
At the hall of her fame, below the blue woods,
she coils sinuously, as if about to speak to you.
Men of Shu vie there, with worshipful thoughts,
To offer her wine to the beating of drums. (Shafer, 1980, 60–61)

But over the centuries, the goddesses increasingly cast off their feathers, their guise as dragons or wild cats, and appeared as charming ladies in fine silk gowns. The goddesses of nature grew less intimidating and more alluring, like perfect consorts of the imperial palace (Chan, 1990, 17–18). In a mixture of dream and vision, countless poets turned their rhapsodies of communion with nature into erotic encounters with the goddesses behind it all. Rather than wild women of primal nature, these goddesses were enchantresses of refined intelligence. So the Maiden in the Mist of the Xiang River reportedly left her admirer a poem:

That red tree—the color of intoxication in autumn
That blue stream—a string strummed at night
A delightful meeting that may not be repeated:
This wind and rain are blurring them, as will the years.
(Shafer, 1980, 125–126)

Some goddesses changed from being powers of nature into beloved daughters of legendary emperors. The goddess Fufei was reportedly a daughter of the snake emperors Fu Xi and Nü Wa. As the girl wandered one day by the Luo River banks, she gazed into the water, and the river's spirit fell in love with her. Over the stream's surface it cast rippling visions of mountain gorges, waterfalls, and pristine beaches. Enchanted, the girl stepped into the water, and the river spirit eagerly pulled her down. There, she became the goddess of the Luo, who has filled the region's folklore down to the present. In 1923, Fufei featured in a Peking Opera production staring Mei Lanfang. In this version of events, the goddess appeared to Prince Cao Zijian, who was staying at an inn by the river, and the two had a long, tender conversation (Huang, 2004, 37). Clearly, the mythical women behind the world retained their romantic appeal.

The Community's Representatives Before Nature

For primitive people, it seemed obvious that shifts in the weather were mood changes on the part of greater beings. Droughts, floods, or typhoons were the work of mighty storm dragons, who could be friends or enemies. To survive in a world of mysterious powers, people needed to befriend these spirits. Without good relations, anything could happen. The seasons could change order, or seas and lands might switch places. The plants people depended on for food might depart like flocks of angry geese, leaving the villagers abandoned in a desert (Gernet, 1962, 197). Of course everyone was responsible for treating the powers of nature well. But in times of danger from disease, flood, or drought, it was the shamans' job to act as the people's ambassadors. Effective shamans performed dances or rites in a way that charmed the deities of earth, water, and sky. In spirit they traveled to meet the deities, and win their affection or mercy. In their tasks of rain making, storm quelling, fertility invoking, or healing, female shamans seemed especially fit for the task.

In North China, where the rainfall came in short seasonal bursts, it was crucial for shamans to determine the right days for planting. It was not just a matter of predicting the weather, but also of winning nature's favor. If the local shamans gave wrong advice and the crops failed, it would seem they had led their community to disaster. We should note that shamanhood was a burden, not a privilege. Where

57

the villagers' survival was at stake, the responsibility was heavy. In times of drought, many shaman women exposed themselves to the sun, fasted, and vowed to die if necessary to bring rain.

On returning from their trance flights from the spirit world, the shamans often brought prophetic messages. They explained which deeds had offended the powers of nature, and how the villagers could make amends (Hayes, 1985, 97). Sometimes the shamans called for rituals to pay the spirits respect. Sometimes they urged practical measures, like protecting trees, conserving water, or blocking soil erosion. They were supposed to speak for the powers of life.

But as early warlords began conquering the villages around them, these strongmen started claiming shamanic authority for themselves. If the warlord held power over the villages and their shamans, then surely he was the one to speak for his subjects. Some warlords reasoned that if the local deity was a goddess, then surely he, as the strongest man of the region, was best suited to win her heart. Maybe it was just a public relations stunt, but King Huai (of the Chu state, late 300s BCE) claimed he had won the love of Yaoji, a celestial maiden who haunted his region's greatest mountain, Wushan (or "Shamaness Mountain"). Reportedly, the goddess gave King Huai an affectionate poem, like a portrait of herself: "On the sunlit slope of Shamaness Mountain, at the steep places of the high hill—your handmaiden is 'Dawn Cloud' in the morning, 'Moving Rain' in the evening. Dawn after dawn, evening after evening, on the sunlit platform" (Shafer, 1980, 45). King Huai dedicated a Temple of the Morning Cloud to Yaoji. His good relations with the goddess seemed to ensure all would be well under his rule—despite the advancing enemy armies which soon crushed his state.

As military rulers expanded their domains, they moved to directly usurp and suppress the role of village shamans. They claimed central authority for mediating with deities, and ordered local shamans to cease doing so. Of course such presumption had its price. In taking power to speak for the deities, the rulers became accountable for appeasing nature. According to legend, Lord Dang (Tang), first emperor of the Shang dynasty (ca. 1700s BCE), let himself be sacrificed to end a terrible drought. And in 30 BCE, a provincial governor reportedly rushed to the banks of the Yellow River as it threatened a disastrous flood. To appease the river's spirit, he generously sacrificed a gray horse. But neither this nor the incantations of priestly officials halted the rising water. Finally, the governor and one assistant resolved to stand before the waters as everyone else fled. The river reportedly crested at their feet, then receded in respect for true leadership (Lowe, 1968, 113).

In the Confucian *Classic of Rites*, we read of early Zhou princes trying to play the shaman's role, not by dancing and going into trances like shamanic women, but through presiding over dignified court rituals. It seemed civilized to replace the unruly rites of shamanic wild women with pompous offerings or proclamations. And such reforms did bring order from chaos, especially because only one set of ruler-appointed priests now spoke for the deities. When state-employed priests read the signs and omens, they almost always predicted success and long life for the ruler. The traditional shamans were not nearly so reliable. Still, the court priests retained some aspects of shamanic tradition. They often made a show of urging respect for nature's powers. So the *Classic of Rites* advised that during the first month of spring,

> *The rules for sacrifices shall be reviewed and orders given for offerings to the spirits of the mountains, forests, rivers, and lakes, but for these sacrifices no female creature may be used [that is, killed].*

> *It shall be forbidden [in the first month of spring] to cut down trees, to destroy nests, to kill young insects, the young yet in the womb, or the new born, or fledgling birds. All young of animals and eggs shall be spared. (De Bary and Chan, 1960, vol. I, 209–210)*

Later, as all China came under centralized rule, the emperors claimed to represent the whole Middle Kingdom before the Lord of Heaven. They became China's fisher-kings, symbolically responsible for environmental problems, and in charge of adjusting the calendar. In august rites at the celestial court, the emperors served as intermediaries to interpret Heaven's will. They usurped the role of all village shamans, saying that only one man had "the Mandate of Heaven." So, the emperors presided over rituals to open the seasons, calling for nature's goodwill. Their ritual performances still involved beautiful women, but only as gracious servants of the court, not as shamans in their own right. During the reign of Emperor Wu (141–87 BCE), the official rites of spring included the *Songs for Suburban Sacrifice in Nineteen Parts*. This was an outdoor performance, in which gorgeously dressed female dancers invoked the "green and yellow" of new life:

> *The Gods are now enthroned,*
> *the Five Tones harmonize.*
> *Happy till the dawn,*
> *we offer the Gods pleasure.*
> ....
> *The Gods serenely linger,*
> *we chant "Green" and "Yellow."*
> *All round mediate on this,*
> *gaze at the green jade hall.*
> *A crowd of beauty gathers,*
> *refined, perfect loveliness:*
> *Faces like flowering rush,*
> *rivals in dazzling glamour,*
> *wearing flowery patterns,*
> *interwoven misty silks,*
> *with trains of white voile,*
> *girdles of pearl and jade.*

They hear Blissful-night and Flag-orchid,
iris and orchid perfumed.
Calm and peaceful,
We offer up the chalice. (Birrell, 1988, 35)

These women were still ambassadors to nature, but only if they worked for the emperor. Their powers to evoke blessing were now tools in service to their patron. But if most villagers had accepted the emperor's claim to be their sole representative before nature, they would have simply let him intercede with the deities for them. As it was, the villagers continued their own appeals to local deities, as they had the past (Wu, 1982, 16–17). They continued invocations like this one, from a ritual text of the Laku people:

Three times in one day, three times in one night, ensure that the lives of the animals suffer no decay; let the animals' hairs not fall out; you who watch over all our animals, you all-true, all-seeing blesser of this house ... watch over all the animals ... this boon order and bestow on us.

Oh blesser of this house, within the four corners of this house may the womenfolk and the menfolk, the big and the small, enjoy easy thoughts; let there be no troubled thoughts either behind or in front; let men of evil intent not prevail against us, let malicious spirits not harm us; at this one corner within the four corners of this house [where the house's alter is located], I once again search for this boon. (Walker, 1996, 334)

Likewise, the people of Longwanggou village in Shaanxi appealed directly to their local Black Dragon King, as they do today: "Oh Dragon King your Highness, we beg you to bless us. We beg you to grant us some rainwater, otherwise, the crops are going to dry up and die" (Chau, 2006, 78–79).

Of course many people rejected the superstitious notion of contacting spirits or deities. Already back in the first century CE, Wang Chong (Wang Ch'ung) argued it was foolish to think that storms, droughts, or floods, were divine punishments for human misdeeds. Natural disasters were not judgments on the emperor for mismanaging the world. Nor were people's fortunes in health or wealth related to their moral conduct (Lowe, 1968, 101–102). Wang urged people to liberate themselves from such misconceptions. But most people remained superstitious. They believed that their conduct affected the environment, that nature was alive, and every deed had consequences in a living world.

Many people think that shamanism is a dead religion, which belongs to the prehistoric age of wandering tribes. But in China, shamanism never died. There are still traditional shamans in remote places like Manchuria. And in most communities, the shamanic role of contacting spirits simply passed to modern specialists. Almost every village has its spirit mediums for contacting ghosts or deities. Almost every community has geomancers or fengshui specialists for relating to the spirits and energies of the earth. Probably most modern shamans are women, and some of them make good money.

Fighting the Forces of Nature

Of course the powers of nature were destructive as well as life giving, and ruling men often sought to simply suppress them. So we hear that when the first emperor of China tried to cross the Yangzi (ca. 219 BCE), he faced furious storms which nearly sank his boats. Clearly, the river goddess had tried to kill him. To punish such treason, the emperor ordered destruction of the goddess's temple on a nearby mountain. As if to strip and humiliate her, he ordered 3,000 convicts to cut down every tree on the mountain, leaving the slopes above the river bare (Cotterell, 1981, 156).

By Han times (206 BCE to 220 CE), many Confucian officials viewed the traditionally female powers of nature as threats to their own power. They even regarded rainbows as ominous signs. Such appearances of water power in the sky seemed to be "wanton and depraved." They were signs of disorder, in which "the wife mounts the husband: a manifestation of Yin dominating Yang." So at the death of Emperor Zhongzong in 710 (CE), one of his wives tried to place her young boy on the throne, and then rule as a regent for the child. At this, "manly" men overthrew and killed her. The dynastic historians claimed it was all foretold in a dangerous omen: "A double rainbow dragon traversed the sky ... The omen reads: 'King-bearers and consorts coerce the kingly one by means of their Yin.'" Later, as the empire suffered catastrophic floods in 813, court officials convinced Emperor Li Chun that the problem was an excess of Yin influence. To solve this, they expelled 200 wagonloads of women from the emperor's courts (Schafer, 1980, 24, 28, 8–9). It was almost like the time the Roman church expelled all wives of priests (in 1074 CE), and then accused village wise women of conjuring the forces of nature.

Even village people sometimes used coercive measures to control their goddesses of nature. In Song times (900s to 1200s) we hear of villagers whipping sacred stones, to punish the local earth deities for bringing flood or drought. In one case, the villagers threw worn-out women's shoes and dead pigs into a deep pool. They meant to show their anger at the pool's divine dragon, for refusing to heed their pleas for rain (Gernet, 1962, 207). So, people saw their deities as a mixture of good and evil. If the gods and goddesses were like parents, they could be cruel parents. If nature was a beautiful mother, she could easily kill her children.

In modern times (1958), another Great Helmsmen, Mao Zedong, declared war on the "four evils" of nature, namely birds, rats, insects, and flies. The people were instructed to exterminate these creatures. Within a year the villagers quit the battle. They said it did more harm than good, especially since birds ate the insects (Li, 2000, 113). People resumed their normal attitude, that nature was a power to befriend, not an enemy to defeat.

The Community of All Creatures

Like ancient Egyptians or Native Americans, early Chinese tribes commonly saw animals as their ancestors. In Yao tradition, people evolved from the bees. The Yao goddess Milotou trained the bees three times each day, and breast-fed them till they grew into human beings. Myths of the snake deities Nü Wa and Fu Xi probably came from tribal groups who claimed descent from snakes. The Naxi of Yunnan claimed to be tiger people, and forbade killing their ancestral cats. Many old clan names are written with the radical *chong*, which means "[of] insects and other creatures" (Cai, 1995, 37–38, 41, 72). In general, many of China's tribes claimed ancestral lineages longer than those of biblical patriarchs. Until the recent past, most Westerners thought that such legends of animal ancestors were superstitions.

Naturally, the belief that animals or plants were ancestors made those creatures seem like relatives of the village community. This suggested a need for good family relations. To get along, there had to be mutual respect. Abuse of helpful creatures was bound to bring bad results. We see this attitude clearly in many aboriginal cultures of South China, Tibet, or Taiwan, but it's also present in mainstream Han Chinese traditions.

In the Ne culture (of Sichuan and Yunnan) native tradition and Buddhist morality seem to complement each other, as shown in a scripture called the *Book of Good Deeds*. The text is partly about good relations with farm animals, so that big and little help each other. To some Western farmers and ranchers this advice may seem uneconomic, but here it is:

> *There are common people who let their cattle and horses wallow in dung. One should not let the dung in a cowshed to be too deep and watery. Though the dung may be deep and watery, they [the animals] still let people ride upon them and use them for draft purposes. They do such good things and are without sin, so we*

should cherish them. How could one lock them up to soak in the ooze of watery dung? The Han people lock up those who have committed great crimes in watery prisons.

Next we see Ne attitudes toward killing farm animals. The Ne have not revered cows in a Hindu way, but they generally found cows more helpful as draft animals and fertilizer producers than as meat. Maybe they've felt for cows like most Westerners feel for horses. At any rate, the *Book of Good Deeds* warns against cruelty:

If you have a cow and kill its calf, you will cause the mother to go crying from the tops of the hills to the bottoms of the valleys in search of it, a most pathetic state of affairs.

The better people among the Han who do good deeds will not have eaten the meat of cattle or horses for thirty generations of their ancestors. When a Han person who kills lots of cattle to make beef jerky is about to die and thinks back on all the cattle he has killed, he cannot help but cry out like all the cattle as they were dying. And when he dies, he will certainly turn into an ox or cow.

Did such regard for non-human life extend to insects? Over much of South China and Tibet it did. For those who respected even the insects, the Ne scripture said the rewards were enormous:

In olden times in the land of Han there was a man named Song Jiao who saw an ants' nest that was being flooded, so he used a bamboo strip as a sort of bridge to let the ants go across to dry land, thereby rescuing tens of thousands of them. The Lord of Heaven, recognizing that he had done a good deed ... gave him blessings and grain and made him a prime minister of the emperor.

But for those who greatly offended nature, the punishments would be horrid:

When spring arrives, the wild creatures are pregnant, birds lay their eggs, and so do bugs and ants. When we hunt wild animals or shoot flying birds, fires are set in the wilds to capture the animals. They burn in the hills and burn in the valleys, burning tens of thousands of bugs and ants. This should not be. Therefore, it is said that those who set many fires in the wilds have no hidden virtue and their descendants will get leprosy.

Any creature could be a powerful spirit, and it would be unwise to make enemies. So the Buddhists of northeast Shanxi believed that their region was ruled by the bodhisattva Manjushri. A visitor reported, "When one enters this region of His Holiness Manjushri, if one sees a lowly man, one does not dare to feel contemptuous, and if one meets a donkey, one wonders if it might be a manifestation of Manjushri" (Campbell, 1986, 449).

The Ne, and probably most ancient Chinese, believed that the living spirits of each place saw everything that happened. Any secret selfishness was known. All good or bad deeds brought their own response from creatures all around. Therefore: "Do not cheat in a dark room ... If you do something in the dark, thinking that no one will know, the spirit of the room knows" (all quotes from the *Book of Good Deeds* cited by Mair, 1996, 412–419).

Did this regard for other lives extend to the plant kingdom? In many primitive communities it did. The aboriginal people of Taiwan had strict rules concerning the humane treatment of food plants: "In the swidden rituals, the people had direct transactions with the foxtail millet, which they treated as if it were a being equipped with human sense organs ... To mistreat ... plants demonstrated disrespect toward the ancestral spirits. For this reason it was taboo to beat the foxtail [millet] with a stick or flail, [or] harvest en masse as with a sickle" (Fogg, 1983, 108–109).

Most Han Chinese villagers didn't display obvious reverence for plants or animals. But they commonly felt that success on the farm required people, plants, and animals to get along in a mutually beneficial way. The domestication of crops and animals was a process of forming friendships, as in the rather stunning friendship of rice farmers with water buffaloes. As for plants, domestication of grains multiplied the progeny of grain plants, so agronomists wonder whether the humans or plants benefitted most. And then there were symbiotic relations between non-human creatures which the villagers encouraged, as when they learned that rice, beans, mulberry trees, ducks, and carp fish all helped each other to grow. The humans in this landscape were not just takers, using up a finite resource. They acted like matchmakers, trying to foster cooperation between creatures.

In 1149 (CE), Zhen Bu (Chen Pu) summed up many centuries of farm experience in a treatise on Chinese multicrop aquaculture. He described how the villagers made each creature help the next: "On the embankments [of ponds] plant mulberry and pomegranate trees on which cows can be tethered. The cows will be comfortable under the shade of the trees; embankments will be strengthened because the cows constantly tread on them; and the mulberry trees will grow beautifully because of the nourishing water" (Ebrey, 1981, 110). In the flooded rice fields, a symbiosis of fish, grass, rice, and algae produced the most efficient farming system in world history. The output of energy is about 50 times greater than the input (Ponting, 1991, 291–292).

Naturally, the more successful this farming civilization grew, the more people it supported. And the greater the population, the more challenging it was to feed them all. On top of this, society added the burdens of taxes, tribute to lords, subdivision of land, interest on loans, confiscation of debtors' property, etc. Over the centuries these combined burdens tended to increase, till villagers across China were reduced to impoverished misery. But despite all these burdens, most villagers tried to manage their orchestra of living things sustainably. In many cases they achieved a balance we call permaculture, where the land could produce thousands of harvests, and its fertility remained undiminished. As Sir Alfred Howard reported, "The agricultural practices of the Orient have passed the supreme test— they are almost as permanent as those of the primeval forest, of the prairie, or of the ocean" (Shiva, 1988, 105). Maybe this is actually the crowning achievement of human civilization to date. And maybe the future of humanity depends on spreading such village wisdom around the world.

In the Confucian version of Golden Age dreams, emperors of perfect wisdom once governed the land as if tending a garden of human souls. Confucian sages hoped to cultivate human potential, as if this was the greatest crop of all. As the *Great Learning* said: "From the Son of Heaven down to the mass of the people, all must consider cultivation of the person as the root of everything besides" (Mote, 1971, 48). But most ordinary villagers had a more inclusive, less human-centered hope. Like mothers and fathers of the world, they hoped that the whole environment of lands, plants, animals, and humans might grow ever more fruitful and beautiful.

The Cause of Natural Conservation

For hard-headed villagers, it was a disgrace to waste good plants and animals. People who took more than they gave were wastrels, just as drunkards waste their families' means of life. Most Chinese villagers felt that greed was the greatest evil. The popular image of an evil person was not a female sorceress, but a fat, selfish "big man." This stock figure of evil would hoard food for himself while others starved. He would waste resources on luxuries till the land was ruined. In village-style common-sense, the rules of farm management, civil society, and religious morality were all basically the same. As the Lingbao School of Daoism explained,

To all students of the Dao and all lay followers! You must not commit the following sins:
The sin to covet personal profits without ever being satisfied ...
The sin to take pleasure in grabbing the valuables of others ...
The sin to slaughter the six domestic animals or kill any living beings ...
The sin to cut down trees or idly pick leaves or flowers ...
The sin to eat all by yourself when among a group, without thinking that they might be hungry too. (Kohn, 1993, 102–103)

Confucianists said the same: taking must be balanced by giving, and the aim should be mutual gain. As Mengzi (300s BCE) said, "If nets that are too narrow are not allowed in ponds and lakes, there will be more fish and tortoises than can be eaten. If the axe and the hatchet can only be taken into the mountain forests at the proper time, there will be more timber than can be used" (Bauer, 1976, 24). According to such logic, land could be managed, not just sustainably, but ever more fruitfully. If things were done right, both the villagers and the land would grow richer over time. And century after century, local communities all over China achieved that goal. But they couldn't control what the rulers demanded. And the greed of overlords was their greatest problem since empires began.

In an early morality tale, an evil Shang dynasty emperor named Zhou Wang (reportedly ca. 1100 BCE) heaped demands for tribute on the villagers. Zhou seemed to assume that the people, crops, and forests existed in order to serve his own desires. For example, he had his chopsticks made from ivory. And concerning this seemingly minor extravagance, the court tutor Jizi said,

Now he has made ivory chopsticks. It is not likely that he will continue to have food contained in earthenware; to be sure he will have bowls made of jade. With ivory chopsticks and jade bowls, he will certainly not be content with coarse fare, rough

clothing, or thatched dwellings. He will have garments of many layers of silk, high pavilions, and spacious halls. And he will demand everything in similar measure; and the whole wide world may not be enough to satisfy his wants. How much do I dread the end! (Wu, 1982, 259)

With his inflows of revenue, Zhou built a huge new pleasure palace called Deer Terrace. It sounds like a modern exclusive suburb. The palace itself was said to cover over a square mile, with marble archways and gem-studded walls. Its highest towers were over 1,000 feet tall. And rather than viewing this great expression of national culture with pride, the local chieftains were horrified. They especially objected to using wood on such a lavish scale. Even over 2,000 years later, the Daoist scholar Wang Zhe (ca. 1200 CE) felt it was only common sense:

It is not the habit of the superior man to live in great halls and lavish palaces, because to cut down the trees that would be necessary for the building of such grand residences would be like cutting the arteries of the earth or cutting the veins of a man. (Ebrey, 1981, 76)

In the famous debates "on salt and iron" of 81 BCE, the Han emperor heard heated arguments against ruling class greed. The advocates of restraint were called "conservatives," because at that time conservatism meant what the word literally means. These mainly Confucian conservatives aired their disgust for lavish silk robes and fur-lined coats. They heaped scorn on the eating habits of rich people, who took game out of season with no thought for the stock (Lowe, 1968, 140). *The Daoist Record of Rites of the Elder Tai* (from ca. 100 CE) made similar protests:

If a human ruler likes to destroy nests and eggs, the phoenix [of the South] will not rise. If he likes to drain the waters and take out all the fish, the dragon [of the East] will not come. If he likes to kill pregnant animals and murder their young, the unicorn [of the West] will not appear. If he likes stopping the watercourses and filling up the valley, the tortoise [of the North] will not show itself.

Thus the (real) king moves only in accordance with the Dao, and rests only in accordance with li (the principles of life). If he acts contrary to these, Heaven will not send him long life, evil omens will appear, the spirits will hide themselves, wind and rain will not come at their usual times, there will be storms, floods, and droughts, the people will die, the harvest will not ripen, and domestic animals will have no increase. (Needham and Wang, 1956, 270)

Unfortunately, these predictions were accurate. Over the next 1,700 years, the imperial court usually consumed around one-fourth of all revenue from the most populous country on earth. And even at the village level, the very success of traditional agriculture gradually generated its own imbalance. China's standard of living was still probably the highest on earth till about the 1500's (CE). But the combined pressures of taxes and rising population were more than the land could sustain. Already around 1075 (CE) the Confucian official Cheng He (Ch'eng Ho) demanded conservation controls:

The [ancient] sages followed the will of Heaven and put things in order through the administration of the six resources ... There were fixed prohibitions covering the resources of hills, woodlands, and streams. Thus the various things were in abundance and there was no deficiency in supply.

Today the five duties of the Five Offices are not performed and the six resources are not controlled. The use of these things is immoderate and the taking of them is not in due time and season. It is not merely that the nature of things has been violated, but that the mountains from which forests and woods grow have all been laid bare by indiscriminate cutting and burning. As these depredations still go uncurbed, the fish of the stream and the beasts of the field are cut short in their abundance and the things of nature are becoming wasted and exhausted. What can be done about it? These dire abuses have now reached an extreme, and only by restoring the ancient system of official control over hills and streams, so as to preserve and develop them, can the trend be halted, a change be made, and a permanent supply be assured. (De Bary and Chan, 1960, vol. I, 402)

Cheng assumed that the government must restrain villagers from foolish land management. But most villagers thought the worst pressure on their land came from the demands of rulers and landlords. Village people were usually devoted to keeping their land alive. While meeting the production quotas of their lords (and living on what remained) they did what they could to sustain it. They formed neighborhood groups to make dams or plant trees. They held festivals to invoke help from the local gods and goddesses.

Most of the village deities in traditional China were gods or goddesses of the local earth. The names of their temples were typically names of the deities' places: Blue Cloud Mountain, Dragon King Valley, Serenity Mountain, Ancient Spring (Chau, 2006, 49). The deities of these environments gave or withheld their bounty according to how the villagers behaved. And to renew relations with these deities, the temple associations held annual festivals, which were normally the high points of village social life. As far back as records go, these annual festivals involved drama productions, or operas. Usually, the plays featured heroic defenders of ancient values. The plots commonly involved rebellion or ridicule toward rapacious overlords. These productions were staged before the village temples, as tribute to a local god or goddess. And since everyone was gathered for the shows, the festivals were also occasions for a village assembly. Between performances, the local leaders discussed issues like protecting the forests, water sources, or adjusting the division of fields. People reported any recent abuses such as over-cutting trees, polluting ponds, or allowing animals to damage crops. The leaders reached agreements for the coming year, and pledged to uphold them. They solemnized their decisions before the local deities. Anyone who violated these agreements had to bear expenses for the next year's festival (Issei, 1985, 144–145).

Traditions like these have survived to modern times. During the Maoist Cultural Revolution (ca. 1965 to 1976), the annual drama festivals were no longer held at village temples, and were not explicitly devoted to local deities. But the same troupes of actors performed similar operas, devoted to similar heroes and values. The village assemblies discussed similar issues, which often concerned conservation. In Liu Ling village of Shaanxi, Jan Myrdal recorded some of the local leaders' reports: "Last year [1961] the [village] militia caught a man cutting firewood in the [forestry] plantations. He was taken to the commune's office; we criticized him and he was allowed to go home after signing a paper in which he promised not to do this again. We read it out to him, and he put his fingerprint on it" (Myrdal, 1965, 372).

Over the course of the twentieth century, China's villagers came under enormous political, economic, and cultural pressure. Both their rulers and modern economic forces pushed the context of maximizing production, regardless of environmental balance. The villagers were forced to subsidize urban development, including industries that polluted whole regions of farmland. It became "revolutionary" to say "the environment isn't as important as making money." Later, it became "conservative" to say that, and vast areas were ruined for short-term profit. But as the villagers reverted to dividing their land among families in the late 1970s, their traditional concern for long-term balance tended to revive. Most villages reopened their temples, and resumed devoting annual festivals to their local gods or goddesses. It grew normal to say "I believe in superstition." With a mixture of new and totally ancient values, the village councils or temple committees launched tree planting programs, some of which were effective. During the first decade of the twenty-first century China led the world in reforestation.

The Journey of All Beings

In the "Western religions" of Islam, Judaism, and Christianity, it's usually been orthodox to believe that sub-human creatures have no souls. By comparison, Chinese religions have been more inclusive toward "kindred of the wild." In their myths, animals are often fellow pilgrims on life's quest. Some stories about this are basically barnyard humor, like the tales of Daoist sages gaining immortality, and bringing their farm animals with them. So it reportedly happened to Cao Guojiu.

Cao was the brother of a Han dynasty empress, who fled from the court and joined the clap-trap band of Daoists known as the Eight Immortals. After Cao overcame his aristocratic pretensions and learned the Way from the locals, he managed to wheedle a bottle of the elixir of immortality from the other Daoists. As soon as he drank the elixir, his body shed its mortal nature. He started floating up into the sky like the moon goddess Chang'e, and hardly noticed as the elixir bottle dropped from his hand. Adjusting his flight pattern, Cao arrived at the heavenly palace of the Jade Emperor. Meanwhile, the bottle of elixir fell back into Cao's farmyard, where his dogs, pigs, and chickens eagerly licked up the spilt juice. Just as Cao was about to address the Jade Emperor, all his barnyard animals flew in squawking, barking, and grunting, to join their farm-mate. Following this rapture, they all returned to their earthly abodes. Everything was basically the same, except now these companions were free from all care.

In a Buddhist view, the relation of people and other creatures was a matter of common destiny. Reginald Ray put it like this:

We might consider all beings as having, like us, membership in the same great family—just as we view our children and our parents equally as family members, even though they are at earlier or later stages of life than we are. In a similar way, we are at a certain stage in our spiritual evolution. Others in the vast sea of being are at other stages in the very same process. Insects, for example, represent an earlier phase in this process, fully awakened buddhas a later one. But fundamentally, we are all made of the same stuff, so to speak. (Ray, 2000, 48)

Probably the most famous story of animals and humans on a common journey is the quasi-Buddhist classic, the *Journey to the West* (written in the 1500s CE). Here, a group of animals and one human set out in quest of enlightenment. One of these heroes was Sandy the fish. Sandy was suffering from bad karma through a fishy incarnation in the River of Sands, where he could barely find enough food to survive. But the goddess Guanyin took pity, and offered Sandy a chance at redemption through joining a pilgrimage to India with the human monk Tripitaka. Sandy was responsible for leading the monk's horse and helping to fight off evil demons. He managed this while constantly complaining. But by the journey's end, our fish overcame his limitations, achieved enlightenment, and received his title of "Golden Bodied Arhat."

The next animal disciple was Pigsy the pig, who was totally given to gluttony, drunkenness, and lust. Pigsy was also suffering a demotion for bad karma. He'd become a pig after a drunken sexual assault on the goddess of the moon, Chang'e. But again, it was the goddess Guanyin who offered him a chance at salvation by joining the pilgrimage. The pig was in charge of carrying baggage, and also helped battle evil spirits. But his own degenerate spirit was probably his worst enemy. He repeatedly embarrassed the other pilgrims with his unbridled debauchery. Eventually however, Pigsy's efforts won him enlightenment. His reward was to become "Cleaner of the Holy Altar." In other words, he got to pig out on the wealth of offerings presented in the celestial temple.

The third animal pilgrim was the notorious Monkey, Sun Wukong, also known as the Trickster God, or the Great Sage Equal of Heaven. Monkey had emerged from a stone egg on the Mountain of Fruits and Flowers, which had soaked up the goodness of natural Qi energy from the beginning of the world. His spirits were high, his ego knew no bounds, and nothing was safe from his irreverent pranks. The problem remained, however, that Monkey was deathly afraid of death. He therefore sought guidance from a sour-puss Daoist sage, who endowed Monkey with the title "Disciple Aware of Emptiness." The monkey was unaware that this referred to the vacuum in his head. Still, he ambitiously learned supernatural powers from his teacher. Then he invaded the heavenly court of the Jade Emperor, stuffed his face with the peaches of immortality, and made himself the terror of heaven. Only the Buddha was able to halt his effrontery, and sent him to be buried under a mountain for 500 years. Finally, after his ego had cooled a bit in the rock pile, Guanyin invited him to come out and join the pilgrimage to the West. And in the end his story was quite hopeful. Even the Monkey King's level of monkey-mindedness was overcome. He reached enlightenment and received his title of "Buddha Victorious Against Disaster." Which goes to show that all sentient beings, even the most depraved, shall be guided by the goddess to reach life's goal.

Religious Doctrines of Life's Organic Unity

Of course many early Buddhists were anti-worldly, and many Confucianists were only concerned with human beings. But over time, popular culture slowly pushed all Chinese religions toward a similar attitude concerning the natural world. As the monk Zongmi

(780–841 CE) explained his doctrine of the Tathagatagarbha (the womb-embryo of the Lord Tathagata), "There is not a single sentient being that is not fully endowed with an enlightened nature, which is numinous, bright, empty and tranquil, and which is no different from the Buddha" (Gregory, 1996, 380–382, 384, 388). All living things had the nature of Buddha from the beginning, and only needed to realize it. Therefore, Zongmi explained that all living creatures were equally "the one son"—evidently of the one mother.

The Daoist disciplines of spirit-body calisthenics such as Tai Chi (Taijiquan), which were Chinese equivalents of yoga, probably rose from watching animals. The tiger, crane, bear, monkey, or deer, did exercises that people could follow to enhance their vitality (Wong, 1997, 223). This was a culture of nature appreciation, in which calisthenics, gardening, or flower arranging could become spiritual practices. In Chinese gardening, the aim was not to "domesticate" the wilderness, but to welcome it into the family space. Just as village women raised baby animals to domesticate them, so they made gnarled forest trees and rugged mountain rocks into members of the household. Daoist texts taught that the human body "includes Heaven and Earth, the sun and moon ... mountains and streams, rivers and seas" (Bokenkamp, 1996, 268). And some teachers took this to shocking extremes, as when Liu Ling was chided for going naked around his house. He replied, "I take heaven and earth for my pillars and roof, and the rooms of my house for my pants and coat. And now, what are you gentlemen doing in my pants?" (Kohn, 1993, 301).

Confucian scholars were less playful and more abstract about this. They stressed that all life arose from a common primordial substance, namely *qi* —the "psycho-physical stuff" from which all things evolved (Teison, 1996, 32–33). So we find in the discussions of Neo-Confucian philosopher Zhu Xi (1130–1200 CE):

Houzhi asked: There's probably no principle for a man's dying and becoming a wild animal. But personally I've seen a son in a Yongchum family who had hog bristles and skin on his ears. What do you make of it?

Zhu said: This shouldn't be considered supernatural. I've heard that a soldier employed in Jixi had hog bristles on his chest and when asleep made hog noises. This is simply because he had been endowed with the psycho-physical stuff of a hog. (Gardner, 1996, 115)

The concept of one variable substance for all creatures seemed a great heresy to Jesuit missionaries in the 1600s. Father Longobardo complained that the Chinese had no notion of a spiritual substance separate from matter (Gernet, 1996, 519–520). Of course some physicists now claim that the concept of *qi* resembles modern ideas of a relativistic universe. But most old-fashioned Confucianists, Daoists, farmers, and shaman women just thought we all have a common mother.

During the Song period (900s to 1200s CE), "Neo-Confucianism" became a medieval synthesis of Buddhist, Daoist, and older Confucian wisdom, all woven into one Chinese culture. For the rulers, this was a project of cultural imperialism to unite the empire. But for many others, Neo-Confucianism was a Way of compassion for all creatures. Zhu Xi claimed that the highest spiritual value was universal harmony, which perhaps sounds like a pious line from Augustine or Thomas Aquinas. But Zhu Xi stressed that universal harmony was not a matter of all creatures conforming to one superior will. Like his mother probably told him, real harmony was the cooperation all would share if they followed their own instincts to honor one another. Living well was a matter of building good family relations with the universe:

*If there is a single thing not yet entered [by an outreaching
spirit], the reaching is not yet complete, and there are things
not yet embraced. This shows that the mind still excludes
something—for selfishness separates and obstructs, and
consequently the external world and the self stand in opposition.
This being the case, even those dearest to us may be excluded—
therefore, the mind that excludes is not qualified to be one with
the mind of heaven. (De Bary and Chan 1960, vol. I, 497–498)*

In this high-minded philosophy, morality flowed from identifying
with other creatures, and acting as if they were part of the greater
self. Maybe this sounds uselessly sentimental to modern minds.
But Joseph Needham asked his fellow modernists, "What, in terms
comprehensible to us, were these Sung [Song dynasty] philosophers
affirming? Surely the conception of the entire universe as a single
organism" (Needham and Wang, 1956, 465).

Such ideas didn't come from "enlightened rulers" or priests of
the court. They came from commonsensical village elders, traditional
farmers, and local wise women. And as the world's image of progress
evolves, maybe these people's sensibilities will yet prevail.

6: The Goddess Realms of Prehistoric China

How old are China's goddess traditions? Apart from famous legends of the Golden Age, what's the evidence that any civilization existed before the age of warlord empires? Until the past several decades, there was virtually no evidence. Now we have quite a lot. Fortunately, the Communist government sponsored major efforts in archaeology. And though many Communists wanted to dump the past, the Party still wanted to affirm China's greatness through scientific confirmation of the nation's antiquity. So a new age of Chinese archaeology began. No more would expeditions of foreign tomb raiders loot the treasures of ancient rulers. Now China's own scientists sought to map the whole picture of antiquity. Rather than focusing on palaces or tombs of ancient "big men," they tried to gather evidence on the lives of ordinary people. In a so-called golden age of modern archaeology, they dug up hundreds of sites dating back to Neolithic times.

This new archaeology pushed the horizons of history backward, beyond the Shang emperors of ca. 1300 BCE, to early civilizations of the 5000s BCE or older. Many of these primitive communities were almost as old as the settlements Marija Gimbutas was discovering in Eastern Europe. It was gratifying to Chinese national pride. The myths of China's vast antiquity were partly confirmed, since *some* civilizations existed in those times. But was this the age of unspoiled nature, and uncorrupted human virtue? Naturally, the bones, buildings, artwork, and pottery gave only hints of cultural history. There were grain crops and storage bins, but it was unclear who did what work, or who got what share of the produce. There were goddess images, but these were also found in historic times, when serious gender inequality prevailed.

In the Marxist view of ancient history, the dawn of civilization was an age of "primitive communism." Later, economies based on slavery and feudalism arose, which involved an "historic defeat of the female sex." Marxists usually dated the fall of women to around 2000 BCE. As Min Jiayin explained, "About 4,000 years ago China turned into a patriarchal society, which can be symbolized as blades in the hands of male warriors, as was the case in Europe. Women's status suffered a dramatic decline as the patriarchs dominated and oppressed women, and it became an unalterable principle that man was superior to woman" (Min, 1995, 555).

Sure enough, most excavations of Neolithic settlements revealed clusters of roughly equal-sized homes, suggesting a rough equality of wealth and status. Most graves were also roughly equal, in both size and in value of items buried with the dead. Only later did large "chieftain graves" appear, with their complements of slaves and women buried along with their lords. The Neolithic artifacts included crude farming tools, and often "goddess figurines," but rarely any signs of war weapons or defensive walls (Min, 1995, 554–555). Some villages had shallow trenches around the parameters, but these would only serve to keep animals in (or out), and probably couldn't block a military attack. The sites were usually out in the open, fronting on the shorelines of rivers or bays, rather than perched on defensible hilltops. Such remains seem basically similar to those of Old Europe's pre-militarized cultures, as described by Marija Gimbutas, Merlin Stone, or Riane Eisler.

All these discoveries of ancient cultures were impressive to the world's scientific community. But they were probably no surprise to most Chinese people. Most villagers already believed that before the age of emperors, armies, or great helmsmen, there was another kind of culture, based on another kind of power. Their folk tales and religious texts already described that pre-dynastic society in some detail. Now, many who had dismissed traditional beliefs wanted to know more.

In evaluating the pre-dynastic cultures, a number of Chinese experts grew enthusiastic. Some believed these remains suggested an age of female power, and even used the "matriarchy" word. In the light of accumulating evidence, it grew common for academics to speak of a primitive "matriarchal age." As Min Jiayin claimed, "a matriarchal society which may be symbolized by the chalice in the hands of goddesses once existed in prehistoric China, just as it did in Europe." Min said it was a society where "females enjoyed high status and prestige, and were the masters of society," while "goddesses were enshrined and worshiped" (1995, 12, 553). Of course "matriarchy" is a loaded term, implying an age of female superiority. And most experts soon backed away from such claims. Probably Riane Eisler's term "partnership" fit the evidence better. There's been no hard evidence from Neolithic huts or graves that women ever ruled by birthright, as if the roles of superiority and inferiority had been simply reversed. Instead, most experts feel the evidence suggests primitive sexual equality. That would complement the myths of co-creation by gods and goddesses.

For many Chinese people, the comparison of myth with archaeology holds a powerful fascination. It's similar to the fascination of Western archaeologists, historians, and biblical scholars, who have pooled their efforts to uncover the original face of biblical traditions. So, I want to look at the archaeology, while keeping the mythology in mind. I want to give an overview of major archeological discoveries, along with evidence of China's prehistoric environment. This should give a glimpse of the early culture centers in the age before warlords. The main "goddess realms" described will be the southern coasts, the Yangzi River basin, and the Yellow River basin.

The Climate of Prehistoric China

After the last Ice Age (ending around 10,000 BCE), it seems that sea levels slowly rose and flooded China's lowlands. The geological evidence suggests several major incursions by the sea, most recently after 3000 BCE. (Min, 1995, 558–559). Inland from Shanghai, low ridges of sand and sea shells mark some of the higher coastlines, and similar inland beaches appear in Japan and Southeast Asia (Pearson and Lo, 1983, 131–132). On the mountainous coasts, rising seas filled the seaside valleys, leaving numerous peaks isolated as rugged islands. In Shandong province, Mount Tai was an island. The lower Yangzi and Yellow River basins became huge bays stretching inland. Fat rainclouds rose from the vast sparkling bays, bearing their loads deep into Inner Asia. The now desiccated Lop Nur basin swelled to a vast inland sea (Cheng, 1959, 67, 60).

China's ancient myths seem to record such ancient floods. In one myth, the springtime goddess Ma Ku saw her mulberry fields sink and rise from the sea three times. In another story, the water demon of bad floods, Gong Gong battled the god of fire, Zhu Rong. The fire god was victorious, and in furious despair, Gong Gong killed himself by smashing his head against a pillar of heaven. This knocked the sky askew and caused the great flood. It took the snake-goddess Nü Wa to patch the sky and save the deluged planet. Other legends say that prehistoric emperors faced an epic flood, and Emperor Yu spent his whole career draining the waters.

When the seas rose, of course it meant that the ice caps were melting. And according to evidence from both organic deposits on land and oxygen isotope data from the sea beds, average annual temperatures rose from around four degrees centigrade colder than present (during the Ice Age) to near four degrees warmer than present before 3000 BCE (Treistman, 1972, 9). The warmer temperatures meant more evaporation off the sea, more clouds, and more rain. Then, by around 2000 BCE, the climate started shifting back toward cooler temperatures and less rainfall. The seas slowly fell to their present levels. The lakes of the Lop Nur basin gradually dried to salty sand, and the Gobi Desert began advancing across Inner Mongolia. According to legend, the Gobi Desert retained a Holy Lake, made by the tears of a Mongolian princess. She was married off to another tribe's headman, and missed her home so much that she cried a lake of crystal-clear water, which has saved many travelers in the desert (Wang, 2002, 37).

On this oscillating curve of planetary seasons, the legendary Golden Age seems to fall in the period of optimal warmth. In that lush environment, tropical forests stretched well north of the Yangzi delta. Elephants roamed the Yellow River basin. Wild rice, tropical banyan trees, bamboo rats, salamanders, tapirs, and rhinoceroses left their remains in the northern province of Shandong (White, 1983, 11). This could be the backdrop for the seemingly exaggerated legends of a remarkably abundant, strangely beautiful ancient landscape. Even in Mongolia, the present sand dunes cover layers of black soil from wetter times. In many areas, Mongolia's soil contains Neolithic hoe blades, pottery, meal grinding stones, and bones of oxen. These remains of a seemingly pre-nomadic Mongolia date from between 5000 and 2000 BCE (Cheng, 1959, 141–145). Near Baiyinchanghan, in Inner Mongolia, a site from near 5000 BCE holds a series of houses built halfway into the earth. Near one fireplace, the archaeologists found a stone statue of a woman with enormous belly and swelling breasts (Jiao, 1995, 122). Perhaps this is a relic of Mongolia's age of the goddess, before the desert came.

What kinds of communities and cultures rose during this warmer, wetter age? Over the past century, several major "cradles" of Chinese civilization have come to light. Each of these, in its own way, resembles an original earthly paradise.

Overview of Prehistoric Cultures in China

	South China	Yangzi River	Upper Yellow River	Northeast China
Before 6,000 BCE	Caves and shell mounds (10,000s to 5000s) Sites at Shi Weishan, Guangdong, and Spirit Cave, Jiangxi **Zengpiyan culture** (8000s to 7000s, Guangxi)	**Pengtoushan culture** (7000s to 6000s, Hunan)		
5000s and 4000s BCE	**Hemudu culture** (5000s to 4500s, Zhejiang) Chongzuo, Guangxi Hedang, Guangdong Dau-duong, Vietnam Sham Wan, Hong Kong	**Daxi culture** (5000s to 3000s, centered on Three Gorges region, mid-Yangzi) **Majiabang culture** (5000s to 3000s) South of Yangzi delta to Lake Tai, to near Hangzhou Bay, (S. Jiangsu, and N. Zhejiang) **Qingliangang culture** (Ch'ing-lien-kang) Near Yangzi delta in ca. 4600s to 2600s)	**Cishan-Peiligang culture** (5500s to 4900s) Sites at Cishan, Henan, and Peiligang, Hebei) **Yangshao culture** (ca. 5,000s to 3000s) Sites of Banpo (Shaanxi), Jiangzhai, and Dahecun (Henan) (4800s to 3600s)	Baiyinchanghan, Inner Mongolia (ca. 5000 BCE) **Dawenkou culture** (4500s to 2500s, Shandong)
3000s and 2000s BCE	**Sidun culture** (3000s to 2000s, Jiangsu) **Fanshan culture** (3000s to 2000s, Zhejiang) **Shixia culture** (3000s to 2000s, N. Guangdong)	**Liangzhu culture** (3400s to 2200s, Lake Tai area of Zhejiang, Jiangsu, Shanghai) **Qujialing culture** (3000s to 2600s, middle Yangzi, Hubei and Hunan) **Shijiahe culture** (2500 to 2000, middle Yangzi, Hubei) **Baodun culture** (2500 to 1700, Chengdu plain of Sichuan)		**Hongshan culture** (3800s to 2700s) Sites at Dongshanzui and Niuheliang (Liaoning) **Longshan culture** (2500s to 1700s) Sites at Chengziya (Shandong) and Pingliangtai (Henan)
1000s BCE	**Ningxiang** (1200s, Hunan) **Wucheng** and **Xin'gan**, (1200s BCE, Jiangxi)	**Sanxingdui** (1200 to 1000, Sichuan)	**Shang culture** (1700s to ca. 1050)	**Shang dynasty** center at Anyang (1400s to ca. 1050, Henan)

The South Sea Goddess Realm

As the world warmed to a climatic peak around 3000 BCE, rising seas flooded a coastal strip of perhaps 100 miles beyond the present shores. The first villages may therefore lie submerged on the continental shelf (Meachum, 1983, 153–154). The ocean pushed coastal tribes to higher ground, flowed around seaward mountains, and created a galaxy of islands. The south coast people still use the same word for "mountain" and "island." Their coastline became a jagged tangle of sandy inlets, rocky peninsulas, islands, and harbors. Later it would be a smuggler's paradise. But first it was just an aquatic paradise. This was a realm of mountainside rain forests, tidal pools filled with shellfish, estuaries of wild rice, and countless islands dotting the tropical Pacific.

Southern China is probably the oldest zone of sedentary culture in the country. Early Neolithic sites date between 10,000 to 5000 BCE at sites like Spirit Cave in Jiangxi, Zengpiyan in Guangxi, or Shi Weishan in Guangdong. Shoreline settlements are found in the Pearl River delta, on sand bars near Fuzhou, or old beaches on Taiwan (Jiao, 1995, 96). A Hemudu culture surrounded Hangzhou Bay from the 5000s to about 4500 BCE. But these villages were then abandoned, probably because rising seas pushed salt water up the local rivers. Later sites of the 4000s to 3000s BCE include Chongzuo in Guangxi, Hedang in the Pearl River Delta, and Sham Wan on Hong Kong's Lamma Island. In a survey of Neolithic sites across China as of 1989, *The Times Atlas of World History* listed 29 archaeological sites occupied between the 6000s and 4000s BCE. Of these, 21 were in the southern half of China, and only 8 in the northern Yellow River basin (Barraclough, 1989, 62).

The typical houses of early coastal villages were similar around the Pacific Rim, from Japan to Melanesia. They were generally built on wooden stilts, with walls of woven reeds, and large overhanging roofs of thatch or palm fronds. The woven wall mats could be rolled aside to let the sea breeze through, while the roof was like a large umbrella

(FitzGerald, 1972, 124–126). As the *Yi Jing* (*I Ching*) explained, "In the earliest times men dwelt in caves and lived out in the open. But the sages of later times substituted houses with ridgepoles and roofs to protect them from wind and rain" (Xi Zi 2, De Bary, 1960, vol. I, 198). In the morning, people probably rolled a wall mat aside for a view of the sun on the eastern sea. In the evenings, smoke from the cooking fires mingled with the ocean mist. On Hainan Island, a modern tourist guide recently explained that people of the ancient Li culture "lived naked in the forests and hunted with poison arrows and bows made from bamboo. The Li ... say the Thunder Spirit took an egg high into the mountains, and that the Li Mother hatched from it ... she gave birth to the Li tribe. We know this is a myth" (D'arcy Brown, 2003, 108–109).

Most coastal villages accumulated heaps of discarded mollusk shells near the huts, and the dead were often buried in these shell middens. Many of the skulls had incisor teeth removed, as was a custom in many cultures south of China (Cheng 1959, 131–132). A few of the skulls were bashed in, probably with clubs, and these skulls usually show an age at death of over 50 years old. It looks like the ancients had little filial piety, and practiced killing the elderly (Hsü, 1991, 28). For grave goods, the villagers generally placed a few clay pots with the bodies, and often items of jade. Later cultures would explain that jade was special, because it was a substance combining the elements of rock and water, and therefore the qualities of male and female (Treistman, 1972, 118).

The coastal people were beachcombers. Every day they could combine work and play, diving in the sea, collecting mollusks and catching fish. The jagged coastline made a greatly lengthened boundary between sea and land. And this boundary is generally the most ecologically fruitful in nature. The underwater topography was also uneven, and creatures preferring various depths of water, from oysters and crabs to sharks, lived in close proximity. To primitive people with myth-making minds, the whole realm seemed magically alive with deadly or beneficial powers. The South Chinese word for "dragon" (*jiao*, or *chiao*) referred to a range of aquatic monsters, including crocodiles, sharks, and rays. A ninth-century (CE) poet caught the old sense of wonder while speaking to a crab: "Long before I traveled the watchet sea I knew your name. / You have bones— grown outside your flesh. / Say nothing of mindless fear of thunder and lightning! / There, in the abode of the sea dragon king, may you sidle!" (Schafer, 1980, 26–27, 21). One item people collected in great numbers was the cowry shell. And down to historic times, these shells were literally used as money over much of the country. As usual, things had economic value for cultural reasons, and the choice of items valued was a clue to people's values. As many ancient people valued gold because it looks like a piece of the sun, so the ancient Chinese valued cowry shells because they look like women's vaginas.

At some point in pre-history, primitive boats let the fisher people hop down chains of islands over the sea. The Hemudu people colonized islands of the Zhoushan archipelago by the early 4000s BCE. And probably on some shoreline around the South China Sea, the first outrigger canoes were built. The ancients then evolved their ways of weaving sails, steering with rudders, or navigating by winds, currents, and stars.

Later, the legends of South China were filled with sacred islands, depicted as the paradise realms of immortals. These myths resembled tales of Avalon, or the Isles of Women, except that China's isles of the blessed seem more beautiful. The mythic island of Penglai Shan was reportedly carpeted in flowers, with trees of coral and pearls. Its streams flowed with the dew of eternal life, down to beaches unchanged since the world began. A Tang dynasty poem by Li Ho embellished old legends of immortal boys and girls, playing in the surf: "At Cyan Peaks, where the sea's surface hides numinous texts, the Supreme Therch selected and made transcendents' dwellings. Pure and bright, their laughter and talk is heard in empty space; they race, riding huge waves or mounting whales. On spring-netted gauze they write graphs inviting the Queen Mother" (Cahill, 1993, 103). Among the 400 islands of the Zhoushan archipelago, Putuo Island later became a legendary home of the goddess Guanyin.

Inland from the coasts, the mountains were washed in rain off the ocean. The peaks drew mist and thunder, and served as the source of rivers. All this made the highlands seem to be places of power, haunted by deities of water and life, which seemed to be naturally female. Later, popular imagination turned the powers of mountain peaks into mysterious spirit women, such as Lady Youying, otherwise known as Lady Right Bloom of the Palace of Cloud Forest. The goddess Wei Huacun resided on the eminence of Lojiang in Fujian. The goddess of Hengshan [mountain] in Hunan was titled "Primal Mistress of the Purple Barrens" (Shafer, 1980, 32–33). A prominent rock in the Yellow Mountains of Anhui became "The Fair Maiden Pointing the Way."

The rugged landscape of South China is still among the most biologically diverse on the planet, and depicting its beauty became a central theme of classical Chinese painting. On the ancient hill slopes bloomed jungles of bamboo, chrysanthemums, peonies, orchids, jade flowers, jasmine, magnolia, plum blossoms, and lilies. The early natives found an enormous potential for domesticating forest plants. In the jungles and marshes they discovered ancestral forms of bottle gourds, cucumbers, peas, beans, taro roots, wild rice, and hot peppers (Treistman, 1972, 37–38). They used bamboo for food, utensils, building materials, and musical instruments. We may never know how early such tools were invented, since wood doesn't last. But little by little, the tribes moved beyond hunting and gathering. They started managing the landscape with a mixture of gardening and sylviculture. According to a Fujian legend, Lady Taimu led her followers to open the land for farming, and became the earliest ancestor of the Min and Yueh people (Gernant, 1995, 22).

Over several thousand years, a common culture evolved along the entire South China Sea coast. The villages with shell mounds, polished stone adzes, spindle whorls, and corded pottery with chalky paint appeared from north of the Yangzi down to Vietnam. The sites along the Tonkin Gulf in Vietnam are among the oldest, dating from around 9000 BCE. By 4000 BCE, a Vietnamese site at Dau-duong displayed wheel-made pottery, dugout canoes, and fishing nets, with evidence of domesticated rice, tea, sugar cane, water buffaloes, chickens, pigs, and cattle. In historic times, the tribes of the whole China-Vietnam coastline were described as the "hundred Yueh" (Meachum, 1983, 152, 158, 161). The name "Viet" is a southern version of the Chinese ethnic term "Yueh." In the 300s BCE, Zhuangzi recorded an account concerning Yueh people:

> In the southern state of Yueh, there is a fief called "the land of established virtue." The people there are stupid and simple. They have little private property, and hardly any desires. They are familiar with work, but know nothing of thrift. They enjoy giving, but do not demand gratitude. They do not know when "righteousness" is called for, or when to observe "ritual." They conduct themselves like savages or mad people, yet they follow certain important rules. (Bauer, 1976, 91)

Most linguists agree that China's languages originate mainly in this southern realm. They belong to the Austro-Asiatic or Tibeto-Burman group, and are more akin to Thai or Vietnamese than to northern languages like Mongolian (Pulleyblank, 1983, 416; Maspero, 1978, 12–13). It seems the Chinese come mainly from the South Sea zone.

Over the past 2,000 years, as dynasties rose and fell, the south sea people repeatedly rebelled and declared independence from the warlord rulers of North China. The southern "nations" called themselves Yueh, Yueh Min, Min, Wu, Chu, Eastern Jin, or Southern Han. And down to the present time, southern Chinese cultures remain profoundly different from those of the North. The prejudice between them is commonly mutual. The novelist Fan Wu has a student from the North remark, "I heard the Cantonese ancestors are snake-eating barbarian natives. How could such a backward people have developed such a complicated dialect?" (2006, 66). But the southerners' outward-looking reliance on maritime activity, their relative safety from drought or invasion, and their comparatively high status for women, helped make their coastline the richest part of China. In a monograph called "Goddesses Worshipped by the Chinese," Zhou Zewei explains it in economic terms:

> *[The provinces of South and East China] are the original Wu and Yue culture areas, which are quite different from the Central Plain regional cultures. The social status of women in the South used to be higher than of women in Northern China as they were active in social production and often replaced men in all kinds of economic activities. So female worship became one of the main features of the local cultures in these areas. (1995. 414)*

The Yangzi River Goddess Realm

The Yangzi River formed another vast string of shorelines, stretching along tributaries, lakes, and marshes for over 50,000 miles. In Neolithic times, the lower reaches of the river were far wider, as higher seas created a vast bay of mixed fresh and salt water. The ocean probably pushed the river delta inland as far as Hubei province. Then, as the seas crested and gradually declined, the river's vast load of mud began refilling the bay (Cheng, 1959, 112). Civilization in the Yangzi valley has a long history. We can start by mentioning that a cave upriver from Chongqing, called Dragon Hill Cave, has yielded hominid jaw fragments which date to 1.9 million years ago (Winchester, 2004, 281–283). But that's pretty much off the chart of early civilizations.

No doubt many ancient village sites were deeply buried in deposits of river mud, or erased by constant re-dredging of canals and rice fields. Besides that, the Yangzi commonly rose by 50 feet or more in the season of rain and melting snow. But starting in the middle reaches of the river, many early villages of "Mound Dwellers" can still be found on small hills among the wetlands. The oldest settlements (such as the Pengtoushan culture of roughly the 7000s to 6000s BCE) appeared around the great Yangzi lakes of central China. Later, the Majiabang culture (5000s to 3000s BCE) or the Liangzhu culture (3000s to around 2200 BCE) appeared further down the river, around Nanjing or Lake Tai. It seems that people followed the advancing delta, which was the richest environment in all China. But the delta's progress wasn't smooth. Paleogeologists detect perhaps six major epochs of higher seas (Zhang and others, 2004, 105–112). Villages of the Liangzhu culture (southwest of the modern delta) were abandoned around 2200 BCE, and the sites covered by sea-borne silt up to one meter deep.

The early Mound Dwellers set their villages where higher ground approached the water. Their optimal sites were in the delta, within reach of both fresh water channels and salt water bays. On these borders between forest and waterline, they built tropical-Pacific-style houses, often on wooden stilts. They usually had heaps of discarded mussel or oyster shells off to the side. The refuse pits held bones from pigs, dogs, fish, water buffaloes, deer, turtles, rhinoceroses, and elephants (Pearson and Lo, 1983, 123). In northern Zhejiang, the large numbers of water buffalo bones suggest domestication, which is a major accomplishment (Ho, 1975, 99). Wild water buffaloes are dangerous. In Africa they were never domesticated, and are feared as deadly enemies. If Yangzi villagers were the first to tame water buffaloes, they had a remarkable capacity to befriend dangerous animals. Some Yangzi people even trained otters to bring them loads of fish.

The ancient tools scattered over Yangzi village sites include sinker stones from fish nets, and pots of coarse sandy clay. The stone axes and adzes seem to be woodworking tools for making dugout boats.

Probably bamboo provided most of the hand tools, but these would have decomposed long ago. Some garden hoes of stone or animal shoulder blades remain, and some sites had earth embankments, for holding water in the hillside gardens (Treistman, 1972, 38–39, 64–65). In Pengtoushan culture sites, some of the rice stored in pots may date to the 7000s BCE.

The dead in these villages were buried individually, usually in the yard outside their homes, with their heads pointing east. In some sites the skulls have missing incisor teeth, especially the female skulls. Perhaps they removed teeth for initiation rites. The gifts buried in graves were usually different for men and women. Men were buried with stone axes and bone harpoons. Women generally had bracelets, spindle whorls, and jade ornaments. Some jades appear to be worn like badges, or signs of rank and honor. In the Qingliangang culture (near the present delta, around 2700 BCE), jade objects appear concentrated in graves of the influential people, be they men or women. But Min Jiayin claims that in over 7,000 Stone Age burial sites in China, the general pattern is that women were buried with more symbols of honor and status, while men were buried with more tools of production (Min, 1995, 554).

In later mythology of the region, most local goddesses were spirits of the rivers. The goddesses might have been real women who drowned in the rivers and were fondly remembered, or general personifications of the living waters. They could have been spirits of Baiji river dolphins, which were known as "Yangzi goddesses." The rivers were just as full of mythic dragons as the southern sea. They were infested with water snakes and alligators, as if the age of dinosaurs never ended. Each tributary of the Yangzi had its patron goddess, such as the Xiao River goddess, or the three sister goddesses of the Jinjiang, Jinling, and Ciyum Rivers. There were two goddesses of the Xiang River, Ehuang and Nüying, whose tears reportedly made the water patterns in bamboo. And in the *Classic of Mountains and Seas* (from between the 200s BCE to 100s CE) the Xiao and Xiang goddesses wander the great confluence of tributaries around Lake Dongting:

> They often wander over the depths of the river in the breezes blowing from the Li and Yuan rivers, where they meet in the deep waters of the Xiao-Xiang confluence ... And every time the waters of these rivers ebb and flow, there is always a raging wind and driving rain. And there are many strange spirits who look like humans and wear snakes on their heads, and they hold snakes in their left and right hands. And there are many strange birds there. (Birrell, 1993, 169)

A unique system of aquatic agriculture emerged in the Yangzi region. In sites of the Hemudu culture (ca. 5000 to 4500 BCE) in Zhejiang, people harvested the swamps. They gathered lotus roots, water chestnuts, wild rice, water spinach, cattail, arrowhead, water caltrop, water shield, water dropwort, and swamp reeds. A poem by Qu Yuan from around 290 BCE describes a woman of that floating countryside:

> I made a coat of lotus and water chestnut leaves,
> And gathered lotus petals to make myself a skirt.
> I will no longer care that no one understands me,
> As long as I can keep the sweet fragrance of my mind.
> (Treistman, 1972, 135)

Since these people used so many forest plants, they showed little or no desire to level the forest. In other areas of the world, ancient forests were often burned to make way for crops or ranches. The modern migrants to forest zones of North America or Brazil often viewed the riot of native plants as a mass of useless weeds, and presumed the whole indigenous bio-system should be eliminated in favor of something else. But Ping-ti Ho says, "One peculiar trait of the prehistoric and early historic Chinese was their unwillingness to destroy forests by such a simple and wanton method" (1975, 41). The aboriginals generally assumed they must "discover" uses for each plant, rather than eliminate all species whose benefits they didn't understand. And they made use of almost every plant they found, whether for food, medicine, clothing, or building materials. From the wetland forests they domesticated rice, beans, mung beans, adzuki beans, and peanuts. For fibers they wove kudzu roots, ramie, and chu. For vegetables they ate Chinese yam, edible amaranth, mustard, gourds, day-lilies, and bamboo shoots. This Yangzi farming culture emerged at roughly the same time as farming in the Yellow River valleys, but the cultivated plants in each region were totally different (Hui, 1983, 42–50).

Later, the great Han dynasty historian Sima Qian was moved to complain that the Yangzi people were lazy. Their land was so abundant in plant and animal foods that they had little incentive to break the soil and tame the wilderness:

[People there] are able to gather all the fruit, berries, univalve and bivalve shellfish they want without waiting for merchants to come around selling them. Since the land is so rich in edible products, there is no fear of famine, and therefore the people are content to live along day to day; they do not lay away stores of goods, and many of them are poor. As a result, in the region south of the Yangzi and Huai rivers, no one ever freezes or starves to death, but on the other hand there are no very wealthy families. (Sima, 1961, 490)

In the warm Neolithic period, wild rice grew all over the Yangzi wetlands, and even northward to Japan. Another phrase for wild rice was "divine rice," which sounds rather like the biblical "manna." Administrative records mentioned it as a major boon to the food supply down to dynastic times. A Tang dynasty official in Hebei

Province wrote in 874 CE, "Wild rice ripened in an area of more than 200,000 mu [about 30,000 acres] much to the benefit of the poor of local and neighboring counties" (Ho, 1975, 67–68). People collected divine rice in boats, beating the stalks with sticks, then straining fallen grain off the water in sieves of cloth. We can imagine the likely stages of evolution in rice farming, from gathering wild rice, to sowing it in rice-less swamps, and from scattering seed, to hand-planting the seedlings. Each step involved more work. But even in the 1100s CE, a government official described the luxuriously easy conditions of southern swamp agriculture:

> *Of all the boundless land that lies beyond what the human eyes can reach, not one percent of such land has been brought under cultivation. In preparing the fields for rice planting, the peasants choose only the kind of land that is evenly submerged under water all year round. If the land is a bit too high they would reject it. Even when they do cultivate, they would barely break up the ground, without deep plowing and hoeing. They simply broadcast the seeds, never transplant the shoots. After the seeds are broadcast, they do not water the fields during drought: nor do they drain off water after excessive rain. Caring nothing about manuring, deep plowing, and weeding, they leave everything to heaven. (Ho, 1975, 72)*

Starting in early historic times, some farmers extended the natural rice swamps by digging water channels. Then they slowly embarked on the massive task of sculpting the landscape into contoured rice paddies. They started digging the irrigation canals which honeycomb the lower Yangzi region. But these laborious innovations came only when the need was pressing, after masses of migrants arrived from the north, and the natural forests were largely consumed. The great irrigation system which now feeds hundreds of millions was a product of harsh necessity, long after the Golden Age.

Where did the first recognizably Chinese culture appear? Recently, archaeologists in Zhejiang Province exposed a ritual center of the semi-legendary Xia dynasty (reportedly of ca. 2100 to 1700 BCE). The buildings contained nine large tripod pots, an image of a human body with an animal face, some long hollow pieces of jade, tablets of jade, and a jade board inscribed with the Xia calendar. Similar ceremonial objects are described in ancient writing as instruments in the Xia emperors' sacrifices. In Min Jiayin's opinion, "These finds disproved the previous belief that the first native Chinese civilization—the Xia civilization—originated in the Yellow River Valley." Min also claims that Daoism originated in the Yangzi region, and argues that Daoism was "a philosophy of the female sex," which rose from "the matriarchal society of the southern Xia nationality living in the Yangzi basin" (Min, 1995, 558–593).

But then, toward the dawn of historic times, the middle-Yangzi people formed a Shijiahe culture (ca. 2,500 to 2,000 BCE), which showed signs of centralized military power. Their main city in Hubei was surrounded by walls and a moat, forming an almost perfect kilometer-wide square. Clearly, new authorities were starting to command the villagers' resources.

The Upper Yellow River Goddess Realm

As archaeologist J.G. Anderson described it, the Yellow River region of North China has always been a battleground between "the God of Rain" and "the God of Wind." The god of wind swept down from the north, bearing clouds of dust off the Gobi desert. In cold dry periods, when the god of the north wind prevailed, this yellow dust from the skies accumulated as deposits of "loess" up to 50 yards deep. This was free-falling fertilizer, seemingly enough to last forever. But after the Ice Age, the god of rain grew stronger. In a warmer climate, fat rain clouds from the southeast began washing the yellow loess away much faster than it could accumulate. Soon many thousands of ravines cut through the light yellow soil, sucking it away to the Yellow

River. The modern villagers of that region still watch this battle of wind and rain. From January to June the north wind blows from Mongolia, bearing its mixture of snow and dust. Then the summer monsoon clouds move in like dragons to counter-attack. Above the villager's heads, clouds of dust and rain collide, and fall as drops of mud (Cheng, 1959, 10, 30, 64–65).

During the period before 2000 BCE, this zone was also a borderland between southern forests and northern grasslands. Further to the north, deep accumulations of loess prevented tree growth. The rainfall sank through the loose soil for yards, and tree seedlings could never reach the water table unless irrigated to maturity (Ting, 1931, 267–269). Ancient people were drawn to the forest-grassland boundary, because it allowed them to live from both environments at once. And sometime before 5000 BCE, a small galaxy of farming villages appeared along this border. First a Cishan-Peiligang culture (ca. 5500–4900 BCE) grew along the tree lines of Henan and Hebei. Then a similar Yangshao culture spread westward up the Yellow River basin, especially along the Wei River tributary (Debaine-Francfort, 1999, 43–44). Since these villages were better preserved, and less buried in flood sediments than villages downstream, they became the best explored sites of Neolithic culture in China.

Most villages in the Wei valley were fairly high on slopes above the river. The ground there was safe from periodic floods, but within walking distance of water. Ideally, villages sat on a ridge above a curve in the river, with a vista view in at least three directions. Here, the people had sunny loess terraces for gardening, with nearby wooded hills (Hui, 1983, 28). For a combination of grain-growing, wild plant gathering, and animal hunting, this valley was among the best in North China.

The most famous excavated site of the Yangshao culture is Banpo, in Shaanxi Province. The village dates from soon after 5000 BCE, and is one of the smaller among hundreds of similar Yangshao sites. At the time of its excavation in the 1950s, perhaps most

Marxist archaeologists saw this culture as the nucleus of Chinese civilization, and a probable example of "primitive communism" in the "matriarchal age."

The ancient village at Banpo lay on a loess terrace about ten yards higher than the river. It was surrounded by a shallow ditch enclosing about 11 acres. The village had some 40 houses, arranged in two rows, with a narrow plaza up the middle. The houses came in two main types, either pyramid- or cone-shaped. The pyramids were of thatched straw, and the cone houses had walls of plastered clay. In a later development, some villagers built a third sort of house—a long-house structure about 20 yards long, divided into compartments. Probably the village held different clans, each with its own type of house. According to housing capacity, archaeologists estimate the village population at five or six hundred.

In the central plaza were several large pits, probably for animal pens and grain bins. Remains of food in the pits and pots show a heavy reliance on millet and pork. There are pig bones in almost every ash pit, and an unnaturally high number of these pigs died at about one year old, which suggests domestication. The remains of millet seed also strongly suggest domesticated crops, starting soon after 5,000 BCE (Ho, 1975, 93, 18). Local pollen profiles for that period show lots of pollen from the wild millet family (*Gramineae*). And gathering this grain from the wild probably led to concentrated plots of millet around the village. As people brought the grain home, the fallen seeds tended to sprout around their houses. So, the food gatherers found their food plants coming to them, and they soon saw that this happened through the seeds.

The villagers had polished stone adzes and hoes, which suggest digging and planting as we know it. The surrounding loess soil was easy to dig, but the mat of grass was probably thick. Possibly the villagers burned the grass off rather than plowing it under, but no evidence of ash layers remains. Nor is there any sign that wheat, barley, or legume crops were known in this early period. At another

Yangshao site, however, Dr. Li Chi found a silkworm cocoon that had been sliced in half. Perhaps the cultivation of this insect had already begun. (Li, 1983, 21–64). Such signs of early agriculture seem to mark the birth of civilization. But the Yangshao ash bins show that much food was still gathered from the countryside. The gatherers brought hazelnuts, celtis seeds, pine nuts, chestnuts, jujubes, peaches, and plums, while the hunters brought plenty of wild animals (Ho, 1975, 60–73, 87, 94).

Near the east side of Banpo stood a cluster of pottery kilns. And like other Yangshao sites, this seemingly communal workshop turned out reddish pots, usually painted with geometric designs. The designs include zigzags, triangles, net patterns, or concentric bands, which are remarkably similar to the pottery art of contemporary Old Europe, as catalogued by Marija Gimbutas in her book *The Language of the Goddess* (Blumenburg, 2006, 10). Some pots have rough pictures of people, fish, animals, or flowers. The images of people show elaborate headdresses, perhaps of feathers. And the pot lids are often shaped like women's heads. By implication, the pots themselves represent women's bodies (Jiao, 1995, 122–123). Many items of pottery show small pictographs. A 1970s survey of 113 Yangshao potshards yielded 22 different pictograph symbols (Cheung, 1983, 324). These could be marks of ownership by various families, but many of the symbols look familiar to readers of old Chinese. The marks may have had different meanings for Yangshao people, but several recurring symbols are roughly the same as later pictographs for "one," "two," "five," "seven," "eight," "people," "grass," and "sacrifice" (Ho, 1975, 223–230).

Outside Banpo's enclosing ditch, a cemetery area holds about 200 graves in neat rows. And like other Neolithic skeletons found across China, the bones are most racially akin to samples from Southeast Asia or Polynesia (Pearson and Lo, 1983, 125; Ho, 1975, 342–343). The graves are clustered in groups, which may correspond to the clans living in pyramid, cone, or longhouse type houses. Most graves contain five or six ceramic pots, and often a pig. This "grave wealth" is generally equal for men or women. Professor Yan Wenming did a statistical analysis of grave goods in all known Yangshao culture sites, and found an average of 2.09 pottery pieces per male grave, and 2.17 per female grave (Jiao, 1995, 111). Perhaps the most luxurious grave in Banpo is for a young girl, who has a wooded coffin. Most of the bodies have bone necklaces or jade earrings. Many are sprinkled with red pigment, which probably symbolized the blood of new birth. Dead babies and small children are buried elsewhere, in clay jars beside their mother's houses (Ho, 1975, 273; Cheng, 1959, 81).

In some areas of Banpo's graveyard, the bodies are all of one sex. And this pattern is found at many Yangshao sites. Most Chinese archaeologists think the clusters of female graves represent matrilineages. Professor Zhang Zhongbei claims that the clusters of female and male graves indicate a culture where mothers and daughters were buried together, and lineage was reckoned through the mother (Jiao, 1995, 108). If so, perhaps it was as Zhuangzi (Chuang Tzu) reported concerning the Golden Age: "In the days of Shennong [the legendary "Divine Farmer"] ... They knew their own mothers but not their fathers. They lived with deer, they fed on the food they grew, wore the cloth they wove, and harbored no ill will against one another. This was indeed a supremely ethical society" (Min, 1995, 592).

What do these remains tell us about the Yangshao culture? Obviously, not a lot. It appears the villagers lived and worked like a big family, but this is unproven. Still, we can imagine life in a Yangshao community by reference to villagers of historic times. Likely they went to the fields almost every day. They probably worked in groups of friends or relatives, gardening or roving the fields for wild plants. In the evenings they sat in the doorways talking, as smoke from their fires sifted through the village. Jiao Tianlong feels that the physical arrangement of Neolithic villages shows a casually communal way of life. Speaking of the Yangshao site at Jiangzhai, Jiao argues, "The pottery-making workshop by the river obviously belonged to the whole settlement ... All large houses and stock pens were collective property. Grain storage pits were distributed around the complexes [about one grain pit for each five houses] ... These repositories evidently did not belong to particular small houses, and their stores were gens [or clan] owned" (Jiao, 1995, 102).

In later times of the Shang dynasty (which ruled the same area ca. 1700–1050 BCE), the oracle-bone pictographs illustrated several early Chinese concepts. The character for "deity" included a picture of a plant calyx, apparently symbolizing the source of food and life. And the character for "woman" showed a person squatting at work. Probably she was preparing food. If prehistoric China was like many other aboriginal societies, women were the major providers of plant food (Ho, 1975, 247–249). The pictograph might seem a lowly image for womankind. But through historic times, many people felt it portrayed women's importance. Throughout recorded history, female shamans were commonly masters of plant lore, and served as emissaries to the plant world. Most of China's tremendous diversity of foods was likely discovered by mothers. In searching for food, they probably tried eating new plants, then shared them with their families if results were good. Of course later legends compressed this gradual process into a single episode, and gave all credit to a male emperor. So, Shennong, the Divine Husbandman (reportedly 2737–2698 BCE), taught the people which plants to eat. In his diligent experimentation, it is reported he tasted 70 poisonous plants in a single day.

As in Old Europe's "civilization of the goddess," the remains of early Yellow River villages suggest there was little need of defense or weaponry. The trenches around Yangshao villages probably helped with drainage, and to keep the pigs from rooting in the gardens. The first archaeologists to excavate Banpo presumed the trench was a "defense ditch." But a one-meter ditch would hardly deter a human enemy. As Min Jiayin sees it, the Yangshao culture was a pre-military society: "Art was on its way to maturity, but there are no signs of weapons of war. That was indeed a time of peace and tranquility, a time symbolized by the chalice in the hands of goddesses" (Min, 1995, 554–555).

The Yellow River Flood Plain Goddess Realm

Where the Yellow River descends from the loess-covered highlands, it quite suddenly emerges onto a vast flat coastal plain. The velocity of the river slows, and a massive load of yellow soil sinks to the riverbed. The deposits of mud grow over time, till the river shifts course. So in the past 2,000 years, official records list at least 400 major floods and course changes across the Yellow River flood plain (Cheng, 1959, 65–66). The river's delta has fluctuated from close to the Manchurian border in the north, to south of the Shandong peninsula. And over that whole region, the coastal plain is buried in river mud. With so much sediment deposited, many ancient sites may never be found. And as the river slowly wanders about, few places on the flood plain are safe from periodic destruction. Still, the river mud is fertile; the sun is warmer than further inland, and the rains are better. The soil of the lower flood plain is denser than the light loess found upstream. Though it is harder to dig, it is more often wet.

The lower Yellow River is like a larger version of the erratic Tigris-Euphrates system in Iraq. Both regions have their legends of "the Great Flood." Both saw their earliest villages appear around the upper tributary streams. Then, at near the same time in both North China and Mesopotamia (around 3,500 BCE), farming villages mushroomed to life on the flatter coastal flood plains. And as in ancient Sumer, those rich but dangerous plains soon supported China's largest towns to date. These sites were commonly as large or larger than nearby modern villages. In eastern Shandong during the 1950s, the village of Liang Chengzhen covered about 88,000 square yards. Beside this, the remains of a prehistoric village covered around 1,090,000, square yards. (Cheng, 1959, 69–72, 87). Usually the villages were placed on hills, or between the river and a hill, to which the residents could flee from floods.

On the northeast edge of the flood plain, in Liaoning Province,

Chinese archaeologists made their first discoveries of ancient "goddess figures" in 1979. First, at Dongshanzui village they found a group of stone altars with two nude female figures of clay, dating to around 3000 BCE. Later digs found a pattern of goddess-like figures near the hearths of cottages from prior to 3,500 BCE. In younger sites, such figures were increasingly found in non-residential buildings with stone platforms. Jiao Tianlong feels that over time, worship of these deities passed from the hands of families at fireside shrines, to community leaders or religious specialists in public temples (Jiao, 1995, 124–125). Along the Niuheliang ridge, archaeologists found ten temple and tomb complexes, one of them with five or six broken female statues, but no male ones (Jiao, 1995, 117–120). The sculptures struck dramatic poses, with clenched fists or arms akimbo. One life-sized clay head had inlaid jade eye pupils, a looped head dress, and a frightfully grim mouth (Debaine-Francfort, 1999, 41–42). Overall, these figures resembled wrathful goddesses of Daoist or Buddhist history.

Between about 2500 to 1700 BCE, a Longshan civilization emerged in regions around the Yellow River delta. It's a culture famous for distinctive pottery. Many wheel-cast pots have hollow tripod legs, for standing in a fire and conducting heat to the food or drink inside. And as J.G. Anderson found obvious, "the apparent likeness of nearly all the tripod legs to a woman's breast ... can hardly be unintentional." The tips of the "legs" resemble nipples (Blumenburg, 2006, 10–11). The Longshan villages also produced numerous clay phalluses, and this combination of phalluses and breasts resembles the mixture of lingams and yonis often seen in India. Many Chinese experts feel these clay phalluses show a growing respect for the male role in reproduction. Ping-ti Ho points out that the classical-age Chinese pictograph for "ancestor" *is* an image of a phallus (1975, 282).

The earliest Longshan graveyards had rows of individual graves, buried with their heads pointed east, often with a few pots or pieces of jade. Then in later centuries, graves of male-female pairs started to appear (Ho, 1975, 280–281). It seems people were starting to think that couples belonged to each other forever. But as of yet, there were no graves of men buried with several women.

Over time, the graves of northern China started to show serious inequalities in grave wealth. In Shandong's Dawenkou culture (early 2000s BCE), one lavish tomb held a coffin with about a hundred valuable pots, jades, and items of carved ivory. For near the first time, we find men buried with their weapons of war, including stone yue axes and leather body armor. Such "aristocratic" graves are segregated from the graveyards of ordinary villagers. With the late Longshan culture after 2000 BCE, we start to find true "chieftain graves." Some of these grew monumental; with mounds of earth several tens of thousands of cubic yards in size (Jiao, 1995, 104, 106–107).

The mature Longshan villages were increasingly built with major earth-works. The Pingliangtai site in Henan had large platforms of tramped earth, perhaps designed to rise above minor floods. And as in ancient Sumer, rammed earth walls started to appear around the towns. The Chengziya site in Shandong had walls over three yards high, enclosing an area of 495 by 430 yards (Jiao, 1995, 105). These walls were raised around 2300 BCE, and they signal an appearance of militarized society. Then, around 2000 BCE, in a Longshan site at Handan, Hebei, two abandoned village wells were filled with human bodies, probably from a battle over land (Chang, 1980, 339). As when Sumerian towns started conquering each another in ancient Iraq, the age of rising warlords had begun.

For the centuries before 2000 BCE, archaeology shows that the Yellow River basin was densly packed with villages. Then arid conditions set in, and the numbers of archaeological sites fell drastically by 1600 BCE. North China became a zone of recurrant dought, famine, and war, as we've known it for most of the past 4,000 years (Fagan, 2008, 218–219). In a land of frequent scarcity, competition to control the means of life grew merciless. A vast gulf emerged between the values of ruling men and those of local women or elders.

7: Confucian Myths of the Golden Age

When Confucius tried to reform the warlord rulers of his day (500s BCE), he claimed that their ancient ancestors had been paragons of virtue in the Golden Age. He implored the present princes to drop their violent, corrupt ways, and return to the values of the ancients. This argument involved idealizing the founding fathers of the Zhou dynasty, who lived around 1000 BCE. And Confucius seemed to seriously believe that the first centuries of Zhou rule had been a Golden Age of virtuous benevolence. The "Confucian classics" he edited were reportedly records from the court scribes of early Zhou princes—in which case the scribes were enormously flattering to their lords. Or maybe, as Kang Yuwei argued in the late 1800s (CE), Confucius made up all these records, and just ascribed his own ideals to ancient rulers in order to make his writing sound authoritative. But either way, these records describe the first Zhou lords as repeatedly denying their own originality. Instead, they constantly claim that they are mere students, following the examples of far more illustrious "emperors of perfect virtue," who lived in a much more distant past. The *Classic of History* gives mythical records of these primordial emperors, and places their reigns in the centuries prior to 2000 BCE. In that case, it seems that the real Golden Age of Confucian legend was set in prehistoric times, before the first recorded kingdoms.

The Daoists also placed their legendary Golden Age in the pre-dynastic past. And their descriptions of those times sound even more primitive. The Daoist scenes of "unspoiled nature" and natural human simplicity bear a rough resemblance to what historians call the Chalcolithic age, of about 3500–2000 BCE (Jiao, 1995, 106–107). And where Confucian records claimed there were great "emperors" in that age, the early Daoists pointedly said that the Golden Age had no rulers at all. Most likely, the truth lies somewhere in between.

Probably there were leaders, but not "emperors." Most likely, the "emperors of perfect virtue" were just village elders or clan mothers. This is how the philosopher Deng Mu (1247–1306 CE) described the first "kings":

> *In the beginning of mankind, probably no one was pleased*
> *about becoming king. If someone was unlucky enough to win*
> *the hearts of the people, he could not really refuse the throne*
> *… In those days the kings ate mostly unhusked corn [millet?],*
> *bean pods, and coarse vegetables. They did not indulge in eating*
> *fancy foods. They wore linen garments during the summer and*
> *deerskin in winter; all men dressed the same. Their palace*
> *and the earthen steps leading up to it rose no more than three*
> *feet above the ground, and with its roof of uncut straw, it was*
> *anything but luxurious. (Bauer, 1976, 236–237)*

Of course Deng Mu had no real evidence about leadership in prehistoric times. He was just going by popular folklore, common sense, and his own moral outrage toward the rapacious rulers of his own time, who were Mongolian conquerors from the horde of Genghis Khan.

Joseph Needham also trusted popular folklore in describing the leaders of primitive China. But Needham also had evidence from ethnographic studies of traditional communities around the Pacific Rim. He felt that ancient legends and living traditions both suggested that early village leaders were respected according to their personal generosity. They were people of the potlatch ethic, in which the greatest leaders in the village were those who gave the most to others: "Their chiefs half-apologetically exercised leadership from within, and vied with one another in the distribution of the products of the chase or of agriculture in potlatch ceremonies; unlike the feudal lords whose pleasure it was to tyrannize from above" (Needham and Wang, 1956, 104–105).

In much of Native North America a comparable standard of leadership prevailed, which often meant that a chief was one of the tribe's poorest people—from sheer dint of gift giving. These people had a "gift economy." Their assets were counted in favors owed for past good deeds. In modern China this is called a *guanxi* system, in which giving between friends, relatives, or "connections" is often more central to economics than marketing (Baptandier, 1996, 128–129). If we can trust these memories and traditions, the most respected kind of power for primitive Chinese villagers was the power to give, not the power to take. The greatest givers were parents, elders, and probably clan mothers.

According to the Mengzi (3A:4), many villagers of the 300s BCE still expected such leadership. A man named Xu Xing, who claimed to follow the ways of legendary divine farmer Shennong, expressed his amazement at the new breed of force-backed rulers:

> *The ruler of Theng is indeed a worthy prince, but nevertheless he has not heard of the Dao. Real leaders cultivate the ground in common with the people, and so eat. They prepare their own morning and evening meals, carrying on government at the same time. But now the ruler of Theng has his granaries, treasuries and arsenals, which is oppressing the people to nourish himself. How can he be deemed a real leader? (Needham and Wang, 1956, 120–121)*

A real leader was someone who did what the other villagers did, and more—not someone privileged to work less. Real leaders were the first in giving. The taker-leaders of later times struck traditional people as the very opposite of what they claimed to be. Mengzi demanded to know: "Now, [to be a sovereign] is to be a father and mother to the people. If the sovereign causes great distress to the people—[who are] toiling for a whole year and yet unable to feed their parents; driven to borrowing till their old and young lie dying in ditches or water channels—how can he justify his claim to be father and mother to the people?" (Wu, 1982, 134–135).

So long as ordinary people expected their leaders to act like parents, they continued speaking of a Golden Age in which society was like a family. And if people couldn't have a full return to "the Great Equality," at least they called for simple fairness. As Dong Zhongshu (ca. 179–104 BCE) argued during the Han dynasty,

> When the five sage emperors and the three sage kings governed, no one dared take the attitude of a "prince" or of a [subject] "people" … The tenth [of crops] was raised for taxes, teaching was done with love, and orders were given with loyalty. The ancients were honored, relatives had feelings of kinship for each other, and showed respect to those worthy of it. The people were not robbed of their time and not used for compulsory labor for more than three days a year. Since families were given all they needed, the grief born of excessive hopes or furious disappointment did not exist, nor were there problems in relations between strong and weak. (Bauer, 1976, 79)

So in the Confucian legends, primordial father-figures exuded the virtues of compassion, generosity, and nurturance, for which the Golden Age was known. And these legends appealed to the present rulers' vanity. The Confucianists presented idealized pictures of the ruler's forefathers. Rather than rejecting the rulers' authority altogether as some Daoists did, the Confucianists tried to flatter politicians into emulating their supposedly more-compassionate ancestors.

In later classical art of imperial times, the Yellow Emperor and other mythical emperors of perfect virtue appeared seated on ornate thrones, dressed in flowing robes of finest silk, their faces blank masks of regal pomposity. These images portrayed ultimate authority vested in one man, as if that was a religious ideal. Supposedly, these were the ultimate patriarchs from which later warlords inherited their power. So the Qi clan claimed descent from Emperor Yao; the Feng clan came from the snake-god emperor, Fu Xi. The Ji clan (which was the royal house of Zhou) claimed a lineage from Hou Ji, or Lord Millet (Maspero, 1978, 73). The pompous pictures of divine patriarchs seemed to set a context, like the covers of a book. But inside these Confucian books, the stories told of values from a pre-patriarchal age. The folk tales of how these emperors *behaved* showed values so different from those of imperial times, that Westerners might term them "other worldly." These "emperors" were described as leading citizens in a meritocracy of spiritual virtue. In legends like these, we see the ambitions of monarchs projected backward onto the past. But we also see the values of pre-patriarchal times coming forward to claim the future.

The Legendary Emperors of Perfect Virtue

The Confucian classics suggest that in the beginning, ordinary people were totally ignorant. As the *Spring and Autumn Annals* report, "Princes did not yet exist in remotest antiquity. People lived together in herds and groups ... Names designating relationships, or concepts for above and below, old and young, did not exist. Nor did they know the various forms of politeness, the advantages of clothing and dwellings, or the use of tools, means of transport, or protective structures" (Bauer, 1976, 132). Then, a series of five to ten perfect emperors arrived to show the villagers what to do. It sounds completely authoritarian. But at least the primordial emperors behaved like hard-working leaders rather than superhuman deities.

The first emperors are described as "culture heroes," who bestowed useful inventions on the early tribes. It's true the Jade Emperor seemed rather impractical and aloof, bearing titles like "Highest Jade Emperor of All-Embracing Sublime Spontaneous Existence of the Heavenly Golden Palace." But Emperor Fu Xi (supposedly ruling ca. 2850 BCE) reportedly gave the people hands-on instruction, teaching them the arts of hunting, fishing, animal husbandry, and the eight trigrams of the *Yi Jing* (*I-Ching*). Emperor Shennong (reportedly ca. 2740 BCE) then invented agriculture and discovered the uses of medicinal plants. According to the *Huainanzi* (compiled ca. 139 CE), this "emperor" had to work very hard: "The Farmer God [Shennong] taught the people for the first time how to sow the five grains and about the quality of the soil ... He tasted the flavor of every single plant and determined which rivers and springs were sweet or brackish, and he let the people know how to avoid certain things" (Birrell, 1993, 49).

The Yellow Emperor (ca. 2700 BCE) then gave people boats, fire drills, and musical instruments. In the *Records of the Grand Historian* (of ca. 100 BCE), the Yellow Emperor is credited with providing almost everything for his infant people, maybe even the air they breathed: "He made it possible for the hundred grains and the grasses and trees to be planted and sowed, for the birds, beasts, insects and reptiles to multiply, for the sun, the moon, and the stars to appear across the sky, and for the soil, stones, metals and jade to be moistened" (Neinhauser, 1994, vol. I, 4). So the creation of the Chinese world was presented in a biblical style, with history drastically foreshortened from now-known archaeological facts. The founding wisdom for civilized life was simply handed down "by immaculate conception," from Confucian-looking sage-kings to the ignorant commoners (Keightley, 1983, xix).

Of course a probably older set of myths ascribed similar accomplishments to the snake goddess Nü Wa and her husband Fu Xi. And where the Yellow Emperor's legend spoke of his providing "the hundred grains," it was probably primitive women who gathered hundreds of wild plants, and started growing them near their homes. Concerning the accomplishments of Shennong, the divine farmer, we know from studies around the world that it was mainly mothers who tested what plants to eat, and took the risk of poisoning themselves before deciding what was good for their children. And Shennong's supposed discovery of Chinese herbal medicine was obviously the accomplishment of traditional village healers. Maybe these legends show that prehistoric people made culture heroes of inventors. But the actual developers of plant and animal husbandry, pottery, or herbal medicine, were almost certainly common villagers, both men and women. By making these inventors into primordial emperors, the Zhou princes claimed that all gifts of civilization came from rulers like themselves. The people depended on their rulers, and not the other way around. The Golden Age was ideal, not because the villagers were free and natural, but because they willingly obeyed their masters.

Confucius apparently accepted that rulers were the main agents of creation. At least his records from the court scribes said so. But the early Daoists drew on village folklore rather than court records, and their versions of pre-history were probably more accurate. In all probability, the age before empires had no emperors at all. Most likely there were only farmers, village elders, and clan matrons, without any perfect lords to teach them common sense. According to Min Jiayin, the primordial emperors such as Huangdi (the Yellow Emperor), Zhuanxu, Diku, Shun, and Yao, all bore their mothers' clan names (Min, 1995, 556). They were not heads of royal patrilineages, but members of important matrilineal clans. The good works ascribed to them were the kinds of work ordinarily done by old-fashioned village leaders. Surely it was the village elders and matrons who actually built the culture, economy, and religion of the Golden Age. They were the ones who passed on village wisdom about the way of fairness, good work, and partnership with nature, which was later called the Dao. If Daoists and ordinary villagers knew this but Confucianists did not, then these traditions might seem diametrically different. But there was one thing they both agreed on: A real leader was a servant to others, and a defender of ancient village morality.

The Selection of Servant Leaders

The legends of perfect emperors claim that ancient leaders were chosen by virtue alone. As Mozi (ca. 400 BCE) put it, the sage rulers "took great pains to honor the worthy and employ the capable, showing no special consideration for their own kin, no partiality for the eminent and rich, no favoritism for the good looking and attractive" (Watson, 1963, 25). Of course it's always possible to claim that the best man won after any contest for power. But the legends of primordial emperors describe a process of leadership selection in some detail, and this seems to roughly accord with old village traditions. Most likely, the earliest local leaders grew from the ground up. If they set an example for generosity and harmony in their family, then they might serve as an inspiration to the hamlet. And the perfect emperors are also described as "rising" from ordinary families, step by step. The most detailed account concerns "Emperor" Shun, who allegedly ruled in the 2200s BCE. His story probably telescopes a long process of evolution, from early gift-giving village heads, to state ministers offering lip service to ancient values.

When Emperor Yao grew old, he sought a leader to replace him. And feeling his own son was unqualified, he asked his ministers of the four mountains to rule jointly. The ministers consulted each other and declined. Instead, they recommended a virtually unknown villager named Shun, from "among the poor and mean" (Campbell, 1986, 386). They said this man had the true ancient virtues of leadership, and he should lead the country.

Shun was described as an eighth-generation descendant of the Yellow Emperor. However, as the Yellow Emperor reportedly had 24 sons and each of those begot many more, by the eighth generation this would have been an extremely distant relation. Possibly, mention of this "relationship" was added later, to accord with dynastic sentiments. Mengzi simply said that Shun was a man of the Eastern Yi Barbarians, a statement which later imperial historians found "startlingly iconoclastic" (Ho, 1975, 344).

Why did the ministers notice Shun? Basically, he was a faithful supporter of his family, regardless of how they treated him. His father was a half-blind, embittered old man, known as "blind oyster." This father repeatedly beat Shun. As the time of great floods began, the family had to move several times, and with each move Shun did most of the work. He was the one who found a new place, built a new house, and found work to support his abusive relatives. But despite his efforts, the other family members blamed Shun for their hardships, and the beatings from his father grew worse. Shun avoided resisting the blows, feeling that a father should be respected. If the attacks grew serious, he just left till the storm blew over (Wu, 1982, 71–73). For him it was a kind of game—like an exercise for strengthening his capacity to overcome resentment.

Word of all this got around the nearby villages, and reached the ministers of the four mountains. And though the court officials of later times would probably view Shun as a pathetic do-good fool, the ministers for the legendary Yao were looking for just such qualities.

Yao decided this was a man worth testing. He sent Shun a series of challenges, to see how he would respond. The tests he imposed suggest a shifting culture, where servant leaders were starting to turn into patriarchal headmen. First, Yao bestowed *two* of his daughters, named Ehuang and Nüying, as wives to Shun. (Later these wives became goddesses of the Xiang River.) Naturally, the arrival of two royal princesses caused a great stir in Shun's family and the surrounding village. The royal ministers watched from afar to see how things played out.

In no time Shuns' brothers and other relatives got greedy. They made a plan to murder Shun so they would inherit the wives and their wealth. The brothers came to Shun and asked him to dig a new well for the family. He did so, but when the well was nearly finished, the brothers poured dirt down the shaft to bury him alive. Fortunately, Shun had seen through the plot with the help of his wives, and had already made an escape tunnel out the side. As the brothers celebrated their success, Shun appeared, looking calm as ever. He gave them a knowing glance, but lodged no accusation against them.

Next, the emperor summoned Shun to serve as a teacher of the five codes. These concerned the five human relationships—between friends, lovers, parents and children, elders and juniors, or leaders and followers. Shun was supposed to teach the art of honoring these relationships to the emperor's relatives, to show if he could pass as a councilor to powerful families. Once again Shun proved helpful. It seemed there was no contradiction between what he advised and how he lived.

Last, Yao asked Shun to perform some difficult tasks in the wilderness, to test his resourcefulness like in a game of Survivor. Basically, all these tests were far more practical than the purely literary exams given to candidates for office in dynastic times.

Finally, Yao decided to offer Shun the top position. Shun accepted the responsibility, but at first avoided taking center stage. For several years he acted only as Yao's assistant. He didn't take the throne openly till after Yao was clearly too old (Wu, 1982, 74–76). Then, predictably, Shun soon had trouble with the royal relatives of previous emperors, who expected to inherit wealth and influence. One clan of these relatives was called "the chaotic." Others were "the eccentrics," "the rapacious," or "the blockheads." Shun banished these arrogant people to remote regions, to let their fearsome behavior frighten away hobgoblins on the realm's frontiers. In another move, Shun decreed "the game preserves and the mountains were all opened" (Neinhauser, 1994, vol. I, 13, 15–16). This implies that certain princes had begun enclosing common lands and excluding the villagers. Shun apparently reverted to ancient custom, in which all wild lands belonged to the whole community.

Though the classic texts describe Shun as an emperor, the role they show him playing bears no resemblance to that of emperors in historic times. He is described as leading by his own example, not by command. The *Huainanzi* describes Shun's leadership as follows:

The farmers of the Lishan encroached upon each other's
boundaries. Shun went there and farmed; and after a year
the boundaries were correct. The fishermen on the Ho bank
quarreled about the shallows. Shun went there and fished and
after a year they gave way to their elders. The potters of the
eastern barbarians made vessels that were coarse and bad. Shun
went there and made pottery. After a year their vessels were
solid. (Campbell, 1986, 388)

Shun is described behaving like a traditional chief among old-fashioned tribes—like a leader chosen by elder women of the Iroquois confederation. It seems he could only influence others by slowly winning their respect. The stories seem to insult the majesty of later rulers, but ordinary people found them inspiring. No doubt such tales influenced the young Zhou Enlai (Chou En-lai), as he strove to make himself a fit servant for his people.

Leadership in the Mythical Flood

Shun and his followers then faced a series of massive floods, which threatened to engulf China. And here, the tales of exemplary servant leadership get extreme.

Reportedly, Shun appointed a minister named Gun to handle the flood disaster. But Gun kept trying to build up dikes around villages and along the streams. The higher he raised the dikes, the more perilous the dammed-up floodwaters grew. An opposition party argued that dike building went against the flow of nature. It would be better and more natural to improve drainage, and let gravity reduce the floods. Egos were at stake, and Gun defended his record. Shun had to dismiss him, and switched to a drainage-based strategy (Wu, 1982, 85–86).

The next minister, Yu, proved a paragon of the ancient virtues. He led by personal example and did the work himself. Yu reportedly traveled over the nine regions by boat, cart, or foot, carrying a measuring rope and T-square as survey tools. Mengzi says he "dug the soil and led the water to the sea; drove out snakes and dragons, relegating them to the marshes" (Campbell, 1986, 389). According to the *Huainanzi,*

> *Yu himself carried baskets of dirt and led the people in damming up the waters. He drained off the rivers and opened up the nine outlets; he governed their channels and directed them to the nine courses. He opened the five lakes and settled the eastern sea. In those times, though it was burning heat, men had no time to rest; drenched, they took not leisure to dry themselves. (De Bary and Chan, 1960, vol. I, 187)*

Like some hero of the People's Republic, Yu slaved year after year, digging channels, draining swamps, or reclaiming farmland. *The Book of Master Zuang* says that Yu's "long exposure to the wind, the rain, and the parching sun roughened his body" (Min, 1995, 558). After several years of this, no hair remained on his arms or legs. His feet dragged as he walked, and people still call such a gait a "Yu step" (Wu, 1982, 86–87). Confucius reportedly said, "If it were not for Yu, we would all be fishes."

These legends exaggerate Yu's self-sacrifice to almost sadistic proportions. They have Yu boast, "When I married, I remained only four days together with my wife. And when my son wailed and wept, I paid no attention, but kept planning with all my might." He labored for 13 years without ever going home, even when he passed his gate. In addition, this "emperor" is said to have labored "in accord with the natural conditions. When he entered the land of the naked, he stripped himself to accord with native custom" (Campbell, 1986, 389–390). To fund the earthworks, he sold off much of his family's property. It was a tale of selfless service that could hardly be intensified, even by self-sacrificing Confucian mothers. Clearly, the mythical Yu was not the kind of role model most future rulers wished to copy. And by imperial times, the virtues attributed to Yu would be deemed more appropriate for women. But the legend recalls a time when service to others was a virtue for both sexes. And throughout history, such legends formed the popular standards by which ordinary people judged their leaders.

Shun reviewed Yu's performance and decided to promote him. Though Shun had at least one son, the boy was "not like" his father, and Shun didn't consider appointing him as chairman. That would have been nepotism, which the classic texts actually opposed. So when Shun retired, he gave his job to the most virtuous leader in the land, namely Yu. The only problem was that Yu was too modest. He withdrew to his own estate when Shun died, feeling he should give Shun's son a chance to rule. This didn't last, because the tribal leaders kept coming to Yu with their problems. Finally, seeing that everybody regarded him as the leader regardless of his position, Yu returned to his office (Wu, 1982, 100). The legend probably suggests how ancient villagers choose their leaders. They let several people try to lead, and found out who the people followed. Maybe the locals in ancient Jerusalem could have tried that, to see if the people of Judah preferred to follow the High Priest Caiphas, or Jesus. But of course, as in later Chinese history, that would be out of the question.

Recent geological studies date the greatest period of flooding and incursion by the sea to the centuries around 3000 BCE. This seems earlier than the legendary dates of Yao, Shun, and Yu (around 2200 BCE), but the folklore could easily be off on dates. Min Jiayin suspects there were indeed leaders who organized villages of the Yangzi and Yellow River basins to build dikes and drainage channels (1995, 558–559). It's quite possible the villagers had to coordinate efforts on a regional scale, perhaps for the first time. They probably had to choose inter-tribal leaders, and give them practical as well as symbolic powers. At first these leaders would have led by personal example. Later, the region-wide importance of the work probably fostered certain abuses, in which local people were pushed to work against their will. The accomplishments of the embryonic state may have fostered pride and ambition—to use the villagers for further great works.

The Confucian *Classic of History* gives the Zhou princes' version of the story, in which the point is "how the state was built." Their princely records claim that after the floods were drained, Shun and Yu had sufficient prestige to assume administrative roles, survey the lands, and compose tithe registers. They reportedly set out a governing structure, with a minister "of the hundred affairs," plus departments of justice, works, animal husbandry, sacrificial ceremonies, music, and a chief secretary to record distributions of land. (Wu, 1982, 92–98). Min Jiayin claims, "It was this battle to harness the rivers that prepared the way for the great change of replacing matriarchy with patriarchy after Yu's death" (1995, 559).

The Leadership of Those Willing to Learn

In dynastic times, teaching was almost always a top-down process, where superiors taught, and inferiors learned. But the myths of the Golden Age say that real leaders were eager to learn from others. Of course this suggests leaders who could admit to having weaknesses and making mistakes. And such admissions would be basically out of the question in the later competitions for supreme power. But willingness to listen and learn from neighbors was what the ancient villages expected in a leader, and the Confucian legends met the demand.

The folk tales of early emperors seeking teachers resemble old Indian stories of quests for gurus. And in many cases the emperor's guru was a woman. For example, the Yellow Emperor went to the holy Tai Mountain seeking guidance about conflicts with his half-brother, Ji Yu (Chi Yu), the Flame Emperor. An encyclopedia from around 400 CE reports:

The Yellow Emperor and Chi Yu [Ji Yu] fought nine times,
but for nine times there was no winner. The Yellow Emperor
returned to Tai Mountain for three days and three nights. It was
foggy and dim. There was a woman with a human head and a
bird's body. The Yellow Emperor kowtowed, bowed twice, and
prostrated himself, not daring to stand up. The woman said,
"I am the Dark Lady. What do you want to ask me about?" The
Yellow Emperor said, "Your humble servant wishes to question
you about the myriad attacks, the myriad victories." Then he
received The Art of War from her. (Birrell, 1993, 137)

In addition to this, the Yellow Emperor got at least seven other sages to advise him. His guides included a Wind Prince, a Mighty Shepherd, a Great Swan, a Beast of the White Marsh, and a Woman of Profound Mystery of the Nine Heavens. A woman named Sunu helped him stimulate the crops by inventing and playing her 25-string *qin* instrument, to orchestrate the growing seasons. As if the Yellow Emperor was Harry Potter, the Queen Mother of the West taught him magic, awarding him a powerful foot-long talisman of jade and cinnabar.

The *Bamboo Annals* (discovered in the 200s CE) say the Queen Mother taught Emperor Shun as well. She reportedly gave him a white tube to regulate the seasons and share her power over time (Cahill, 1993, 45–46). Another myth says that Emperor Yu appealed to the Jasper Lady for help with the floods. He approached her palace, which was guarded by intimidating lions, vicious dragons, horses of heaven, and lightning animals. The Jasper Lady received Yu in her hall, as if she was a more elegant version of the Great Oz. In response to Yu's request, she opened a box of jade and cinnabar and gave him a scroll called the *Book of Rules and Orders*. She issued commands for spirits of the elements to help Yu, by reshaping huge stones to unblock the floodways (Birrell, 1993, 157–159, 176–178). How did Yu win such support from powerful women? Probably it didn't hurt that, as the legend says, he never heard anyone criticize him without bowing low in appreciation (Mengzi, 3:2; Wu, 1982, 111–112).

Some of the later rulers of early dynasties were said to follow this tradition. Lord Dang (Tang), the founder of the Shang dynasty (ca. 1700 BCE), reportedly searched for a sagely teacher, and found a village farmer called Yi Yin. As the *Dao De Jing* put it, "When it comes to governing the people, there is no one like a farmer" (LaFargue, 1992, 58–59). Dang tried to lure this peasant to court, offering gifts and explaining, "So I have heard, he who finds teachers for himself will end up becoming a king: he who says that others are not equal to himself will come to ruin. He who likes to ask becomes enlarged, and he who uses only himself is small" (Wu, 1982, 157). At first, Yi Yin turned him down, saying "What use have I for such gifts?" But later Yi thought it over, and reasoned: "Instead of abiding in these plowed fields and regaling myself with the principles of Yao and Shun, would it not be better for me to make this prince [Dang] a prince like Yao and Shun? Would it not be better for me to give the people a chance to live like people under Yao and Shun? Would it not be better for me to see these things happen in my lifetime?" (Wu, 1982, 133).

Clearly, this was how the later followers of Confucius hoped to be employed—by leaders eager to learn. In that case, the teachers of Golden Age values would not be forced to sell their wisdom in the courts of dismissive tyrants.

Maybe the real Lord Dang was just a petty despot, who barked orders and assumed his subordinates were blockheads. Or maybe he did show some eagerness to learn from others, and the tale of it was wildly exaggerated in hopes of shaming later royal egomaniacs. Maybe the story has nothing to do with the historical Lord Dang, and simply restates what the village elders and clan mothers expected of a leader, namely a willingness to learn from neighbors, Dark Ladies, and Queen Mothers.

The Law of the Village

In dynastic times (after about 1000 BCE) rulers generally tried to control the villagers by intimidation, using threats of horrible penalties. As in ancient Rome, law enforcement was haphazard. The authorities hoped to inspire obedience, less by efficient crime detection than by making a terrifying example of those they caught. In Zhou times the usual penal codes listed "five punishments": death, castration, amputation, cutting off the nose, or marking the face with a black tattoo. By the 200s BCE, there were about 2,500 legal bans carrying one or another of these penalties (Maspero, 1978, 47). A Chinese equivalent of crucifixion was the Qin dynasty penalty of the "five-pains," which involved (for a male offender) cutting off the victim's nose, then a hand, a foot, castrating him, and finally chopping him in half. Later dynasties tried the famous "death by a thousand cuts." Worse yet, the emperors imposed collective punishment on the relatives of offenders. In cases of treason or peasant revolt, entire communities were presumed guilty by association and massacred.

Supposedly, the worse the punishments, the fewer would be the offenses. But somehow it never seemed to work that way. By the Ming dynasty (1328–1644), Emperor Zhu Yuanzhang could report, "In the morning I punish a few; by evening others commit the same crime. I punish these in the evening and by the next morning again there are violations. Although the corpses of the first have not been removed, already others follow in their path. The harsher the punishment, the more the violations. Day and night I cannot rest" (Ebrey, 1981, 125).

This was *fa*, or law, as both rulers and subjects knew it. Basically, fa was simply the will of the powerful. And for the villagers, law was a thing to be avoided—the way they hoped to evade taxes (Ching, 1990, 164–165). Such evasion of fa law seemed subversive and anarchic to the rulers, but the villagers had standards of their own. In general, they hoped to preserve the peace though neighborly care, rather than force-backed control of inferiors by overlords. Just as the village elders and local wise women had countercultures, so they had customs of counter-law.

The early village leaders probably had no authority of life or death over their neighbors. They had only powers of persuasion, without real means of enforcing obedience. Besides, violence had long-term costs. If a local conflict led to "mob justice," then the relatives of both killers and victims would have to face each other the next morning, and maybe for the rest of their lives. For some such reason, the legends of Golden Age emperors urged extreme caution in using force. Emperor Shun supposedly told his justice ministers, "Be reverent! Be reverent! Be ever sparing of punishment!" Shun reportedly advised symbolic rather than literal penalties, such as wearing a black headband instead of a facial tattoo, being covered in red mud rather than having a nose cut off, etc. (Wu, 1982, 83–84). Likewise, the Confucian scholar Xunzi (Hsün-tzu, 200s BCE) tried to argue with his warlords, "One who truly understands how to use force does not rely upon force. He is careful to ... create a fund of goodwill ... his benevolence is the loftiest in the world ... He need not wear out his men and arms, and yet the whole world is won over to him" (Ching, 1990, 164).

Such traditionalists made an argument that is still rejected by most rulers, but accepted by most mothers, families and communities— that renouncing the threat of violence against other people is mature rather than weak, and enforcing demands by violence is depraved rather than moral. The first Confucian scholars were evangelists for such impractical values. As I will argue later, they were "mama's boys," loyally defending values that originally came through their mothers.

Rather than resisting warlords by force, most Confucianists argued like women, trying to flatter their "lords" into behaving with "humanity." Rather than opposing the warlords' power directly, they claimed that previous warlords had relied on benevolence, and benevolence would actually increase the warlords' prestige. But aside from claiming that past emperors had been despots of a kinder sort, what did the Confucian books say about village government in the Golden Age?

When Confucius or his followers edited a compilation of old laws called the *Zhou li* (*Rites of Zhou*), they published a mixture of old village customs and policies of early Zhou princes. And these records say that in older times, both villagers and princes wanted the local people to handle their own affairs.

From the prince's side, the *Zhou li* says that the Duke of Zhou (ca. 1050 BCE) tried to discourage villagers from bringing criminal charges against each other. It required feuding parties to each deposit 100 arrows in order to appeal their case to a district official. That was costly by the standards of ancient times, and few people were willing to pay so much to take a complaint beyond the authority of the village. Besides, both parties had to be willing to pay 100 arrows, or else the case would not be heard. It was therefore impossible for one party to drag the other into court against his or her will (Wu, 1982, 409). Even if local disputes got violent, the book of customary law urged villagers to settle it themselves: "If a fight has resulted from an outburst of angry passions, the arbitrator shall do his best to seek an amicable settlement. If no settlement can be reached, the whole proceedings shall be entered into the [public] record. Thereafter, the party that strikes the first blow shall be punished" (Wu, 1982, 410). Concerning these traditional laws, Jacques Gernet says "it was a system of justice apparently designed to discourage people from acquiring a taste for legal proceedings" (1962, 107). Instead of urging warlords to restrain their own powers over the villagers, the *Zhou li* argued that village autonomy was best for the princes themselves. With a certain self-contradiction in terms, it claimed that the wisest rulers taught their villagers to be self-governing.

The Zhou princes liked to take credit for their people's virtues. They praised the organization of traditional villages, implying that this order came from the prince. Most villages had associations for mutual help in planting, harvesting, house building, or holding weddings and funerals, much like villages do today. No doubt the women especially worked together, weeding or weaving in groups, singing songs and making up stories as they went. As the old saying about good neighbors goes, "two donkeys gnaw each other's neck" (Chau, 2006, 40–41). The *Zhou li* and other sources made general statements about local organization, saying that five families made a neighborhood, and five neighborhoods a village (Wu, 1982, 252–253). Many sources also say that village land was divided equitably between families, according to some standardized formula. Probably the formulas were mathematical abstractions of a type well loved by officials. Actually, the divisions of land were different in each place, according to the landscape. But however untidy things may have been, it seems most ancient villages did divide land equitably among families, as they do in modern post-Mao China today. Whatever the family feuds, the village mothers generally urged sharing enough land to feed the local children.

In urging their warlords to respect village traditions, the early Confucian preachers credited the warlords' ancestors with inventing village law. So we picture the first Zhou princes busily commissioning village associations, and overseeing divisions of farmland across North China. But those mutual-help associations were almost certainly formed by the villagers themselves, and the divisions of land were probably simple agreements among village families, according to their numbers of mouths. In praising these local structures, the Confucianists seemed to congratulate the rulers for letting local people do their work. They seemed to encourage warlords to claim credit for their villagers' decency.

Where old-fashioned people handled their own affairs, the law of the village could be arbitrary. The villagers could be personally vicious. But personal animosity was usually tempered by accepted values, which the locals evolved from living together over centuries. The punishments recommended in the *Zhou li* reflect those handed out by traditional villages. One common penalty was for offenders to have a wooden plaque fastened on their backs, listing their crimes for all to see (Wu, 1982, 411–412). The idea was to make criminals accountable to those they harmed. A modern description such village-style justice appears in Jan Myrdal's *Report from a Chinese Village*, which was written in the 1960s but probably represents ancient tradition more than any new Communist ideology:

> We ... captured a thief ... who had stolen a two-wheeled cart ... He was taken to the office of the people's commune, and we had a serious talk with him. He was severely criticized and also criticized himself. After that he signed an undertaking that he would never do such a thing again and was then allowed to go home. We never let such matters go up to Yenan [or Yanan, the district center]. We can deal with them ourselves. (Myrdal, 1965, 372)

If this sounds like a traditional "justice circle" in a Native North American community, maybe the roots of both traditions are related.

Sometimes local justice involved beating or flogging, which many modern westerners would consider barbaric. But the ancient Chinese would probably be more horrified by the modern prison system. Their justice usually took a few minutes. Then the criminals were reintegrated with their community, hopefully on a better basis. That was the way mothers disciplined children. To isolate people from their families for months or decades seemed the cruelest, most mentally damaging punishment short of death.

In general, the villagers tried to manage their own affairs with as little interference from "higher authorities" as possible. Just as the villagers wanted their grain to stay in the village and not be taxed away, so they hoped to settle their own problems. They wanted to work things out face to face with people they knew. They wanted local leaders accountable to their neighbors, not to some distant power. As Mozi explained in the 400s BCE, the origin of social authority was consent among the villagers, who gathered together to prevent injury or disorder, and elected the wisest among them as leaders. This ordinary desire for self-determination didn't originate from contact with Western democracies. It was the desire of most local people from the first village cultures forward. For example, when students made demands for greater local autonomy to Shanghai mayor Jiang Zemin in 1986, they were outraged by his excuse—that he had no mandate to respond to their requests, since his position was by appointment from above rather than from the community below.

The legends of Golden Age leaders have had scripture-like status in popular culture for nearly 2,500 years. They have formed a standard for moral expectations by which all rulers have been judged, at least in the court of public opinion. It took considerable textual engineering to make these legends of Golden Age leaders into pillars of support for absolute monarchy and male superiority, since these stories were basically a standing rebuke to most later rulers, who simply seized or inherited power. Partly due to stories like these, ordinary people across China were outraged over Deng Xiaoping's 1980s nepotism in naming numerous relatives to high office. Their anger was not just imported from foreign cultures; it was traditional in China's own counterculture.

The Survival of Traditional Leadership

The virtues praised in these ancient legends seem patriarchal because they are typically ascribed to men. But actually these virtues resemble a list of traditional Western ideals for women. The virtuous in these tales are those who nurture others. They embody "feminine" qualities of kindness, harmony, and selfless giving (and giving, and giving). These values are more in line with those of ancient clan mothers than warlord patriarchs. And in reports of the Golden Age, the same values are expected of both women and men. To many Western readers, the men in these ancient accounts seem effeminate. Later, China's rising warlords would set new standards for real manhood.

But probably most local men and women were repulsed rather than impressed by the warlords' powers to take and intimidate.

During the first years of the modern twentieth century, a woman calling herself "Guardian of Modesty" wrote a series of articles for the *Magazine of the New Chinese Woman*. She argued that since Confucius praised the virtues of women (at least occasionally), that it was only after Confucius, "from the Warring States period [of 475 to 221 BCE] that women's rights began to deteriorate." The task for women, therefore, was not to initiate women's rights in opposition to the whole of Chinese tradition, but to *recover* the legal rights and powers women had in the deep past (Judge, 2008, 211–212).

Naturally, the traditional "laws" of ancient villagers tended to focus on face-to-face relations, family values, and personal morality. Most village traditionalists seemed to assume that if personal relationships were proper, then the problems of society would be solved. But of course China's villagers had to cope with far greater problems than personal or communal disharmony. The real outlaws these villagers faced were like "corporate criminals," whose extortion and abuse were mainly imposed from above, through impersonal higher institutions or foreign invasions. At first, Confucian moralists aimed to defend village people from abuse by these higher authorities. The Confucian sage Mengzi even cited the *Classic of History* to justify killing tyrants. Much to the horror of his contemporary war-monger princes, Mengzi claimed there was an important legal distinction between "regicide" and "tyrannicide."

To deal with such critics, the first emperor of China (200s BCE) simply massacred any Confucianists who dared criticize present rulers by standards from the past. Then he burned all known copies of their books. And this persecution was largely effective. As Christian critics of Roman tyranny tended to become loyal citizens in response to deadly persecution, so Confucianist would-be officials tended to change their tune. In later centuries they increasingly taught that duty to superiors was more important than defense of subordinates.

In that case, most Confucian scholars stopped speaking for local people. And the local people increasingly looked elsewhere for leaders.

Daoist folklore upheld a different kind of nostalgia. For early Daoists, the Golden Age was not a time of benevolent dictators, but of no dictators at all. The old Daoist writings were almost Luddite, with back-to-nature, utopian-anarchist sentiments (Ching, 1990, 90–91). As a zither-playing member of the Eight Immortals reportedly said, "Musicians who pander to the tastes of the leisure class are no different from dogs who wag their tails in the presence of their masters" (Wong, 2007, 63).

But many Daoists were basically wish-dreaming escapists. Their legends often concerned escape to alternative worlds. And in a sense this reflects actual history. Because over the centuries, vast numbers of villagers fled the domains of abusive warlords, hoping to find autonomy elsewhere. The rulers condemned such disrespect, as the *Guanzi (Kuan Tzu)* advised, "A ruler should not listen to those who believe in people having opinions of their own and in the importance of the individual. Such teachings cause people to withdraw to quiet places and hide away in caves or on mountains, there to rail at the prevailing government, sneer at those in authority, belittle the importance of rank and emoluments, and despise all who hold official posts" (Campbell, 1986, 423).

Most refugees went south to where life could be marginally better. But in many Daoist legends, there were actually parallel realities (known as *beyul*, or hidden lands) where people lived as they had in the Golden Age. For example, Kang Yuzhi (1100s CE) wrote of discovering a secret cave, which opened into an underground world. There, people lived in an idealized dream of long ago. As Kang had the cave villagers explain,

> *It is true that the people here come from a great many families, but they all have absolute trust in each other, and live together in the most marvelous harmony you normally find among members*

of a single family. That is why they can live together without distinctions. But we don't like people who cannot reconcile their interests, let alone those who have disputes or quarrels ... It is a principle among us that there should be no private property, and that includes clothes and foodstuffs, cattle, silk, and hemp. Everything is owned communally. That is also the reason we can all live together without distinction. If you really want to settle here, you must not bring any gold, pearls, brocade, embroideries, or other valuables. They would be useless here, and only provoke quarrels. It would be best if you came with empty hands. (Bauer, 1976, 232–233)

But whatever the escapist, primitive communal sentiments of many village Daoists, the leaders of Daoist sects eventually joined the Confucian scholars in seeking employment from their rulers. They began claiming to represent the wisdom of past perfect Daoist emperors such as the Jade Emperor. They tried advising their rulers in a slightly less manipulative approach to absolute power. When Daoist priests gained high office, they generally served their patrons well. The priest Kou Qianzhi (early 400s CE) felt moved to proclaim that the emperor of the Northern Wei state was the incarnation of a Daoist deity. He was rewarded with an appointment to head a new Daoist state church (Hawkins, 2004, 205). Once again, the weakness of organized religion was its need for patrons.

It was the "popular religion" of ordinary village men and women (be it Daoist, Confucian, Buddhist, shamanic, or all four) which remained a largely independent force. And popular folklore was never successfully controlled by any set of rulers. It could be traditional, but anarchic. It was often moralistic, but also irreverent and comical. In the view of the villagers' superiors, popular "superstition" was often heretical and traitorous. But nothing could stop the villagers from making their own myths, songs, and dramas. They imagined or remembered a pantheon of "real leaders." They created a folklore of secret societies, heroic bandits, goddesses of mercy, or rogue deities who defended village people.

In one popular legend, the goddess of the moon, Chang'e, looked down upon the earth and saw that a cruel tyrant had taken the emperor's throne. Chang'e had once been a mortal woman, but after stealing the elixir of immortality from her husband, she had floated into the sky and become the moon goddess. Now she was horrified to see her former people oppressed without mercy. In hope of helping them, she let herself be reborn on earth as a human girl. While she was growing up, the emperor's agents enslaved or killed all the other members of her family. Chang'e alone escaped and managed to survive in the wild countryside.

Meanwhile the emperor was growing old, and became obsessed with finding the secret of eternal life. He ordered sages and shamans from across the kingdom to report to his palace. One after another he demanded they tell him the secret and give him a magic potion. When they failed to deliver it, he killed them.

Back in her forest Chang'e was pondering what to do, when Guanyin, the goddess of universal compassion, appeared before her. She gave Chang'e a small bottle of elixir for the emperor. Chang'e traveled to the imperial palace and claimed to have what the emperor desired. Naturally, the emperor was suspicious, since many had tried to kill him. He required that Chang'e taste the elixir first. She complied, and stood before him smiling. At this, the emperor seized the bottle and drank it down. Within moments he gasped and fell over dead. Chang'e also collapsed and died as the poison elixir took its delayed effect. Then, freed from her mortal body and having accomplished her mission, she rose to resume her place as goddess of the moon.

8: The Fall of Chinese Women

In Communist-era China, most historians believed that the rise of ancient states involved an "historical defeat of the female sex." As Engels and Marx felt it had happened in Europe, so it seemed to be in China. The initial age of "primitive communism" gave way to force-backed regimes of slaveholders and feudal lords, with dire consequences for most women. Some people argued that this was no tragedy, but simply an inevitable march of progress. Others felt that social inequality was always a choice, and other options were always possible.

If the fall of women wasn't inevitable, how did it happen? How was it different in cause or effect in China compared to what happened in Europe?

In Europe, the early "civilizations of the goddess" excavated by Marija Gimbutas and others show signs of almost total destruction during several periods of warfare. It looks like these ancient villages were burned and plundered by several "waves" of invaders, called "Kurgan waves," after the Russian word for their warlords' earth-mound graves. The first Kurgan wave came around 4400 BCE, leaving the ruins of plundered villages across the Ukrainian steppes and into Eastern Europe. The next wave arrived around 3500 BCE, and pushed further west into Germany or Serbia. The Old European villages in these regions were destroyed, and often turned into nomadic camps for people with animal herds. Possibly most of the village men were killed, and the women absorbed into the invader's clans. Graves of the Kurgan warlords commonly contained a heavily armed male body, surrounded by several dead women and slaves. Kurgan wave III came around 3000 BCE, as a "Battle Axe Culture" spread westward to the British Isles. After that, the tempo of invasions stepped up, and the migrations of groups like the Indo-European Celts or Dorians grew too numerous to clearly count. A later cluster of invasions from Inner Asia overran most of Europe as the western Roman empire collapsed.

Probably the last pre-warlord cultures in Europe held out on islands such as Crete, or Ireland, with Crete's Minoan culture being overrun around 1450 BCE. All this happened so early that previous cultures had basically faded from living memory by the time written history began. Concerning Europe's first cultures, only vague myths and some vestiges of folk tradition survived, until the remains of Minoan and Old European cultures were excavated in recent decades.

The Historical Defeat of Women, Chinese Style

A few differences in China's situation are obvious. First, China's age of autonomous village cultures lasted around 2,000 years longer, often down to the 1000s BCE or later. And while Europe's "cultures of the goddess" were conquered long before the dawn of recorded history, China's early cultures survived as a powerful counterculture in popular memory. More recently, however, China suffered from warlord invasions even more than Europe. It was conquered by several nomadic groups, including the Mongol horde and the Manchus. Basically, warlord states and empires arose later in China, but then lasted longer—until the fall of the Manchurians' Qing dynasty in 1911.

Besides these differences in timing, most Chinese historians claim that the "defeat of women" happened for different reasons in China than it did in Europe. Liu Ruzhen says that, unlike Riane Eisler's model of patriarchy and militarism in Europe, "The transition from the matriarchy to patriarchy [in China] took place naturally" (Liu 1995, 355). Min Jiayin basically agrees:

> *The dramatic change in the status of and the relationship between the sexes in China was not caused by the invasions of barbarous and violent nomads; instead ... the patriarchal society and the dominator model took shape in the process of gradual*

evolution, although the male physical power and forcefulness, the blade and war, did play a decisive role ... So far, Chinese archaeologists have not found any signs indicating nomadic invasions on any great scale which could have been the force replacing matriarchy with patriarchy between 5000 BC and 3000 BC. (1995, 555–556)

Some historians say that Chinese men grew economically superior after farmers on the northern plains developed plows, and strong plowmen seemed more important than women as farmers (Barber, 1994, 165). Back in the 1800s, Friedrich Engels speculated that patriarchal culture arose as local leaders took on coordinator roles between communities, and slowly became regional power brokers (Engels, 1987, 25). For some reason, almost all these leaders were male, and the domination of some males over others also involved ranking most men over most women. Some argue this was "natural," even though much of recorded folk sentiment opposed it. Most likely, there was an element of force involved.

If China's early cultures were not systematically destroyed by invader waves, they still suffered a less destructive level of violence, and a more gradual series of invasions. To the north of China prior to 2000 BCE, farm settlements dotted the landscape of Mongolia. The early Mongolian houses held stone slabs, grain-hullers, and grinders of the farmer's trade. But these villages were quite suddenly abandoned, sometimes with signs of violence. To the east, fortified towns on the Amur River (such as Kharinskaya mound or Kirovsk, near Vladivostok), were deserted so suddenly that pots of millet were left to carbonize on the cooking fires. For the next several thousand years Mongolia was a country of nomadic herds people (Walls, 1980, 70–74). They lived in tents, followed the good grass, and became a roving army of horsemen, who regularly raided China's villages to the south.

In Longshan-culture villages of North China from late 2000s BCE, the signs of fortification and weaponry (such as stone battle axes) probably indicate early wars between egotistical village headmen. It seems clear that large settlements were starting to conquer weaker ones (Jiao, 1995, 104105). But at the site near Handan, Hebei, where two village wells were filled with decapitated bodies, six of the skulls bore signs of a kind of scalping. Archaeologist Yan Wenming claimed that these skulls had been used as drinking cups. Yan also noted that from the time of Herodotus, observers regarded drinking from the skulls of enemies as a characteristic tradition of nomadic warriors from Inner Asia (O'Connell, 1995, 162–163). Probably raids from the pastoral country were a factor in the slowly rising level of violence.

Over the next several millennia there were many major or minor invasions of "barbarous and violent nomads," who attacked and often ruled much of China. The early Shang, Zhou (Chou), and Qin (Ch'in) dynasties (of the 1700s to 207 BCE) all likely rose from nomadic tribes on the northern frontiers of China. Then, from 316 to about 580 CE, much of northern China was overrun by "Five Barbarian Groups." Contending warlords captured "enemy people" from other warlords, and took the women as slaves. From 581 to 618, the Toba tribe nomads established the Sui dynasty. Later, from 907 to 1125, Quidan (Kitan) tribes from the Gobi region imposed the Liao dynasty over much of North China. After that the Nuzhen (Jurchin) pastoralists dominated the entire northern half of China from 1125 to 1234. Then the Mongol horde moved in, conquered the entire country, and held it till 1368. Finally, the warlords of Manchuria seized all of China from 1644 until 1911. Min Jiayin says these invaders never successfully imposed their cultures on ordinary Chinese people: "In the outcome of the prolonged struggle against the force of the blade of the northern nomads, the ethnic Han, a farming race, was never conquered culturally, and, of course, was far from being eliminated" (Min, 1995, 575). But as I'll show in a later chapter, the legal status of Chinese women declined most dramatically during the periods of direct "barbarian rule."

In this chapter, I want to look at early changes in leadership and women's power during the first several "dynasties," from the Xia (Hsia) to the Qin, which span a period from around 2100 to 200 BCE. These first dynasties already showed a strong disconnection between the cultures of ruling clans and ordinary villagers. Their ruling clans already showed cultural or technical affinities with other militarized cultures across Inner Asia and the Middle East. For example, excavations of the Shang capitals in North China (from around 1300 BCE) show artifacts typical of dominator cultures: bronze weapons, horse-drawn chariots, and monumental graves of male rulers, buried with their servants and women. The chieftain graves resembled those of earlier Kurgan waves across Inner Asia. Their two-wheeled chariots had likely diffused eastward over the steppes from West Asia (Campbell, 1986, 377). Two Shang oracle inscriptions mention getting "chariots of the Gong (Kung) people," or capturing horse chariots from the Weifang people. Both the Gong and Weifang were Turkic tribes, and such tribes left remains or rock drawings of similar chariots all the way across Inner Asia (Ho, 1975, 355–366; O'Connell, 1995, 120–121). As in later history, it seems that the strongest Chinese rulers took their arts of war from the nomadic raiders.

But China's myths of the first strong-man rulers concern an even earlier period, of the semi-legendary Xia dynasty.

Xia Kings (ca. 2100 to 1700 BCE)

Though Min Jiayin feels the Xia state was centered in the Yangzi basin, many other historians identify it with the Erlitou culture, which was a cluster of early Bronze Age towns in central Yellow River valley. Aside from this, the whole dynasty is basically a matter of folklore. It was reportedly founded after Yu, the Golden Age leader who saved China from the flood, tried to pass on his mantle of leadership. Through some traditional tests of ability and virtue, Yu chose a man named Boyi. But unfortunately, Yu's son, Qi, seized the throne by force. Qi then proclaimed a principle of patrilineal inheritance, which founded a dynasty as we know it.

In Chinese folklore, this event is roughly equivalent to the opening of Pandora's Box. Except that in China, the box is opened by a greedy man. Probably the story condenses a long series of developments. But through some such events, the property of matrilineal clans was changed into a patriarchal inheritance (Min, 1995, 556–559). As the *Han Commentaries on the Book of Changes* complained, "The Five Emperors [before the Xia dynasty] regarded the country as belonging to everyone and so they found the ablest men to run it, whereas the Three Kings [after Yu] regarded the country as their own private property and so bequeathed it to their children" (Du Jinpeng, 1995, 129).

This notion of patriarchal inheritance quickly led to further problems. When Qi chose his own successor from among his six sons, the other five sons rebelled and fought a civil war. The winning son, Daigang (Taikang) presumed to rule "without winning the confidence of blood relations or the hundred surnames" (Wu, 1982, 119). While most local villages still had their elders and matrons, the regional leaders were claiming authority by some combination of birthright and force. The "divine right" of rule by male inheritance was being entrenched, but the concept of primogeniture (inheritance by the *eldest* son) was not yet accepted.

According to many legends, the Xia dynasty slowly degenerated into moral depravity. Their last emperor, Jie, was so selfish that popular folklore made him a stock figure of primordial evil. He was insatiable in demands for tribute, which he wasted on sumptuous pavilions and lavish banquets. It didn't help that he kept a dragon woman in his palace, called the "Kraken Concubine," who was a dangerously beautiful maneater. Anyway, Jie and his court grew so corrupt that Heaven and Earth could take no more. According to Mozi, drought scorched the land, wilting the five grains. Winds and demons howled their protests. People muttered that there was not enough to eat. Yet more ominously, the cycles of the sun and moon grew irregular. Obviously, a new pivot of heaven and earth was required. Finally, the nine ceremonial cauldrons in the Xia court, which were tokens of divine favor, vanished in a puff of smoke. They reappeared in the court of Lord Dang (Tang), a heroic leader of the Shang people, who lived on the northern boundaries of China. With this miracle, Lord Dang knew himself divinely chosen for power. He and his loyal men mounted their horses and rode forth to execute the will of Heaven. Like Lord Rama attacking the evil Rakshashas of ancient India, Dang righteously smote his demonic foes, driving them in terror from the field (Campbell, 1986, 393–396).

Clearly, the Xia experience was not an auspicious start for China's dynasties. Popular revulsion against despotic rulers appeared overwhelming, but the remedy at hand was another warlord from the northern frontier, riding in to seize the throne for himself. Before his attack, Lord Deng warned his men like a typical horseback chieftain: "I pray you assist me, the One Man, to carry out the punishment [of the Xia] appointed by Heaven. I will greatly reward you ... [But] if you do not obey the words I have spoken to you, I will put your children to death with you. You will find no forgiveness" (Chang, 1980, 194–195). Joseph Campbell suggests that the legendary Shang victory echoes other victories of mounted or chariot-driving tribes across Europe, the Middle East, and India. At roughly the same time (probably between 1800 and 1700 BCE) both the Harappan towns of aboriginal Pakistan and the Xia towns of northern China were conquered by invaders from the borderlands of Inner Asia (Campbell, 1986, 395, 407). It seems that that dominator civilization as we know it had arrived in the Far East.

The Shang (ca. 1700 to 1050 BCE)

The Confucian classics claim that Lord Dang conquered the land only to restore ancient virtues. Mengzi (Mencius) showered him with praise: "While he punished the [Xia] rulers, he consoled the people.

His arrival was like a timely rainfall." Like the ancient perfect emperors, Lord Dang searched for and found a sagely teacher to advise him, the humble village farmer Yi Yin. Reportedly, Dang was deeply disturbed by his own recourse to violence. Through sleepless nights he worried how it would look to future generations. To show that he fought only for the good of all, he invited all chieftains in the land to a special conference. There, he greeted the other chiefs as equals and sat among them. Up on the dais, the emperor's throne stood empty. Dang explained, "This is the seat of the throne of the Son of Heaven. It should be occupied only by men of virtue. The world is not to be possessed by one house alone. Only men of virtue deserve its possession." As a true paragon of virtue, Dang offered the throne to any who dared take it. None dared. Dang was therefore obliged to make himself the pivot of the universe. He took his seat, and called the chiefs to peacefully settle their land-boundary disputes (Wu, 1982, 139, 158).

After Dang paid lip service to the ancient ways of choosing leaders, he and his family proceeded to rule by patrilineal inheritance for generation after generation. To eliminate disputes over power, his Shang nobles slowly clarified their process of inheritance. The practice of passing the throne to the emperor's younger brothers gave way to primogeniture. Furthermore, the "eldest son" was defined as the oldest boy of the principal wife, not of a secondary wife or concubine. Already we had polygamy for big men, with different legal ranks assigned to their various women. Still, inheritance was not yet everything for a ruler. We hear of Shang rulers upholding the notion of training and testing their sons in preparation for power. Emperor Xiaoyi (1352–1325 BCE) groomed his boy Wuding by sending him out for several years to live with the common villagers, travel about the empire, and learn from a sage called Gan Pan (Wu 1982, 181, 201–202). Likewise, the *Classic of History* reports of Emperor Zujia (1258–1226 BCE),

He would not unrighteously become emperor, and had at first lived the life of the little people. Thus when he came to the throne, he came with the knowledge of what the little people depended on for livelihood. He was able to protect and benefit the masses. He durst not treat with contempt even the widower or the widow. Thus it was that Zujia enjoyed the possession of the empire for thirty-three years. (Wu 1982, 217)

It seems the Red Guards' idea of sending privileged people to "learn from the masses" has a long and dubious history. And though the value of such education for professional civil servants was limited, many of the later emperors' brats might have benefited from such treatment. Unfortunately, most Shang kings preferred to send their sons to be hardened in military service, which conveyed a different message.

In Shang cities like Anyang, the ordinary people's ceramic pots were still covered with spirals, patterns of coiling snakes, or flowing water, like old Yangshao pots from the age of the goddess. Anyang bronzes still commonly featured tripod legs shaped like female breasts, and people still prized cowry shells (Munsterberg, 1986, 226–227). But the artifacts, records, and legends of the Shang rulers suggest a totally different culture. The Shang behaved more like Inner Asian warlords than heads of traditional villages. Their warriors rode horses and took patrilineal names. They buried their leaders in huge earth mounds, full of treasure and sometimes with hundreds of human sacrifices. Their values appear quite directly in their own writing, as found in their massive numbers of oracle bone inscriptions.

The Shang rulers apparently valued militarily capable men so much more than women, that they constantly consulted oracle bones about the sex of unborn children. Their inscriptions used the term "fortunate" or "good" to denote a male child (Ho, 1975, 323). Perhaps they already worshipped the later god Zhang Xian (Chang

Hsien), who is the god of birth and protector of children, but only of the male variety. At any rate, the philosopher Han Feizi explained that the Shang practiced "extending congratulations on the birth of a boy and killing a girl when she comes" (Du Jinpeng 1995, 158). Graveyards dated to Shang times show an adult population ratio of nearly two men for every woman. Du Jinpeng concludes, "The high adult imbalanced sex ratio for the Shang dynasty population must ... be due to some manmade reason" (1995, 159).

Accentuating the imbalance of men and women, the strongest Shang men took many wives for themselves. King Wuding (ca 1300 BCE) apparently kept 64 women, at least 30 of them bearing the title *Fu*, meaning "king's concubine." Some of these women represented marriage alliances, and some were taken in war (Du Jinpeng 1995, 133, 162). We know that such polygamy, plus the general male-female population imbalance, left many men without wives. The unmarried men often served in the army, living a life of tribute collection and state-backed raiding.

The oracle inscriptions also give details on human sacrifices, such as the numbers of human beings offered on specific occasions. When the approximately 2,000 known sacrifice lists (as discovered through the early 1990s) are added up, they total about 13,000 people killed. These oracle records used the same character (*qie*) in referring to female war captives, female human sacrifices, or the ruling men's concubines. Likely these various classes of women were all drawn from the same pool of captives. A Shang slavemaster could apparently use his women for labor, sex, or sacrificial offerings. Modern Chinese historians characterize this phase of history as "the slave age" (Du Jinpeng 1995, 136, 163–164).

The oracle inscriptions and the *Classic of History* both suggest a rising egomania in Shang kings. Both quote the kings referring to themselves as "I the One Man." Over time, the oracle bones increasingly recorded the king as the only diviner, which suggests that predicting the future became a royal monopoly (Keightley,

1983, 550). It seems these kings spent much of their time on the road. To keep control and raise revenue, they came around checking on each part of their empire. The *Classic of History* records whole speeches they reportedly gave, calling on the local leaders for loyalty. Supposedly, the country's welfare depended on the kings' generous service (Ho, 1975, 320–321). But these were taker-leaders, willing to use deadly force to confiscate much of the villagers' produce.

Some pro-feminist observers point out that certain Shang women helped rule their subjects as military leaders. For example, the Shang oracle bones show inscriptions concerning Fu Hao, the powerful consort of King Wuding. Regarding an upcoming battle, the oracle reader asks, "Should Fu Hao follow Gou of Zhi and attack the X tribe, with the king attacking Zhonglu from the east toward the place where Fu Hao shall be?" (Eno, 1996, 50). It seems she was a general over the army. Fu Hao also had one of the grandest graves in the burial ground at Anyang, and was buried with 16 sacrificed servants. In addition to Fu Hao, over 100 other important women are named in the Shang oracle bones, with mention of their roles in religious, political, or military activities (Chau, 1979, 149). Maybe the Shang men still treated women of their own rank as equals. Maybe it was a positive sign that women could be overlords and military commanders. Or maybe it just shows that in the dominator age, women could be dominators too.

According to popular folklore, the last Shang emperor, Zhou Wang, ended up almost as bad as the last Xia king. His deeds of cruelty and debauchery grew notorious. He reportedly forced his slaves to swim naked in a wine-filled lake, which probably struck the villagers as a shocking waste of good wine. In general, outraged critics felt the Shang set a hellish example for their subjects. As the *Classic of History* abused them, "The people of Yin [the Shang capital city], small or great, are given to thievery, to robbery, to all sorts of villainy and wickedness. The officers, high and low, imitate and vie with one another in violating the law. While so many crimes have been committed, there is no assurance at all that the culprits are apprehended and punished. Consequently all the lesser people rise up without restraint to do outrages upon each other" (Wu, 1982, 288).

Clearly such a house could not stand. And once more, Heaven sent a hero to cleanse the land. The righteous Prince Ji Fa of the Zhou tribe launched an overpowering attack, driving the Shang from their palaces. Zhou Wang tried to flee, but was hunted down and killed like a dog. On being dispatched to heaven, he reportedly begged the gods and goddesses for mercy. They considered his merits, and granted him a post as the God of Sodomy.

The Zhou Lords (ca. 1050 to 221 BCE)

Concerning the Zhou dynasty's founder Ji Fa, Mengzi explained, "He is among the great ones of the world who dared, in this age of violence and unbridled appetites, to offer a bold challenge and to return to the humanitarian mode of government of the ancient kings … [He] would provoke a sort of revolution; all the oppressed peoples would run to him as their savior" (Gernet, 1996, 95).

On breaking into the Shang king's pleasure palace, our hero asked, "Where are all these women from?" The retainers said they were taken from many places. Ji Fa ordered them released to go home. Regarding the huge stores of jades and gems, Ji Fa said, "Let them be returned to their original owners" (Wu, 1982, 300). Next, the victors had to decide what to do with all the defeated Shang officials. After conferring with his advisers, Ji Fa announced, "Let us proclaim peace for all. Let each and every man enjoy the safety of his hearth, and the fruits of his labor. There will be no scrutiny of his past conduct, or of his relationship with the old regime. There will be only an understanding that we shall be attached to none but those who will lead a life of virtue and humanity" (Wu, 1982, 298).

It was the job of ancient court historians to make their rulers' ancestors look like saints. And in all probability the Zhou princes were just ambitious warlords from the northwest drylands. They were reportedly descendants of the semi-nomadic Huaxia, Rong, and Di tribes in the Shaanxi region, who expanded southeast into the zone of farming villages (Min, 1995, 560). They were excellent horsemen, and probably well experienced in combat with other frontier tribes. They brought a new kind of chariot which harnessed four horses abreast. Clearly, they outclassed the Shang as warriors (Gernet, 1996, 51). According to the *Classic of History*, Zhou military discipline was fearsome. Ji Fa threatened to kill any of his men who failed to ford a river and reach an attack point on time (Wu, 1982, 284). The Zhou warlord also showed a certain contempt for the non-military female sex. Before the climactic battle Ji Fa told his troops "The ancients had a saying, 'A hen shall not crow in the morning! For a hen to crow in the morning means that a household will become desolate.' Now ... the king of Shang only listens to women's words" (Neinhauser, 1994, vol. I, 61).

After his great victory, Ji Fa (now called Emperor Wu Wang) celebrated in a manner familiar to nomadic warlords. He took his leading men and new subjects out for a glorious hunting expedition. On returning from this male bonding experience, they boasted of bagging 22 tigers, 3,235 reindeer, 118 grizzly bears, 151 other bears, 721 yaks, 352 boars, 12 rhinoceroses, 2 mountain lions, 16 antelopes, 18 sleepy foxes, 30 roebucks, 50 musk deer, and 3,508 other deer (Wu, 1982, 302).

Among later Zhou princes, the practice of passing power to the ruler's eldest son grew firmly entrenched, even though this often meant proxy rule in the name of a boy-ruler. The practice left little scope for rule by the most able men, much less by able women. Still, we hear a legend of two royal sons, Taibo and Zhongyong, who decided that their younger brother was the best fit to inherit power. In order to thwart the inevitability of inheritance to the eldest, these older sons ran away to live among the barbarians on the southern coast. They even had themselves covered with tattoos to fit with the locals, and hide their identities forever (Wu, 1982, 316). Only years after their younger brother was firmly established on the throne did they contact him again.

So the Zhou chose their top dogs by heredity or contests of arms. But at least they claimed to choose their middle- and lower-level managers according to ability. For their bureaucrats and local officers, they aimed to appoint virtuous males to control the villagers. A typical list of qualifications is given for the southern Zhou kingdom of Chu:

> From the descendants of famous surnames were chosen those
> who had the knowledge of cultivation and growth in the four
> seasons, of the diversified nature of animals, jades, and silks,
> of the designs of dresses, and the measurements of utensils
> that were required in various ceremonies ... [many other kinds
> of expertise are listed] ... all these with a mind dedicated to
> the pursuit of past tradition—such men should be made zong,
> "elders." (Wu, 1982, 13)

But here also we see the creeping rise of hereditary power—the men of ability came "from the descendants of famous surnames." And of course the princes were *appointing* local leaders rather than letting the villagers do that. A clearer description of the appointees' duties appears in the *Rites of Zhou* (*Zhou li*), where these officers are called "servitors." The servitors' job sounds like a mixture of tax collector, army conscription officer, preacher of state religion, and informant for the police:

> Each village servitor is in charge of the conscription orders in
> his village [of 25 families]. From time to time in the year he
> shall take count of the inhabitants of the village, distinguish
> who are of conscription age and who are not. He shall assemble
> all the people that should be assembled, for Spring and Autumn

veneration ceremonies, for public works and hunting exercises,
for community gatherings and activities, for funeral services.
After every assemblage, he shall read the law to the people;
he shall also enter into the record which ones of them are
conscientious of duty. (Wu, 1982, 414)

In theory, the Zhou conscripted troops on the basis of one man per family, for a platoon of 25 soldiers from each village. The conscripted men were trained to kill, and held accountable to the usual dominator principles: Unconditional obedience to superiors, duty to rulers before loyalty to wives and children, and a moral obligation to avenge insults from inferiors. As in the Roman empire, the army was a machine for indoctrinating vast numbers of the country's young men.

The Zhou lords apparently viewed themselves as bringers of civilization to the benighted villagers. In newly conquered areas, the peasants were supposedly uplifted culturally by submitting to the new masters. The peasants' lives were made meaningful through association with an empire. By paying taxes to a military state and being conscripted into its armies, they become useful for something more important than themselves. The peasants, however, had their own views on the march of civilization. A song from the *Shi Jing* records local sentiments, from sometime around 600 BCE:

Great rats, great rats,
Keep away from our wheat!
These three years we have worked for you
but you despised us:
Now we are going to leave you
and go to a happier country,
Happy land, happy land,
Where we shall find all that we need. (Needham and Wang,
1956, 106)

And there is historical evidence of significant migration moving outward from the Yellow River zone of Zhou control. Before China was unified under one administration in 221 BCE, the most common form of peasant protest was flight. The early states bordered "untamed" wilderness, into which the peasants could escape. Their saying was, "Northward we can flee to the Xiongnu [nomads], southward we can run to the Yueh." Also, "of the 36 options available, running away is the best." Most refugees moved south toward the wetter, warmer country of rice and fish, leaving the harsh northern plains with their grasping warlords behind. But escaping the warlords was not so easy. When large numbers of their taxpayers moved south, the rulers simply sent soldiers and tax collectors after them. In hindsight, the Zhou princes even regarded their fleeing subjects as obedient colonists, going forth to settle rich new lands for their rulers.

Having divided up their empire among noble families, the Zhou princes slowly began squabbling over their boundaries. By the time of Confucius and Laozi (500s BCE), they were attacking each other like sharks. Both Daoism and Confucianism rose in a time of slowly escalating war, and both movements protested the rat race for domination. According to the *Classic of Rites*, Confucius bemoaned that princes had long ago departed from the ways of the Golden Age: "By now the Great Tao [Dao] is disused and eclipsed. The world has become a family inheritance. Men love only their own parents and their own children. Valuable things and labor are used only for private advantage. Powerful men, imagining that inheritance of estates has always been the rule, fortify the walls of towns and villages and strengthen them by ditches and moats" (Needham and Wang, 1956, 168).

Likewise the early Daoists observed,

So long as the court is in order,
(rulers are content to) let the fields run to weeds
and the (village) granaries stand empty.

They wear patterns and embroideries, carry sharp swords,
glut themselves with drink and food,
have more possessions than they can use ...
These are the riotous ways of brigandage;
they are not the Tao [Dao]. (Dao De Jing, chap. 53)

Reportedly, Confucius met a woman in the forest near Mt. Tai, who was weeping beside a new grave. The woman was burying her son, who had been killed by a tiger. Before that she said, her father-in-law and then her husband had been eaten by tigers. When asked why she remained in the dangerous forest, the woman said "There's no tyranny here." When Confucius told the story he said, "Remember, tyranny is fiercer than a tiger" (Li, 2000, 121).

Confucius urged the warlords to reform, but they found him useless for their purposes. And they treated village Daoists as rustic fools, whose shamanic powers should be suppressed. In that case, village folklore imagined other solutions to the warlord problem.

Xi Shi (Hsi-Shih), the daughter of a tea merchant in the Spring and Autumn Period (770–476 BCE), was a woman of stunning beauty. But being such a goddess was not necessarily good for a girl, since even the prince of the realm heard of her. The world's traditions of women hiding their beauty in public generally involved a need to avoid the warlord's evil eye. And when the typically corrupt Prince Wu learned of Xi Shi's elegance, he ordered her to appear in his court. At this point, we could consider her stolen from her loved ones.

It seems, however, that Xi Shi was not just a helpless victim. When she appeared before Prince Wu, her dignity and charm took his breath away. He promptly added her to his collection of wives or concubines. But it seems she had a plan. Where Prince Wu had been aggressive in wars and revenue collection, he suddenly seemed to forget all else but Xi Shi. Affairs of state ground to a halt—which was good, because the villagers suffered less abuse. Best of all, the charm-smitten Wu neglected his army. This allowed a more righteous prince, the virtuous Yue, to move in and overthrow the oppressor.

As a reward for service to her people, Xi Shi was appointed the goddess of women's beauty secrets, including facial creams, cosmetics, and perfumes. No nation should be without such a goddess. And however silly this story sounds as a solution to tyranny, its chain of events is so probable that it's almost certainly based on any number of real situations. The dream is also real, that women's powers may bring the warlords under control.

Possibly the advice of sages and the influence of women did have some effect curbing the rising egomania of princes. Because it took several hundred years for the competition among Zhou states to escalate into general war. The slow acceleration of violence can be measured in the shrinking numbers of independent states. When the legendary emperor Yu (ca. 2200 BCE) called a meeting of all chieftains, it is said that 10,000 tribes attended. When Lord Dang overthrew the Xia dynasty about 1700 BCE, some 3,000 tribal heads came to meet the new emperor. After the Zhou revolt of around 1050 BCE, the new lords counted 1,753 tribes and princedoms (Wu, 1982, 383). During the Spring and Autumn Period (775 to 476 BCE) around 140 states remained. And finally, in the Warring States period of 475–221 BCE, the last seven or eight remaining kingdoms entered an all-out battle for survival of the most vicious. Mengzi protested that "death is not enough for such a crime" (Hawkins, 2004, 221–222). But the warring states fielded armies averaging over 200,000 men. They had crossbows, and built walls around some 700 cites. This was the age of Sunzi (Sun Tzu) and *The Art of War*. It only ended when the most ruthless state of all, Qin, led by the greatest egomaniac, Qin Shihuang, eliminated every rival in 221 BCE.

The First Emperor's Dominator Dream

According to later critics, the Qin descended from horse dealers in the far northwestern region of Gansu. Their customs resembled those of the nomadic Jung and Ti tribes. As a nobleman of the Wei state put it, the Qin rulers had "the heart of a tiger or a wolf" (Cotterell, 1981, 61–64, 97). Over several centuries they encroached eastward into the Wei River valley, first raiding and then dominating the farming areas.

As the Qin warlords grew powerful, their courts attracted would-be consultants, who tried to sell their advice for patronage. The most cunning consultants, like Shang Yang (ca. 390–338 BCE) or Han Feizi (Han Fei-tzu, ca. 280–233 BCE), told the warlords what they wished to hear. Han Feizi advised, "It is important that the prince should be the sole dispenser of gifts and honors, punishments and penalties. If he delegates the smallest part of his authority, he runs the risk of creating rivals who will soon usurp his power" (Gernet, 1996, 90). Over time, the Qin acquired a favored group of the most ruthless advisors, who formed a Qin-backed school of thought. Among the "Hundred Schools of Philosophy" which contended during in the Warring States period, the Qin embraced "Legalism," or "The School of Law."

The term "Legalism" referred to concern for law, but this law was not based on consent of the governed or popular standards of goodness. It was simply a legal principle that inferiors must obey superiors, no matter what the superiors required. According to this philosophy, the strife of the world came from the clash of different wills. And the solution was to subject all wills to one. When all people obeyed one master, and all resistance to the ruler's desires was eliminated, then there would be victory and peace. In a paradoxical way, the greatest violence by the strongest man would actually secure the world's tranquility. The more mercilessly he waged war, the more his rivals would be intimidated to surrender. The more horrible his punishments, the less crime there would be. As Shang Yang explained, "If the punishments are so strict that they even extend to the entire family, people will not dare to try and see how far they can go, and if they do not try, the punishments will no longer be necessary ... and no one will be punished any more" (Bauer, 1976, 58). Basically, there would be harmony because everyone would submit to one top dog. For Han Feizi, it was a matter of facing reality: "What allows tigers to conquer dogs is their claws and teeth. If the tigers lost their claws and their teeth, and if dogs had them, it would be the dogs that would conquer the tigers. As for princes, they control their officials through the punishments and virtue. If they divest themselves of punishments and virtue, and allow them to be used by their officials, it will be the ministers who control the princes" (Maspero, 1978, 325).

In answering the primary question of "Who's on top?", the Qin prime minister Li Si (Li Suu) felt the options were clear as black and white:

Now, if a ruler will not ... apply the system of censure in order to utilize the empire for his own pleasure, but on the contrary purposelessly tortures his body and wastes his mind in devotion to the people—then he becomes the slave of the people instead of the domesticator of the empire. And what honor is there in that? When I make others devote themselves to me, then I am honorable and they are humble: when I have to devote myself to others, then I am humble and they are honorable. (De Bary and Chan 1960, vol. I, 142)

Of course many people objected that such Legalist ideas contradicted the sages and values of the Golden Age. In the past, leaders had to win respect through generosity and service to others. Han Feizi had to explain that times had changed:

In ancient times men, few in number, found a plentiful living without the need of working. It is different in the present age, in which families have at least five children, population is excessive, and even with the most exhausting labor, they do not get enough. The men of other times, being able to satisfy their needs without difficulty, were calm and peaceable, and there was no need for a very strict system of punishments and rewards. Nowadays,

on the other hand, since they are constantly disturbed, it is
necessary to increase both punishments and rewards in order to
govern well. To imitate the ancient sages' methods of government
without regard to the change in circumstances could only
produce disorder. (Maspero, 1978, 327)

To help eliminate disorder, the Qin introduced new laws. They criminalized remarriage—for women only. Women would now learn to obey their masters, or else the masters could both banish them from their families, and legally block them from ever choosing another man. And to make the males do their duty in war, Han Feizi urged that people must be made to fear their own rulers more than they feared death in battle (Cotterell, 1981, 141).

When the Qin enforced such policies on their subjects, they were gratified by the results. As the teacher Xun Zi (Hsün-tzu) observed around 264 BCE,

[The Qin governors] employ their people harshly, terrorize
them with authority, embitter them with hardship, coax them
with rewards, and cow them with punishments. They see to it
that if the humbler people hope to gain any benefits from their
superiors, they can do so only by achieving distinction in battle.
They oppress the people before employing them and make them
win some distinction before granting them any benefit. Rewards
increase to keep pace with achievement; thus a man who
returned from battle with five enemy heads is made the master of
five families in his neighborhood. (Cotterell, 1981, 125)

In Qin society, people were ranked in 18 levels of status, to which men could be promoted or demoted, usually according to their military performance (Kruger, 2004, 88). And since force was king, warriors were deemed the most valuable members of society. Shang Yang explained that war was the state's main means of progress, because war builds strength and eliminates weakness:

> *If a country is strong and does not make war, there will be*
> *villainy within and the Six Maggots, which are, to wit: rites and*
> *music; poetry and history; the cultivation of goodness; filial piety*
> *and respect for elders; sincerity and truth; purity and integrity;*
> *kindness and morality; detraction of warfare and shame at*
> *participating in it. In a country which has these twelve things,*
> *the ruler will not be able to make the people farm and fight, with*
> *the result that he will become impoverished and his territory*
> *diminished. (Waley, 1939, 236–237)*

With their maze of rewards and punishments, the Qin rulers built the most efficient army, the most effective system of taxation, and the most obedient population on the subcontinent. The clay images of Qin imperial guards buried with their emperor near Xian are mostly over six feet tall. Likely, the core of the army came from nomadic tribes, whose men towered over most Chinese conscripts (Dorsey, 2004, 146). As the Qin war machine began demolishing rival states one after another, the Legalist order seemed to prove its superiority over all weaker societies. With horrific efficiency, the Qin warlords merged vanquished forces into their own, built an army exceeding one million men, and marched to crushing victory over every rival on China's chessboard. For the first glorious or tragic time, they put the whole Middle Kingdom under one man's will. The victorious Qin king took a new title: Qin Shihuangdi. This name involved the words "huang" for "majesty," and "di," for "god." The full title meant "Majestic god of the Qin," which is slightly more grandiose than the usual English translation of "emperor" (Kleeman and Barrett, 2005, 98). And the philosophy of this great new god was close to the perfect antithesis of any popular beliefs concerning the Golden Age.

Naturally, the First Emperor described his role in benevolent terms: "If the whole world has suffered from unceasing warfare, this is the fault of feudal lords and kings. Thanks to my ancestors, the empire has been pacified for the first time. If I restored feudal holdings, war would return. Then peace could never be found!" (Cotterell, 1981, 149). For a short time there was order. The king of kings and his ministers quickly standardized weights and measures, writing, laws, and money across the semi-continent. They also tried to standardize thought. They attempted to wipe the slate of the Chinese mind clean, and write their own doctrine on it. Prime minister Li Si advised burning all copies of books contrary to Legalism, and killing any traditionalists who "criticized the present by the standards of the past": "Your servant suggests that all books in the imperial archives, save the memoirs of Ch'in [Qin], be burned. ... Those who dare talk to each other about the [Confucian] *Book of Odes* and *The Book of History* should be executed and their bodies exposed in the market place. Anyone referring to the past to criticize the present should, together with all members of his family, be put to death" (De Bary and Chan, 1960, vol. I, 140).

Back around 400 BCE, Mozi (Mo Tzu) had asked "If a small crime is considered crime, but a big crime—such as attacking another country—is applauded as a righteous act, can this be said to be knowing the difference between righteous and unrighteous?" (Griffith, 1963, 22). In the early 200s BCE, Mengzi argued that gaining power over the whole world would be unjustified if it involved killing even one person. These comments certainly fell under the Qin ban against criticizing the present by standards of the past. Therefore any surviving copies of Mozi's or Mengzi's works were banned. Copies that survived were hidden from the police, like the Gnostic Christian texts of Nag Hammadi in Egypt. As the Legalist Han Feizi argued, "Literature does not exist in the state of the enlightened ruler. Only the law is taught. Nor do we find the traditional sayings of sage-kings. The functionaries of the state are the only teachers" (Bauer, 1976, 61).

Some historians claim the Confucian literati never joined in rebellions against the Qin or other tyrannical dynasties, and this suggests their timidity towards authority. But clearly the Qin felt a need to kill large numbers of Confucian preachers. The rulers must have feared what would happen if these people were not silenced. If we judged the non-violent Confucian resistance in modern terms, we would say they practiced civil disobedience rather than terrorism. And maybe civil disobedience took more courage.

The Villagers' First Taste of Imperial Omnipotence

Under the unified empire, there were still regions hardly touched by the government's power, where people mostly lived as they had in the past. In seemingly backward areas, the sons of the village might be left to work their fields, rather than being drafted for the army. The leaders were still traditional elders and matrons, who were accountable to their neighbors rather than outside authorities. The crops could still be shared among relatives rather than raked over for the ruler's granaries. But now the state surrounded such islands of tradition, and the One Man was resolved to close every gap. No more should remote villages escape the net of taxation and conscription. Uniform laws, taxes, measurements, rewards, and punishments should be imposed without exception, and with zero tolerance for disobedience. As in other empires across the Old World, if any group of villagers refused to hand over heavy portions of their produce, labor, or manpower to the state, the rulers would unleash the army. The indiscriminate pillage and slaughter would leave a lasting impression.

The Qin empire-building project required an ambitious expansion of roads, irrigation canals, defenses, walls, and armies. The emperor also ordered a monumental tomb for himself, which was an earthwork larger than any Egyptian pyramid, and required the forced labor of an estimated 700,000 conscripts (Debaine-Francfort, 1999, 93–94). Some of these great works were beneficial to both rulers and subjects. But the Qin rulers systematically delegated the benefits to themselves, and the costs to the villagers. For example, the network of rammed-earth imperial roads was deeply resented by villages near the routes. The locals were ordered to repair the roads, supply official travelers with food, and pay upkeep for the postal service horses. Then the road police harassed nearby villages, questioning people about illegal traffic and enforcing road service requirements. We might assume that the primitive villagers would find roads an economic boon. But under the early imperial economy, it seems the villagers felt like trees in a forest when a logging road is put through. In future peasant revolts, the rebels often immediately destroyed these roads and bridges (Cotterell, 1981, 171–172). But for the rulers, the advantages of a centralized empire were undeniable. No dynasty or government after the Qin favored a return to decentralized society.

To secure his northern frontiers, Qin Shihuang reportedly ordered his greatest general to mobilize masses of able-bodied subjects, and build a great wall from the eastern sea to the western desert. The officials rounded up and marched tens or hundreds of thousands of men northward for the work. Among them, according to famous legend, was a villager called Wan Xi Liang, who was forced to leave his new bride, a beautiful woman named Meng Jiang Nu. With other masses of conscripts, Wan had to walk all the way to the northern frontiers, with little food and no shelter. Then the men were set to work, enduring exhaustion, hunger, cold, and abusive supervisors. The supervisors were probably afraid to show mercy for the conscripts. In such conditions, the conscripts' clothes soon turned to rags, leaving them no protection from sun or cold wind.

As months passed, Meng Jiang Nu heard no news of her husband. When winter approached, she decided to travel however far, to bring him some warm clothes and boots. On the way she climbed mountains and crossed rivers. She suffered from blistered feet, hunger, and freezing wind. But finally she reached the place where thousands toiled, and the monstrous construction twisted over the hills like a snake. The men were hungry and in rags, driven in work gangs by the soldiers. Meng passed down the lines of workers for days, asking if anyone had seen her husband. At last she met a crew of workers who knew him. They said he had died of exhaustion and was buried in the wall where he fell.

Meng reached the part of the wall where her husband was buried, and she wept. Day after day she cried, and so great was her grief that it reached up to heaven. In response, a gigantic storm of snow fell, and that section of the Great Wall collapsed. In the rubble, Meng found her husband's body. News spread that the Great Wall had been torn down by Meng Jiang Nu's tears.

When this report reached the imperial court, the second Qin emperor, Ying Zheng, was amazed. He decided to travel north to see this woman himself. He expected to punish her for sabotaging the imperial will, but when he saw her face, words left him. The emperor knelt in the snow and asked her to marry him.

Meng did not answer immediately. She pondered what she might achieve or lose if she accepted the proposal. Finally she said she would marry him if he granted three wishes. First, she wanted her late husband's body placed in a proper wooden coffin. Second, the emperor must give the dead man a state funeral. Finally, all heads of state and generals must come and officially mourn for her husband. The emperor gladly agreed.

The funeral was planned as Meng directed. Following the coffin, the emperor, all his ministers, and his generals walked in procession. The spot she chose for her husband's burial was on a high cliff above a raging river. The entire court stood solemnly as the ceremony concluded. Only then did Meng stop weeping and throw herself from the cliff.

Later, people built a shrine to Meng's memory at the spot where she killed herself. About a thousand years ago, during the Song dynasty, the Temple of Lady Meng Jiang was built at the eastern end of the Great Wall. She is still worshipped at a temple at Qinhuangdao, in Hebei Province.

The First Semi-Continental Peasant Revolution

How could rulers like the Qin be resisted? Certainly not by pointing out flaws in their ideology. Besides, arguing with the Legalists was out of the question. The Qin rulers were so contemptuous of critics that they simply killed anyone who contradicted them. So, since the dominator ideology could not be defeated in debate, it had to fail in practice. And it did fail, because when Legalist ideas were taken to their logical conclusion, the rulers had no enemies left to make.

According to the obviously anti-Qin *History of the Former Han Dynasty*, Qin taxes on farmers rose to half the crop. The Qin drafted "half" the able-bodied men in China for military expansion and works like the great wall. The combined Qin tax in food and manpower brought on a general famine in which "half the population perished" (Cotterell, 1981, 152; De Bary and Chan, 1960, vol. I, 212). The *Huainanzi* says, "Increasing the five punishments to a severity which was contrary to ... the virtue of the Tao, they [the Qin rulers] sharpened the points of weapons and cut down the greater part of the people like straw. Filled with satisfaction, they considered that they had put the world in order. But this was like adding fuel to fire or trying to empty an ever flowing stream" (Needham and Wang 1956, 71).

The revolt reportedly started with a group of conscripted men who were commanded, like Meng Jiang Nu's husband, to appear for work on the frontier by a certain date. Due to floods, they failed to reach the place in time. They therefore stood under an automatic death penalty for disobedience. With nothing left to lose, they decided to fight. As Sima Qian (Ssu ma Ch'ien) described the group's leader,

Chen Sheng [Zhen Sheng]... was a lad from a home with window frames made of broken jars and door handles made of cords, a migrant farm worker, and a soldier sent off [to the frontier], whose talent was below that of the average man ... [He] came forth humbly from the ranks, and ... rose in revolt

from among a squad in a company—led his exhausted and unorganized soldiers, a troop of several hundred, to turn and attack the Qin. They cut trees for weapons and raised bamboo poles as standards. The people of the world gathered like clouds in response and brought their own provisions. (Neinhauser, 1994, vol. I, 167)

When Zhen Sheng died in battle, other leaders took his place, some from the old princely families, and some from the peasants. As the rag-tag rebel armies grew like typhoons, they converged on the Qin capital from several sides. The emperor's aides avoided telling him the bad news.

9: The Goddesses' Outlaws

The peasant revolt that destroyed the Qin dynasty was an event unlike anything in European history. It was as if the slave revolt of Spartacus had spread across Europe and overthrown the Roman empire. At that moment, China's emperors had not yet learned restraint, and the peasants had not yet learned resignation. The age of village autonomy still seemed like a recent memory, and the Qin empire seemed a novel outrage against all that was sacred. The villagers still felt it perfectly possible to seize back the Golden Age.

When the peasant rebel leader Liu Bang (Liu Pang) gained control of the country, he simply cancelled all laws of the Legalists, save for the bans on theft and murder. The rebels moved to eliminate legal distinctions of social rank, asking "Are kings, nobles, generals, and ministers a race of their own?" With the Qin tyrants gone, masses of conscripted workers and soldiers went home to their families. For a time they focused on production rather than conquest. For a few years, it seemed that warlord rulers had been banished back to the frontiers of Inner Asia. In most nations, the founder of a great centralized empire might be hailed as a glorious father of his people, like Cyrus of Persia or Augustus of Rome. But in China, most people remembered the First Emperor as a monster (Mote, 1971, 123). In the future, most rulers would at least pay lip service to their taxpayers' values.

Several of China's later dynasties started with semi-idealistic emperors. The Han and Ming dynasties rose directly from peasant revolutions, and at first they taxed the farmers with moderation. But even Liu Bang kept the first emperor's structures of power, and all future emperors did the same. Liu reduced taxes and conscriptions of labor, but hesitated to abolish them. The flow of resources from such a vast country was huge, and few officials on the receiving end wished to reduce it (Bol, 1992, 23). Predictably, replacing one emperor with another never stemmed corruption for long.

After the first national peasant rebellion, the revolts of later centuries were generally less sweeping. To crush dissent, many emperors imposed collective punishments for disloyalty. A hundred or more relatives could be killed for each individual's act of rebellion, as in Nazi-occupied Europe. Under such policies, only the most savage repression could goad the villagers to risk everything in a revolt. With the passage of centuries, most villagers grew more cautious in the face of their rulers. They resorted to passive resistance, hid their grain and their sons, or fled to other regions. They bribed the stove god not to report their tax evasions to the Jade Emperor on New Year's Eve. Usually they fought only as a last resort. But their last resorts could be earth-shaking.

The Greatest Tradition of Peasant Rebellion in the World

China's popular culture is filled with partly real and partly fictional heroes, who often resembled Robin Hood or Spartacus, and sometimes became gods or goddesses. As the struggles between autocrats and rebels split the world, so rebellion often spread to the heavens. While some deities solemnly upheld the ruling powers, others were divine outlaws. There was the monkey god, Sun Wukong, who proclaimed himself "The Great Sage Equal to Heaven," and embarked on a riotous insurrection against the whole hierarchy of the Jade Emperor. More rebel heroes fill the folklore classics, such as *The Water Margin*, *The Enfeoffment of the Gods*, *The Romance of the Three Kingdoms*, or *The Quelling of the Demons*. There were utterly eccentric rebel deities like the Eight Immortals, the fat cloth-bag Buddha known as Budai Heshang, or Jigong the Mad Monk. In general, the rebellious deities always seemed to be the most popular (Shahan, 1996, 199–201). Goddesses like the Queen Mother of the West, Chang'e, Guanyin, or the Eternal Mother reportedly lent their hands to protect rebels or kill emperors.

Of course China is famous for tyranny, and for thousands of

years tyranny seemed to be a core Chinese value. But China also has the world's greatest tradition of popular rebellion. As Mao Zedong reflected in 1939, "In thousands of years of the history of the Hans [Chinese], there have been hundreds of peasant insurrections great or small, against the regime of darkness imposed by the landlords and nobility. And it was the peasant uprisings that brought about most dynastic changes" (De Bary and Chan, 1960, vol. II, 216). Peasant revolts played a major part in bringing down almost every major dynasty of the past 2,200 years: the Qin, Han, Sui, Tang, Yuan, Ming, and the Qing. Then, a peasant revolution overthrew the Nationalist government in 1949. If we compare this record with Europe's, each major Chinese dynasty is like a reincarnation of the Roman empire. It's as if the Roman empire rose and fell, not once, but about eight times. And several of those rises or falls happened through massive peasant rebellions.

In ancient and medieval Europe, peasant revolts were also endemic. But almost all of them were local affairs, which were quickly crushed by regional militias of the ruling houses. No peasant uprisings grew massive enough to threaten the Roman empire, and few endangered the thrones of medieval kings. Also, the prevailing attitude toward peasant rebels was different in Europe. In medieval European records of state or church, the scribes display naked contempt for rebellious peasants. Villagers who rebelled against church, state, and lord were officially recorded as diabolical heretics and terrorists against God. In 1358, Canon Jean le Bel explained a wave of French peasant revolts as "uncontrolled diabolical madness" and "senseless beastly rage" (Cohn, 2006, 15). Of course Chinese officials also condemned rebels who "form bands and carry out despicable acts as if they were outside the pale of civilization" (Ownby, 2002, 229). And some rebel leaders were basically scourges of the earth, like the almost unbelievably destructive Huang Chao in the 800s. But even the rulers commonly accepted that peasant rebels often had justice on their side. As the *Classic of History* said, "Heaven sees as the people see; Heaven hears as the people hear" (Ching, 1990, 164). A rebellion spreading across the semi-continent could represent Heaven's verdict on an emperor. And the memory of many such verdicts appears in a common fortune-telling poem. According to the number you draw for your fortune at a temple, you could be warned:

> *It is widely known that your sin is as serious as covering the*
> *whole sky,*
> *Yet you still congratulate yourself by claiming that you are*
> *following the examples of sage kings and the virtuous.*
> *If you return the country to its former rightful owner,*
> *You may be able to save your life and home. (Chau, 2006, 106)*

Dr. Sun Yat-sen (Sun Yixian) gave a speech in 1921, explaining the tragedy of Chinese history and the counterculture tradition he hoped to build on. For lack of a better word, he described the popular sentiments of most Chinese people as "anarchism":

> *The history of China, which ... begins with the so-called "Golden*
> *Age," shows the continuous movement of freedom towards*
> *dictatorship ... Our nation had enjoyed freedom for too long;*
> *it became tired of it and destroyed it. Ambitious emperors and*
> *kings took advantage of this opportunity to seize unlimited*
> *power, and in this way the dictatorship of the Ch'in [Qin]*
> *and Han dynasties began ... [But vast numbers of ordinary*
> *people never accepted this.] For indirectly, anarchist theories*
> *were known in China several thousand years ago, and created*
> *considerable interest—or is one going to maintain that the*
> *doctrines of Buddhism and Taoism [Daoism] are something*
> *other than anarchism? (Bauer, 1976, 346–347)*

Anarchism would seem a strange word to most traditional villagers. But they knew the ancient dream of the "Great Peace," the

"Great Equality," or *Taiping*. And to some degree, they expected that kingdom to come.

The Goddesses of Justice

About 200 years after the Han dynasty rose, the slow accumulation of burdens on the peasants reached a new critical point. Around 4 BCE, officials began reporting large meetings of villagers in the fields and roads. At these meetings, local shamanesses spoke of revelations from the Queen Mother of the West. Rumors spread that the goddess was soon to return. At the same time, a drought spread over much of northern China. People claimed it was another sign of divine displeasure with the rulers. If nature withheld its bounty, it was a reaction to the emperor's greed. By 3 BCE, the landlords and officials were alarmed to see that the villagers were neglecting to plant or harvest crops. Huge groups of peasants moved from place to place, beating drums, carrying torches, shouting and singing. Amazingly, they took shortcuts through the fields, trampling the grain as if it was now of no account. Heedless of their appearance, they traveled cross-country in bare feet. (Cahill, 1993, 21–22) At revivalist meetings they sang and danced themselves into ecstasy. Disapproving writers claimed the cult was "orgiastic." All this, the villagers said, was preparation for the return of the Queen Mother, Xi Wang Mu. She would restore the world to peace and justice, avenging all her children who were deprived of the means of life. With her on their side, they confidently defied those who would take their lands and crops.

The year after crops were neglected, widespread starvation set in. In response, the authorities hoarded grain and posted extra soldiers to guard their storehouses. Next, crowds of villagers gathered to take what they felt was theirs. As a rhyming poem described similar riots in 1849,

The village behind beats the drum, the village in front the gong.

Men and women, like wolves and tigers, fierce and strong,
gather together in a tumultuous throng,
and to the gates of rich families move along.
Here, hoards of rice are swept completely clean,
And there, stores of grain are suddenly gone. (Bernhardt, 1992, 62)

Since masses of the Queen Mother's peasants refused to pay tax, the army moved in to collect it by force. As in several later revivalist movements, many believers claimed that a spiritual power made them invulnerable. They passed out talismans from the Queen Mother, claiming that those who wore them would not die. The advancing soldiers met masses of men and women armed with little more than naked faith. The troops proceeded to slaughter the rabble.

Obviously the movement for the Queen Mother showed great devotion to beliefs from a previous age. But by this point in history, belief in the Golden Age was fading to a generalized mystical longing. The rule of the mother no longer meant a practical system of leadership by clan mothers, shamans, and local elders. People imagined it as the return of a celestial mother, like a female perfect emperor, who would come down from on high.

A few years later, a better armed revolt rose in response to a new crisis. In 11 CE, the Yellow River broke its dikes, and flooded a region of perhaps 20 million people. The government opened granaries for famine relief, but this utterly failed to meet the need. Still, there was money for law enforcement when starving people stole food. And when the troops tried to kill the thieves, the villagers committed the capital offense of fighting back. Since the empire enforced collective death penalties on the families of traitors, masses of the refugees found themselves under a death sentence. With nothing to gain from surrender, they formed a rebel army.

It took several years for these bandits to become an empire-threatening force. By about 18 CE, a "woman skilled in witchcraft" called Mother Lu appeared at the head of rebel peasants across

Shandong. We have little knowledge of their beliefs since these people were almost all illiterate. But clearly they felt united by misfortune, and by devotion to simple codes of justice. In areas under rebel control, those who injured others had to pay compensation—not to any authorities, but to their victims. Anybody who killed, was executed. Other rules of fairness were enforced by peer pressure and "village talk." As in most later rebellions, these villagers were not a lawless mob, but a community with leaders and legal standards. Wherever they drove the government forces out, their own organization took over (Gernet, 1996, 150, 556).

The rebel refugees armed themselves as best they could, but had no formal units, flags, or chains of command. Still they fought with greater ferocity than most conscripted government soldiers. The peasants scattered the first major army sent against them in 21 CE. Then, in the following year, a larger army came to kill them. Before facing this force, the rebels painted their eyebrows red, becoming the "Red Eyebrow Rebels." By this gesture they marked themselves with a prominent badge of revolt, and burned their bridges to anonymity. If they lost the battle, it would be difficult to disappear into the general population (Bielenstein,1953, 113–115, 138). As it happened, the Red Eyebrows held off the army, and went on to help bring down Emperor Wang Mang's government. It was a *fanshen*, or overturning of Heaven's mandate. After considerable bureaucratic delay, the new Latter Han dynasty granted new plots of land to many surviving rebels.

Repeatedly in later centuries, the factors of official corruption, natural disaster, and millennial religion converged for new peasant revolts, some small, and some enormous. The villagers' religious visions kept getting political, as in the Yellow Turban revolt of the 180s CE, which was largely responsible for bringing down the Latter Han dynasty. Both the Lingbao and Shangqing sects of Daoism taught that times of hardship foretold a cyclical apocalypse, with destruction of the present order, and a return to the original state. On a certain coming day, the Queen Mother would gather up virtuous "seed people" and restore them to "lands of bliss" (Robinet, 1997, 161–162). Repeatedly, prophet-style leaders rose up to execute this judgment of heaven. After the rebel prophet Li Hong died leading the Yellow Turban revolt, numerous later outlaws claimed to be reincarnations of Li Hong. The last "Li Hong" (unless he returns yet again) died nearly a thousand years later (Hawkins, 2004, 198–199). All these visions may seem like escapist, self-defeating delusions. But sometimes faith in the goddess motivated successful protests, and such faith proved enduring. During the 1500s, Wang Shizhen wrote a dedication to the Queen Mother in his *Bibliographies of the Immortals*:

> *White clouds in the sky,*
> *the forest grows on its own accord.*
> *The road is endless,*
> *between the mountains and the water.*
> *She who will never die,*
> *can still return. (Cai and Lu, 1994)*

The Good Criminals

At some point perhaps 1,000 years ago, a notorious criminal named Song Jiang discovered that crime does indeed pay. After breaking every law imaginable, he died and went straight to hell. The governor of Fengdu hell, Yen Lo Wang, was shocked by Song's utter depravity, and condemned him to round-the-clock agony in the torture chambers. But Song Jiang raised an objection. He admitted his own crimes were despicable, but claimed they were trivial compared to the crimes of every government official in his province. "I was only following their example," he said. And then Song proceeded to divulge the details of all official crimes—names, dates, places, sums of money. Where Dante published the crimes of dead officials who were roasting in hell, Song delivered the goods on living powerholders.

With such a wealth of evidence, the lords of hell were able to convict hosts of high-ranking officials. Soon the prisons and torture facilities of Fengdu were filled to capacity. Yen Lo Wang was pleased. He rewarded Song Jiang with a formal pardon, and elevated him to godhood. To this day people know him as the god of thieves and whistleblowers.

If the emperor and his officials were thieves on a grand scale, then those who stole from the thieves might be heroes. And if medieval England had one Robin Hood, China had hundreds. There were more than a hundred in just one book, *The Water Margin*, in which 108 enormously popular outlaws stood head and shoulders above the lackeys who would punish them. These characters rejected the bond of subject to lord, but vowed loyalty to their friends. They were fugitives from the law, but the readers cheered them on. In doing what they had to do, their cry was "Accomplish the Way for Heaven!" (Ruhlmann, 1960, 168–170). As the hero robber Song Jiang fled from government troops, the Daoist Mother Goddess hid him.

For those who couldn't read, there were the countless local drama troupes which met the popular demand for glorious outlaws. A nineteenth-century official named Cheng Hanzhang was moved to complain,

Local troupes present operas dealing with disloyal servants and rebellious [subjects]. They completely ignore ethics and principle and stress only strength, jumping and fighting throughout the performance ... This is teaching people to be rebellious.

Let the local officials prohibit this. Relay to the troupe heads that they are only permitted to put on uplifting operas, not these lewd, heterodox, rebellious plays ... [And] let the local officials keep an eye on the book markets, where the publishers are coming out with lewd novels and tales of mountain rebels. All these should be burned. (Ownby, 2002, 233–234)

Clearly, there was a serious feedback loop between popular outlaw fiction and real banditry. The fiction reflected countless real situations, in which bands of outlaws were basically small-scale peasant revolts. And some of the real outlaw rebels were women. For example, after China conquered Vietnam during the Han dynasty, two Vietnamese sisters, Tru'ng Thac and Thu'ng Nhi, led a bandit force for independence. And though the rebels were temporarily crushed in 43 CE, the Tru'ng sisters became an inspiration for all future Vietnamese patriots. When the Chinese Communist Premier Zhou Enlai visited Hanoi in the 1950s, he showed his respect for Vietnamese sovereignty by bowing at the altar of the Tru'ng sisters (FitzGerald, 1972, 23). During the Tang dynasty, a woman named Chen Shuozhen set up a rebel peasant government, and ruled as "Emperor Wen Jia." Her state held out only two months against imperial forces, but her example made a lasting impact on future rebel leaders (Wang, 2004, 93–94). As northern nomads encroached on China in the 1100s, a woman named Han Ximeng helped lead the resistance. When the Manchus attacked in the 1600s, the female hero Qin Liangyu led forces against them. In the Taiping rebellion of the mid-1800s, women like Hong Xuanjiao, Hong Xiuquan, and Xiao Sanniang led rebel armies against the Manchus (Judge, 2008, 162). Outlaws like these helped feed the whole genre of Wuxia novels, where male and female heroes joined forces to battle for justice.

All this glorification of criminals seemed dangerously foolish to most government officials. With some justification, they argued it was the government which protected ordinary people from criminal gangs: "In many localities of Shensi [Shaanxi], pugnacious, violent people abound who rely on their strength to tyrannize ... their neighbors, induce [innocent people] to join ... or gather mobs to engage in highway robbery. They do not fear the imperial laws, nor do they submit to the discipline of their fathers or elder brothers" (Ownby, 2002, 228). But even many officials shared the public's sympathy for bandits, accepting that many were decent people, forced by misfortune or official corruption onto the wrong side of the law. A nineteenth-century official in southern China admitted: "According to my humble estimate, among the large number of bandits now existing, two in every ten are roused by their hatred towards local officials, three in every ten are driven to extremity by hunger and cold, and four … are either constrained to join after having been captured … or coerced to follow … after having been driven from their home villages. No more than one in ten … have willingly become bandits" (Ownby, 2002, 227).

Some captured Taiping rebels (in the 1850s) confessed, "We were born in a time of prosperity and we were good people … But because of continuous flooding in our area, we could not get a grain of rice to eat even if we worked hard in the fields, and we could not engage in business because we lacked the funds. As a result we all joined the bandits" (Bauer, 1976, 230–231). Or maybe they were just desperados, like the bandit leader "Sister Lu," who was captured and shot by the Communists in 1947. Her last words were: "I lived a good life. I had the best clothes, and the best horses. I have no regrets. I'll reincarnate and do it all over again" (Li, 2000, 36). Obviously the grey area between criminality, self-preservation, and moral protest was very wide. But many fugitives from the law were wanted for breaking rules that just had to be broken—as in this account from a famine in 1912:

> *I was passing his [the landlord's] place, and paused to watch the demonstration. I saw that many of the men were half-starved, and I knew this man had over 10,000 dan of rice in his bins, and that he had refused to help the starving at all. I became infuriated, and led the peasants to attack and invade his house. They carted off most of his stores. Thinking of it afterwards, I did not know exactly why I had done that. I only knew that he should have sold the rice to the poor, and that it was right for them to take it from him if he would not. (Snow, 1938, 269)*

In 1944, a Communist drama troupe presented a play called *Forced Up Mount Liang*, based on an episode in *The Water Margin*. The hero, Lin Chong, breaks the rules to help his friends, then realizes he has no choice but to flee his home, go up the mountain, and join the bandits. After the play, Mao Zedong praised the performers for "restoring history's true face," in which the real heroes of China were not "lords and ladies," but peasant outlaws (Mackerras, 2008, 258).

Of course Mao was a bandit himself. As he boasted, "I am a graduate from the University of Outlaws." And in sympathy with his kind, he was willing to bless almost any village outlaw in the land. Mao tended to assume that peasants with guns were the good guys. It wasn't always true, because many village thugs took pay from the landlords or officials, and served as goon squads to keep the locals intimidated. Besides, many villagers admired outlaws from a distance, but were terrified of them face to face. Still, Mao was confident that when ordinary village vigilantes took justice into their own hands, they would do what had to be done. Though their verdicts could be arbitrary, Mao trusted them more than the official courts. As he rather optimistically reported in 1927, "The peasants' eyes are perfectly discerning. As to who is bad and who is not, who is most ruthless and who is less so, and who is to be severely punished and who is to be dealt with lightly, the peasants keep perfectly clear accounts and seldom has there been any discrepancy between the punishment and the crime" (De Bary and Chan, 1960, vol. II, 208–209).

The Networks of Secret Societies

When the good outlaws got organized, they generally formed secret societies. Instead of running to the forests (which were shrinking), they blended in with the local population. Secret societies were a more permanent, ongoing kind of resistance, based on furtive organization more than open revolt.

Starting in the 1100s, a hydra-headed "White Lotus Society" began spreading over much of China. It was a movement combining

Buddhist hopes for an enlightened future with political expectations of a new savior—to be sent by the Eternal Mother and the Buddha Maitreya. Various offshoots of the society appeared under different names. But they usually preached a semi-anarchistic message, that "all people big and small shall be equal, there being none treated differently" (Harrison, 1969, 153). Since arms were forbidden to civilians, the secret societies cultivated the martial arts, for turning the human body into a deadly weapon. Rather than confronting mounted armies of the Nuzhen (Jurchin) or Mongol conquerors, the secret societies attacked invader officials in the alleyways. Though it doesn't make the White Lotus look good, the first emperor of the Ming dynasty (1300s) was a former member.

Later, the Ming and Qing dynasties banned the White Lotus as a criminal organization. That's the main reason it was a secret society. The members met in private like outlaw gangs, conducting rituals and offering prayers like this:

> *Having left the magical mountain and lost our way home,*
> *we live in this world of suffering and bitterness.*
> *The Eternal Mother will send a message,*
> *and come especially to invite us to return home. (Naquin, 1985, 279)*

The White Lotus and other secret societies formed a series of networks, almost like shadow governments over large areas. An offshoot society called the Red Turbans played a major role in overthrowing the Mongol Yuan dynasty in the 1300s. The Hung Society reportedly began in the 1600s, with rebel monks at the Shaolin temple in Fujian. When the Manchus burned their temple, some of the monks escaped. They formed a legendary association of Kung Fu warriors, devoted to righteous service of Father Heaven and Mother Earth. And between 1796 and 1804, the White Lotus openly controlled much of China's heartland.

The Taiping rebels (of 1850 to 1864) gave up all pretence of secrecy, and launched a rebellion that drew recruits like a hurricane draws water. The Taipings were semi-Christians, who mixed dreams of the Golden Age with biblical images of God's Kingdom. They proclaimed equality of land holdings: "The distribution of land is to be based on the number of persons in each family, regardless of sex" (De Bary and Chan, 1960, vol. II, 32). They also called for equality of men and women. With such populist slogans they drew female leaders like Hong Xuanjiao and Su Sanniang, who established a women's department of the government, banned footbinding, and fielded whole divisions of female soldiers (Wang, 2004, 93–94). At first, these rebels seemed to live up to their name of "Taiping," as a new Great Equality. If the movement's increasingly egomaniacal "prophets" had honored their promises to redistribute land, maybe they would have overthrown the Qing dynasty.

By the late 1800s, China's outlaw societies had greatly diversified and grown more pervasive. Some of the more famous offshoots of older societies were the Red Scarf, the Eight-Trigram, the Yellow Society (which led the Boxer rebellion in 1900), the Red Spear, the Big Sword, and the Elder Brothers. These societies sometimes acted like witch covens, sometimes like *le resistance*, and sometimes like the Mafia. The equally idealistic and ever-conspiratorial Communists fit this pattern.

Many Communists criticized the other secret societies as "reactionary Daoist cults." But that was assuming that all religion served the establishment. Actually, most secret societies were religious rebels, and they played a significant role in the Republican revolution of 1911. Several leading Communists, including General He Long and General Zhu De (Chu Te) started out in these societies. When the Communist outlaws arrived in Shaanxi from their Long March, they were received and replenished by Liu Zhidan's band of several thousand Elder Brother bandits. Liu's secret society was arming the villagers to defend themselves, and he invited the Communists to help (Thaxton, 1982, 150–152; Naquin, 1985, 258). The Communists willingly formed alliances with older secret societies, but tried to reject the ancient religious context for resistance. Rather than giving credit for past rebellions to believers in the Queen Mother, Mao blamed their failures on superstition: "The gods? They may quite deserve our worship. But if we had no peasant association but only the Emperor Kuan [Guandi, a god of war] and the Goddess of Mercy, could we have knocked down the local bullies and bad gentry? The gods and goddesses are indeed pitiful; worshiped for hundreds of years, they have not knocked down for you a single local bully or a single one of the bad gentry!" (De Bary and Chan, 1960, vol. II, 213).

Throughout his career, Mao encouraged people in "social banditry." He urged the villagers to rise up in true outlaw fashion, take back what was theirs from the local lords, and divide it as they saw fit. "In a very short time," he predicted, "in China's central, southern, and northern provinces, several million peasants will rise like a tornado or tempest, a force so extraordinarily swift and violent that no power, however great, will be able to suppress it" (De Bary and Chan, 1960, vol. II, 207, 205). Sometimes, for all his modernistic atheism, Mao sounded like Mother Lu, the old Han dynasty prophetess of rebels for the Queen Mother.

The Return to Equality in Land

Under protection of the Communist bandit army, villagers across the subcontinent divided up their land in the way of their ancestors. About 50 million previously landless families got a farm—often less than half an acre (Hessler, 2010, 186). And with this, the goal of their rebellion was achieved. After that, most people just wanted to farm their share of land and be left alone. The Communist Party had no further mandate to "modernize production" by imposing initiatives for collectivization, production brigades, quotas, or unsustainable industrialized farming methods. Within two decades, this whole set of "Marxist" experiments on the villagers proved counterproductive, and ground to a halt.

Finally in the 1970s, the villagers redivided their land into family plots. Each family kept or sold its own produce. But this was not really a shift to modern capitalism; it was a return to ancient tradition. As in pre-dynastic times, the land was ultimately owned by the whole community (Milbraith, 1989, 142). According to custom, it was right to share it equally. In post-Maoist China, it's normal for the neighbors in each village to meet yearly, and adjust their field boundaries according to the number of mouths in each family. That's how they believe it was done in the beginning. At present, the villagers' fields cannot be sold or seized for debts. Only the government can buy them out, for declared purposes of urban development.

There's lots more to say concerning the fall and rise of women and their values, especially about the evolution of families. But next I want to focus on women's versions of Chinese religions.

10: Women's Powers in Popular Daoism

Most religions are psychologically split into Janus-faced, contradictory versions of themselves. Usually, one face calls for partnership between equal souls, while the other requires subordination of some souls to others. These faces of religion don't just represent different moods; they uphold different values. And the competition between different values usually makes for ongoing culture wars. China has a reputation for peaceful religious pluralism, with a supposed absence of murderous holy war. But actually, its culture wars have often been nasty. The three main religions (Daoism, Buddhism, and Confucianism) have competed for influence, not always peacefully. And each tradition has always been divided internally over which values, or which people, are most important.

In the general split between organized and popular religion, powerful men have usually controlled China's "official" religious institutions. But outside these organizations, the informal sector of "popular religion" has remained a forest of countercultures, many of them created by women. In organized Confucianism the leadership was all male, so the official goals, values, and rules of that religion were set by males alone. On top of that, Confucianism was the official state-backed religion over most of the past 2,000 years. But even in Confucianism, women's values always contended for influence. After all, obedience to mothers was a fundamental Confucian value.

In Daoism or Buddhism, men have usually occupied around 90% of all formal leadership positions. But at least some women have held every kind of leadership role, be it teacher, priest, abbot, realized master, lineage founder, head of clerical training, or living goddess. And beyond the organizational leaders, perhaps a majority of local holy people have been women. Many male religious leaders lamented the influence of "stupid, superstitious women." But usually they could only complain. According to the *History of the Jin Dynasty* (of 265–420

CE), a Confucian scholar named Xia Tong objected that his relatives hired shamanesses to perform their ancestral rites. He admitted that the shamanesses were beautifully skilled in music and dance. They started their ceremony in a respectable way, playing drums and bells. But soon they were swallowing swords and spitting fire, which reportedly caused a dense fog to envelop the area, punctuated by flashes of lightning. For the scholarly Xia, the whole display was "lewd" and disgraceful, but his foolish relatives were enthusiastic (Chan, 1990, 21). Though Confucian scholars were official guides to the people, the villagers spoke of shamanesses as "the other clergy."

It's commonly remarked that many Daoist deities resemble government bureaucrats. And to a large extent, the emperors and officials did co-opt popular religion and remold it in their own image. It happened in roughly the way that Europe's medieval rulers made Christianity into a cosmic hierarchy to uphold the divine right of kings. In this type of religion, Chinese men increasingly modeled themselves on the rulers, like small emperors over their families. In Daoist sects, the leading men slowly squeezed out female leaders. But where the village wise women in Europe were commonly labeled as witches serving Satan, China's wise women retained a certain popular respect. According to a traditional joke, there are nine kinds of Chinese religious women—the "three aunties and six grannies." These are the Daoist nuns, Buddhist nuns, fortunetellers, matchmakers, shamans, healers, spirit mediums, herb or drug sellers, and midwives (Despeux and Kohn, 2003, 151). As the joke suggests, probably most women doing these sorts of work are mature, and often past child-bearing age. They are common local women, doing common wise-woman work, and the crafts they practice are probably older than recorded history. To this day most Chinese villages have their aunties and grannies, who often do good business. Some of them achieve regional fame as saints or living goddesses, however strange their ways may seem to outsiders.

A Folklore of Women's Spiritual Adventures

In reading the lives of immortal women we find broad patterns and variations on common themes—as in Joseph Campbell's hero journeys. Each immortal has a kind of life story, which tells her deeds and how she attained goddess-hood. The stages of these journeys often reflect the natural phases of women's lives. In youth and child-bearing years, they are often idealistic rebels with a passion for righting wrongs. They often refuse arranged marriages, or defiantly choose their own mates. In maturity they generally turn to disciplines of meditation, fasting, inner alchemy, or sexual abstinence. In old age they might leave home and devote themselves completely to a spiritual quest. After attaining the Way, they become spiritual teachers (Cahill 1993, 240). Some became founders of multi-generational teaching lineages, such as Cao Wenyi's Purity and Tranquility lineage. They sometimes formed associations of female teachers, like the College of Priestesses at Linjin (Blumenberg, 2006, 43). Of course some immortals were child prodigies like Chen Jinggu, who rose through all these phases of inner growth by early adulthood.

These goddesses were usually prodigal daughters, divorced wives, or widowed mothers. Their actions showed strength and independence rather than duty or obedience. They were people with a calling, and if their families could not accept that calling, the goddesses often ran away. So the Han dynasty saint Zheng Wei (Cheng Wei) was abused by her army officer husband, feigned madness, and vanished into a new life as an independent holy woman (Cleary, 1989, 8–9). The Buddhist saint Miaoshan defied her father's orders to marry, and let herself be thrown out of the family. When Qi Xiao Yao's father tried to teach her "rules for women," she said those were for ordinary people. Her focus on spiritual practice caused conflict, and her parents had difficulty marrying her off. After she got married, her husband's family couldn't control her, and said she was possessed by a devil. She ignored them all and became a Daoist immortal. The Holy Mother Dongling studied the Way and gained amazing powers of self-transformation. As a teacher and healer, she spent most of her time visiting and helping other families. But her husband grew jealous of her rising fame, not to mention her neglect of wifely service to himself. In a huff he denounced her to the police for lechery and witchcraft. The authorities slammed her in jail, but she escaped into immortality like a bird through the bars, leaving only her slippers behind.

Such snippets of folklore offer glimpses of the goddess legends. But many stories are far richer in detail and depth. To illustrate the folklore better, let me describe the legends of two South Chinese goddesses, and the religions they founded.

Guanyin's Fighting Daughter

Long ago, in the 700s CE, the prefect of a district near Quanzhou (on the Fujian coast) tried to build a bridge across a tide-swept arm of the sea. The passage was dangerous, and travelers had drowned there every year. But where the bridge was most needed, there it was most difficult to build. The foundations for pilings across the bay had to be huge, and it was bound to be expensive. The prefect therefore prayed to the goddess Guanyin for help in the enterprise. The goddess answered his prayers, appearing wondrously in a boat before the fishing villages. As the local people flocked to the shore to see this marvel, Guanyin announced she would marry whoever could throw a coin and touch her. Hundreds of men rushed forward, throwing coins out to her boat. The coins landed about her feet, filling the bottom of the craft. The fund-raising gambit was working very well, till one vegetable seller managed to hurl a handful of silver powder which touched the goddess on her hair. Realizing what had happened, Guanyin promptly disappeared. Desperate to claim his prize, the vegetable seller hurled himself into the sea after her, and was drowned. At this, the goddess reappeared. Pulling out the silver-coated hair from her head, she cast it on the sea. Then she bit her finger, sucked the wound, and spat blood the water. Unknown to the amazed observers, she sent the soul of the vegetable seller to be reborn, as a scholar in Gutian.

As a chain of results, the bridge was built with the money in the boat. The silvered hair from Guanyin's head came alive as a white female sea snake. The blob of blood floated to the lower ford of the Min River, where a childless woman was washing clothes. She saw the curious red clot in the water, ate it, and conceived a girl prodigy.

The girl, named Chen Jinggu, could talk soon after her birth. She could write soon after learning to walk. A few more years, and she announced herself ready to leave home on a quest to learn magic from the spiritual adepts on Mount Lu. In her apprenticeship as a shaman, the girl mastered every magical art save childbirth. She didn't bother with that because she wasn't interested in getting married.

On returning home, Chen Jinggu rejected her mother's efforts to find her a husband, and set up practice as a professional shaman. She was hired for traditional jobs like rain-making, spirit-calling, or exorcising demons. Beyond that, she trained a group of sworn sisters, forming a shamanic band of heroines. Her *yinbing* (soldiers of yin) helped lift a siege of Fuzhou city, overcoming forces of the king's rebellious brother. The sworn sisters also saved the kingdom of Min from an assault by evil spirits. But of all the enemies Chen Jinggu fought, the worst was the white water snake born from Guanyin's hair. Once it attacked the king's palace, and Chin Jinggu managed to drive it away only after it ate all the king's consorts. Another time it attacked a brilliant young official named Liu Qi, who happened to be the man reincarnated from the drowned vegetable seller. After a desperate struggle, Chen Jinggu was able to save him. The two promptly fell in love, and so the great shamaness married. The vegetable seller was granted his wish to marry the goddess, but only on the other side of death.

Some time afterwards, the Kingdom of Min suffered a deadly drought, and Chen Jinggu was called as chief shaman to invoke rain. This ritual involved the difficult and strenuous feat of dancing on the waters. It had to be done, and couldn't be delayed. But Chen Jinggu was pregnant at the time, and in no condition to undertake the arduous dance. Therefore, she magically took the fetus from her womb, sealed it against injury, and kept it at her mother's house. Then she returned to perform the ritual.

While she was out on the waters dancing, the white snake broke into her mother's house and swallowed the fetus "to feed its life." At that moment, Chen Jinggu began to hemorrhage badly. Realizing what had happened, she staggered back to her mother's house to engage the snake in mortal combat. With her strength almost gone, she managed to kill it. But when it died, she died as well—because it was the other half of her own soul.

After dying at age 24, Chen Jinggu went in spirit back to her teachers on Mount Lu. There she finally learned the wise woman's arts of childbirth. She took back the spirit of her unborn child, and transformed him into the child-god San Sheren, otherwise known as the Third Secretary Who Rides the Unicorn. Chen Jinggu herself received the title of the Lady Linshui.

The first temple to Lady Linshui was dedicated in 792 CE, in Daqiao village. Legend says the temple was built on the site of a cave where an older python goddess had been worshipped. Originally, this python goddess may have been a creator snake-woman, like the goddess Nü Wa. But in some split of roles, this python had become a goddess of death as opposed to birth. Every year it had taken two children back to the realm of death, till Chen Jinggu fought and killed it. And so, in the cave beneath Lady Linshui's enthroned image, the mummified body of Chen Jinggu reportedly lay on the slain serpent's head. So these ancient goddesses of life and death, after their struggle as opposites, lay together in eternity.

Lady Linshui was officially recognized in the emperor's Register of Sacrifices around the year 1250. Perhaps the rulers of the Southern Sung dynasty sought her aid against the advancing Mongol horde. Her shamanic lineage, called the Sannai Lüshan, practiced healing, exorcism, soul-calling, seasonal rituals, and funerals down the centuries. The primary temple in Daqiao burned in 1875, but was carefully restored. Then in 1950, Communist anti-superstition rioters defaced statues of the goddess. The Red Guards inflicted more damage in the 1960s. The Communist government passed laws against feudal superstition, as if all the spiritual heroes of village China had been fronts for the people's oppressors. But most local women trusted their own traditions and values. Since 1980 they restored and expanded the Lady Linshui's temples. Her devotees argued that the laws against superstition did not apply to them, because their goddess is real.

In the past few decades, a number of books and movies about Chen Jinggu sold well. She featured in a 1980s TV series, but her mediums and shamanesses felt it failed to do her justice. In 1993, an organization called the "Association of Research on Civilization and the Association of Research on Popular Literature and Arts of Fujian" hosted an international conference on "Research into Chen Jinggu's Cult." The cult's temples received a rising flow of guests and pilgrims, many of them from overseas. Worshipers of the goddess claim that she and her sworn sisters still rove the world, fighting injustice wherever it appears. It is said they fought in Vietnam against the Americans, side by side with their Vietnamese sisters (Baptandier, 1996, 105–135).

The Queen of the Seas

Another goddess story from South China illustrates the constant emergence of new cults over time. Mazu (Ma Tsu) is famous as a savior of sailors at sea. She saved people in her sleep by the power of her dreams. According to legend, she was a boat person on the coast of Fujian in the 900s CE. She died at age 27 in a hunger strike, because she refused to submit to an arranged marriage.

Mazu's career as a savior started when she dreamed one night that her fisherman brothers were sinking in a storm at sea. She reached out to save them, and stopped the hurricane. The next day her brothers returned, saying they had nearly died in a storm. Then they saw a woman coming to them on the water, quieting the waves.

In medieval Europe, witches were believed to travel by night, and to have power over the forces of wind, lightning, or fertility. The old-fashioned villagers often revered such people as wise women, but the authorities feared them. Women accused of having such powers were commonly killed. But in medieval Fujian, the villagers began turning to Mazu for help. Rumors spread down the coast, that in case after case, this woman saved sailors in distress. It seems that Mazu was an adept in lucid dreaming, like some other Daoist or Buddhist saints who practice healing or teaching from a dream state. Soon she was in great demand, intervening like a traditional trance-born shamaness to deal with droughts, storms, or plagues. Under her protection, sea commerce flourished on the South China coast, despite the emperor's restrictions on international trade (Gernant, 1995, 263–269).

When she was 27 years old, Mazu's parents grew desperate to marry her off. They arranged an engagement against her will, and she defied them by refusing to eat. An inflexible code of family duty met an adamant woman, and neither one budged. Mazu actually starved herself to death, which by the standards of conventional Confucianism was close to the worst of sins. Here was a daughter who would rather be dead than follow her parents' wishes for the family's good. In another culture she might be cursed as a soul bound for hell. But there must have been more than Confucian orthodoxy in the culture of medieval Fujian, because Mazu transcended this death like a saint. She was soon reported appearing to more sailors than ever before. In some accounts she came wearing a red dress, which was a garb associated with suicide. Such an apparition might normally be the stuff of nightmares—yet she was deemed a powerful savior.

Temples dedicated to Mazu soon appeared, and growing numbers of people paid her worship. Her temples were often built over older buildings, stones, or statues, which had been dedicated to more ancient local goddesses. As Mazu literally absorbed these holy places, her folklore picked up the attributes of other goddesses. She became a protector of mothers in childbirth. Both pirates and wealthy traders called on her to protect their ships. She saved the Ming navy in the late 1300s, using miraculous balls of fire to guide Admiral Zhou Zuo's battleships through dangerous reefs. The great explorer Zheng He invoked her protection for his 60-ship, 30,000-sailor expeditions to India, Africa, and the South Pacific in the 1400s. When waves of pirates infested the coast, Mazu helped sink their ships or poison their water. Some researchers, however, claim there was a connection between pirate outposts and Mazu's temples, like the one on Lantau Island. Anyway, even the emperor eventually found it prudent to honor Mazu's cult. He offered her homage, recognizing Mazu with the slightly inaccurate title of Tian Hou—Queen of Heaven (Watson 1985, 294–320). So well was an utterly non-filial shamaness respected.

Today, Mazu's temples are among the busiest in China. She is worshipped by a total of around a hundred million people, especially on the south coasts of China and in Taiwan. From there, immigration spread her followers to perhaps most countries in the world (Zhao Zewei, 1995, 406–415). Her cult is therefore a world religion, which is considerably larger than Judaism.

The Possibilities for Deviant Women

In many other cultures around the world, such deviant wise women were barred from leadership by every means available. For example, in Spain during the 1500s, numerous women took religious vocations independent of the church. These were called "beatas," and they often operated like Mother Teresas in the streets—at a time when church-sanctioned nunneries were carefully cloistered from the world. The church responded to these beatas with cautious concern. The women were usually summoned to public hearings, where priestly psychologists carefully discredited their apparent delusions of grandeur. For presuming to take religious initiative without God's authority, many of these women were taken away, and sentenced to solitary penance for the rest of their lives.

But in China, the authorities never managed such control over popular religion—at least not until the brief Maoist period. Confucian orthodoxy exerted expectations on women mainly through their families. But if a holy woman could avoid domination by her family, she was usually free to build any career the market would bear. If she ran away from home, she was free to starve or found a new religious sect. The public commonly supported independent holy women, and many were able to live on the offerings of their admirers (Gernet 1962, 163–164). If they acquired a reputation and many followers, their leadership was seldom repressed by any civic or religious authority. Under ambiguously "open" conditions, they could teach their own answers to their own questions, with little pressure to fit their teaching to a male-made orthodoxy.

The Spiritual Journeys of Daoist Women

What generalizations can we make about the practices and insights of female saints? Maybe the main thing is that their religions are clearly built from their own experience. For example, they sometimes describe the process of inner growth as spiritual pregnancy and childbirth, or the conception and nurture of an "immortal embryo." The Daoist female sage Sun Buer (b. 1124 CE) described a process which resembles spiritual insemination from a woman's point of view. As her teaching is explained by Chen Yingning,

> *Every morning before sunrise they would still their minds and
> sit quietly, waiting for the sun in a state of empty openness.
> Inwardly laying aside ideas and thoughts, outwardly
> disengaging themselves from objects, all at once they forgot about
> the universe and broke through space.*

> *Then a point of positive energy, like a drop of dew, like lightning,*

would spontaneously appear in the great void and enter their
bellies, passing into the spine and rising to the center of the
brain; there it would turn into sweet rain and shower the inner
organs. The sages would then cause this energy to circulate
throughout their bodies, cleaning them out and burning away
pollution, to change their bodies into masses of pure light.
(Cleary 1989, 43)

If this sounds like kundalini yoga, the parallel is often drawn. But Chinese women often compared their spiritual energy, not to a rising snake, but to an embryo growing in its mother's womb. They described the stages of spiritual development in terms of pregnancy, childbirth, and nurture of an inner child. As the Daoist mystic Wei Huacun (d. ca. 330 CE) explained in her *Gold Pavilion Classic*,

How keep body and mind one?
Be like a child.
Be aware of breathing, soft and pliant.
To see the transcendent Dao, have a pure mind ...
Don't say No.
To receive heaven's blessing,
be empty like a mother's womb.
Give birth and nurture, then let go. (Saso, 1995, 80–81)

Daoists commonly speak of merging male and female energies in a process of "inner alchemy." The practice usually involves controlled breathing, yoga-like physical exercise, and various kinds of meditation or visualization. The type of union it works toward resembles the sense of "ha-tha" (in hatha yoga), which means a union of sun (masculinity) with moon (femininity) in a greater wholeness (Sovatsky, 2009, 209). According to the Complete Perfection (Quanzhen) school of Daoism, the spiritual journey starts with "external and internal strengthening" exercises—to unblock the body, stimulate vitality, and still the mind.

When that foundation is built, a "firing process" of deep breathing and meditation incubates the internal energies. As a text called the "Diagram of the Ascent and Descent of Yang and Yin in the Human Body" explains,

> *Heaven and earth are the great forge, yin and yang are the pivots of transformation, and the unified qi [vital energy] is the great medicine. To refine the elixir, use your inner male and female, yang and yin qi, and circulate them all around the inner stars until they form the alchemical vessel. The Metal Mother [the Queen Mother of the West] resides right there, and through wondrous transformations stimulates the qi of life. (Despeux and Kohn, 2003, 187)*

These exercises are sometimes called "the dragon and the tiger swirling in the winding river." The dragon and tiger are terms for the inner male and inner female, and the winding river is the energy path up the backbone. When these circulating energies rise to the heart, they are called "the sun and the moon reflecting each other in the Yellow Palace." When they reach the forehead, they are termed "the union of husband and wife in the bed chamber." And this is just the beginning. Because then follows an incubation period called "the ten months of pregnancy." It is said that those who embark on this journey cannot simply stop and turn back. Because next comes "the birth of the immortal child" (which happens through the crown of the head as in kundalini yoga), "three years of breast-feeding," and raising the inner soul child to maturity. As the inner child's capacities unfold, it grows capable of leaving its mother's body in a kind of soul projection. Ultimately, the old sense of identity is transcended in a merger with the entirety of life (Wong, 1997, 173–176; Despeux and Kohn, 2003, 19–21). Of course this little outline is simplistic, and for real explanations I'd suggest *Internal Alchemy* by Livia Kohn and Robin Wang, or Eva Wong's *Cultivating Stillness: A Taoist Manual for Transforming Body and Mind.*

In recent decades, many Christian denominations sought to remove sexist language from their worship services, hymns, and prayers. But it is far more than words that accommodate women in some of these Chinese traditions. These are schools of religious wisdom built largely by women, for women. Their poetry and teachings are created through women's explorations of their own inner continents. In surveying their evocative words, we have to wonder what was ever gained by excluding female experience from religion.

The Dao of Sex

Some Daoist adepts include Tantra-like sexual practices among their spiritual disciplines. It's even possible that Tantric practice evolved first in China, then influenced Tibetan Buddhism, and later gave rise to Indian Tantrism (Ching and Küng, 1989, 150). Most texts about these practices are written by men, and these often portray the female partners as a means to the male adept's goals. But though the women's experience is not so well published, certain texts describe sacred sex from a woman's point of view. The following passage from the *Yufang Bijue* describes the sex life of a goddess in terms designed to toy with male fears:

> *The Queen Mother of the West is a good example of a woman who obtained the path of immortality by nourishing her yin. Each time she had relations with a man, he fell sick, while she herself kept a polished, transparent face of a sort which had no need of makeup. She fed herself continuously on milk, and played the five-stringed lute, always keeping harmony in her heart and calm in her thoughts, without any desire. So, the Queen Mother of the West never married, but she loved to couple with young men. The secret could never be divulged, for fear that other women would get it into their heads to imitate her methods. (Baptandier, 1996, 134–135)*

According to legend, sacred sex was first taught to the Yellow Emperor by a series of celestial ladies called the Plain Maiden, the Colorful Woman, and the Mysterious Woman. These teachers reportedly left texts on the "art of the chamber" which were later lost. But other texts abounded on the arts of generating health, vitality, and inner awareness through sex. These include the "Yellow Emperor's Basic Questions," "Secret Instructions of the Jade Chamber," "Ten Rules of the Queen Mother of the West on the Proper Path of Women's Cultivation," or the "Great Unity's Instructions on [Developing] Golden Fluorescence" (which Carl Jung and Richard Wilhelm translated as "The Secret of the Golden Flower") (Despeux and Kohn, 2003, 39, 203–206). We might assume these teachings were hedonistic celebrations of sexual pleasure. But actually most of them were single-mindedly focused on attaining mental and emotional self-mastery. As a Celestial Masters' text (called "Esoteric Rites of the Perfected") instructs, "Do not fail to observe the proper order of attendance in the inner chamber. Do not harbor desire for the ordinary way [of intercourse] nor fail to observe the teachings of control ... Do not lust to be the first nor fail to observe the rules of cultivation of the inner chamber" (Despeux and Kohn, 2003, 107). The "Heart to Heart Transmission of the Mysterious and Delicate" instructed,

[When the Numinous Father and the Holy Mother] are at work, their spirits are in union, but not their bodies. Their qi energies are in coition, but not their forms. The male must not loosen his garb and the female must retain her robe. They mutually respect each other like divine deities; love each other like father and mother. They keep still without moving until they feel moved by each other, and only then become interconnected. (Xun, 2009, 130)

By such methods, the Daoist female adept Nü Ji reportedly attained the Way.

In recent decades, these kinds of teaching were popularized in numerous "Dao of sex" manuals, for general rejuvenation of couples. The popularized versions of such teaching generally omitted guidance from a personal teacher, and made the practice a set of self-help generalities. Modern people heard of such things from couples counselors, or books in the library such as *The Tao of Love and Sex*, by Jolan Chang, *Sex, Health, and Long Life*, by Thomas Cleary, *Healing Love Through the Tao: Cultivating Female Sexual Energy*, by Mantak Chia, *Sexual Teachings of the White Tigress*, by Hsi Lai, or *The Tao of Seduction: Erotic Secrets from Ancient China*, by Liao Yi Lin. Perhaps the most scholarly treatment of the subject is *Sex in the Yellow Emperor's Basic Questions: Sex, Longevity, and Medicine in Early China*, by Jessieca Leo.

Of course most women of past centuries were illiterate villagers, who were consumed in their rounds of daily work. If they learned anything of sacred sex, they applied it in relation to their husbands. Few village women found the time or privacy for any concentrated spiritual practice, at least till their children were grown. But those who did manage it were often able to learn women's wisdom from female teachers.

Women in Primitive Daoism

Like other saviors, Laozi (Lao Tzu) had a mother, and as her son was increasingly deified, she became a virginal mother of the deity. Reportedly, the mother of Laozi was none other than the Jade Maiden of Profound Wonder, who may be the same Jade Maiden who lived with Peng Gu, the first man (Chan, 1990, 39). As first described in Han times, Peng Gu had hatched from an egg, and then wandered the world for countless eons. One day, however, he found he was not alone. With amazement and delight, he discovered the Jade Maiden was also wandering the universe. Peng Gu asked for her love, and the first couple began the lineage of divine ancestors.

According to the *Wide Sagely Meaning of the Perfect Scripture of the Dao and its Virtue,* "The Holy Mother Goddess was the Jade Maiden of Mystery and Wonder as long as she resided in heaven. After she had given birth [to Laozi], she was promoted to Goddess of the Great One. As such she taught Lord Lao the basic principles of reforming the world and spreading the true teaching" (Despeux and Kohn, 2003, 50). She reportedly taught Laozi the cosmic nature of the human body, the course of its spiritual growth, and the arts of inner alchemy. Perhaps this is where Laozi got lines like "Know the eternal and forgive / Forgive and be altruistic / Be altruistic and embrace all / Embrace all and be like heaven" (stanza 16), or "Concentrating the breath to the utmost softness, can you become like an infant?" (stanza 10).

But the Jade Maiden didn't just give away the whole shop. Some of the greatest secrets of life she required her son to figure out for himself: "I am the chief of all the immortals, queen of the wonderful Dao. The mysterious and numinous secret arts are all part of the Great Origin. How could I disgrace myself by revealing them?" After leading her son to the brink of sagehood, she avoided infringing on his own initiative, and made an exit worthy of the Virgin Mary: "She climbed into a jade carriage drawn by eight luminants and, followed by a host of transcendent attendants, ascended into heaven in broad daylight." Later the Jade Maiden became the Eternal Mother, Wusheng Laomu, who spoke to numerous women's groups through spirit writing. She assisted countless women in reaching paradise, and guided religious societies such as the White Lotus or the Unity Religion (or Yiguan Dao) (Despeux and Kohn, 2003, 59–60, 50, 42–43). Those who attained the Way were said to live in "free, spontaneous wandering," like the Jade Maiden herself.

Like other sages of early Daoism, many ancient female immortals were basically yogins, who withdrew to the mountains, practiced strict austerities, and became enlightened wild women. Their independent quests were described as "the path of higher virtue," as compared to the lower virtue of conventional religious practice in temples or nunneries (Wang, 2009, 163–164). The women of higher virtue commonly reverted to a way of life from before farming, replacing a grain-based diet with herbs and minerals gathered from the forest floor. Some lived on pine needles, mushrooms, sesame seeds, or bits of mica. Chang Rong ate only raspberry roots. Yu Jiang became a famous "hairy lady of the forest," who reportedly escaped her role as concubine for Prince Ying of the Qin state, and understandably fled to the wilds. They found her there hundreds of years later, living naked and free on a diet of pine needles and pure *qi* energy (Despeux and Kohn, 2003, 86–91). Likewise, the Tibetan master Yeshe Tsogyal reported going to the caves of Mön "to practice the extraction of the essence of various medicinal plants. I began, however, by taking the essence of minerals, knowing that the quintessence of all these is contained in chongzhi, or calcite." On this primordial diet, Tsogyal reported, "My body became like a diamond; no weapon could harm it. My speech took on the qualities of the voice of Brahma, so that even a fierce tigress, when she heard me, became quiet and attentive. My mind passed into the immaculate vajra-like concentration" (Gyalwa and Changchub, 1999, 78). Though Tsogyal was a Buddhist, her methods were in this case indistinguishable from those of Daoist ascetics, such as the master of medicinal plants, Baogu (300s CE). Another legendary Daoist immortal was Magu, or "the Hemp Lady," who was portrayed wearing a tiger-head pouch, a sword, and a headdress symbolizing the freedom of heaven. She had wild hair and bird-like fangs.

Clearly, some women went beyond romanticized longing for the primitive Golden Age.

Female Teachers in the Age of Organized Daoism

As the Han dynasty started to collapse in the 100s CE, various Daoist leaders began forming organized alternative communities, which soon grew into formal religious denominations. The Celestial Masters sect assigned priests to lead parishes, officiate at communal ceremonies, take confessions of sin, and accept tithes (Ching, 1993, 103). All this gave scope for the rise of patriarchal power in religious garb. But for at least the first one or two hundred years, this sect maintained a certain balance of yin and yang. The priestly leaders claimed that all members of the sect, male or female, were "priests," and capable of receiving transmissions from spirit guides. When a member channeled a text called "Demon Ordinances of Lady Blue," it seems the community respected it (Kleeman and Barrett, 2005, 132–133). Though men prevailed as priests, the ritual guides were written for priests of both sexes: "When a man and a woman receive the registers of the three generals displayed on the altar, the man takes them from the left and the woman from the right." Any member could take formal vows to study under a master. The standard vow for an unmarried girl was as follows: "Grateful for weighty kindness of the Dao from which I obtained life, I, an unmarried daughter, in such and such a year, with a devoted mind take pleasure in the Dao. Although I am ignorant I embolden myself to advance, and now take refuge at the master's gate" (Despeux and Kohn, 2003, 105–112).

All members of the Celestial Masters underwent formal initiations according to age and accomplishment. These included rituals of "harmonization of the *qi*," which involved supervised ritual sex between non-married initiates. The rite required three days fasting, and partners were chosen by ritual supervisors. By all accounts, the men and women were treated as equal participants, and equal beneficiaries of the initiation (Robinet, 1997, 60). It seems these people viewed sexuality as a kind of sacred power, which was a means rather than a block to spiritual growth.

By around the year 200 CE, the growing Celestial Masters' society in Sichuan sought independence from the government. The leader Zhang Lu presumed to halt military conscription, and stopped sending tax revenue to the imperial court. In due time, this quiet secession from the empire was punished. General Cao Cao arrived with 100,000 men in 215, but the Celestial Masters didn't fight. Their leader submitted to imperial authority lest lives be lost. The Han rulers then ordered the community dispersed across China (Wong, 2007, 56–59). That way, they became a China-wide sect rather than a local alternative society. When scattered among ordinary Chinese communities, they increasingly conformed with mainstream patriarchal customs.

Daoism in the Dominator Age

Of course Daoism was subject to all the pitfalls of other organized religions. As the Han dynasty collapsed into chaos around 220 CE, traditional Daoism began changing into a religion of personal salvation from a cruel and violent world. As in other escapist faiths, the portals to salvation were increasingly staffed by religious professionals. Organized Daoism arose to compete with other religions, partly by claiming higher authority. Its theologians developed "a vast system of celestial bureaucracy," reflecting the hierarchical world around them (Needham and Wang, 1956, 161). As in Christianity, some Daoist priests tried to make their founding sage into a superhuman king. They made Laozi a heavenly patron of rulers, who came to earth as a lord visits his subjects. Many people felt this was the highest form of respect, since the emperors demanded such reverence for themselves. But fortunately, this division between mortal supplicants and divine lords never seemed obvious to most villagers. As Ge Hong wrote in his *Biography of Spirit Immortals*, "If one says that Laozi was a man who realized the Dao, then people will be encouraged in their efforts to emulate his example. However, if one depicts him as a supernatural and wonderful being of a superhuman kind, then there is nothing to be learned" (Kohn, 1996, 58).

Like the Confucianists, many Daoist leaders sought patronage from their rulers. Occasionally they received it, and were employed as state priests. Then, instead of upholding ancient village traditions against the cult of state, they began preaching conventional morality to the peasants. Under Mongol rule in the late 1200s, Liu Yu founded a Pure Light Movement (Jingming Dao) which pleased the warlord rulers by pushing loyalty, respect, and obedience as the cardinal Daoist values (Robinet, 1997, 215). Somehow, the Daoist path came to involve concocting potions to ensure the emperors' eternal life.

As in other religious rivalries across the world, many Daoist leaders tried to have themselves patronized by the government. And if successful, they often tried to suppress other religious leaders. This commonly involved discrediting village wise women, while claiming their jobs for professional male priests. But over time, Daoists lost the competition for official status. Confucianism prevailed in the struggle for state backing, and Daoism was demoted to a rustic religion of village people. Popular Daoism resembled the pre-Christian cults of European villagers, which the state-backed church viewed as crude superstition or witchcraft. We hear of Confucian officials righteously destroying hundreds of "unauthorized" shrines, hoping to stamp out "weird and immoral things" that "lead astray the sons and daughters of good families" (Weller, 1994, 169–170). In the Tang dynasty court, formerly celebrated Daoist priestesses like Li Ye and Yu Xuanji were denounced by dour Confucian ministers as "next to prostitutes" (Guo, 1995, 303). Later, the Manchu Qing dynasty (1644–1911) placed all Daoist or Buddhist institutions under government control. The Ministry of Rites outlawed women from becoming nuns until they were past child-bearing age (Despeux and Kohn, 2003, 64–65, 207). The Manchus grew so paranoid about rebellions from "sects," that they actually imposed a penalty of beheading for anyone "employing spells and incantations in order to agitate and influence the minds of the people" (Ownby, 2002, 229).

Still, for all this periodic censorship, popular Daoism usually escaped government control. In the villages, "superstition" prevailed. As a Guangxi province gazette reported in 1897, "When people are sick they do not take medicine but instead invite Daoists to worship the peck measure and pray to the stars, or they call in a sorcerer who wears flowers, waves a sword and dances with plates. They call this jumping demons. There are also sorceresses called devil-women" (Weller, 1994, 65). As Min Jiayin says, "Daoism has always enjoyed the favor of women in Chinese history" (1995, 593–594). As women's wisdom is compared to water, Daoism is commonly called "the watercourse way."

Realized Women of Institutional Daoism

Though the organized forms of Daoism slowly grew to resemble organized Confucianism, a minority of important female leaders maintained alternative Daoist institutions.

In the 300s CE, a woman named Wei Huacun founded a new sect of Daoism, the Highest Clarity (or Shangqing) school. Wei was a devotee of Celestial Masters Daoism, and became a supervisor of training for clergy. She was responsible for drawing up curriculum for the sect's clerical schools. But Wei grew increasingly critical of the whole organization. She said it fostered dependence on professional clergy, and focused on goals of wealth and power, rather than honoring heaven and earth. She decided to resign her position and develop her own approach to Daoism. After a period of spiritual struggle, she received an inner guide—an old man named Wang Bo, who she credited with a new text called the *Great Cavern Scripture*. After that, Wei became an independent teacher and founded her own lineage. Her approach was a new integration of diverse practices, which included meditation, visualization, breath control, and yoga-like calisthenics. (Wong, 2007, 72–76, 80–81). After she died, Wei appeared as a spirit teacher to a male disciple named Yang Xi, who further established Highest Clarity Daoism as a major sect.

Besides Wei Huacun, Highest Clarity Daoism claimed to receive texts and guidance from several goddesses, including the Queen Mother of the West, the Lady of the Purple Tenuity (Ziwei Furen), and the Lady of Highest Prime (Shangyuan Furen). The sect soon developed a series of large monastic communities, which women from all states of life could join. The Highest Clarity nunneries accepted women seeking to avoid unwanted weddings, wives who fled incompatible husbands, or former prostitutes. It was okay to go from courtesan to saint. Around the year 500, the Highest Clarity sect had 57 monastic houses on its holy mountain, Maoshan. Of these, 18 were supervised by female abbots (Despeux and Kohn, 2003, 14, 111–118, 128).

Wei Huacun was an inspiration to women across China, and a challenge to the attitudes of most male Daoist leaders. In one folktale set in Tang times, an 11-year-old girl named Xie Xiran told her tutor, "I have an infinite admiration for Wei Huacun. I want to be like her when I grow up." Later she left her home in Sichuan and went to the eastern mountain of Tiantai, hoping to gain enlightenment. She became the student of a male master named Sima Zhengzhen, but he withheld the more advanced teachings from her, feeling that a woman was somehow unworthy. After several years, Xie went away looking for a more open teacher. When she finally came back, he apologized, saying

> It was my fault that I did not give you the highest teachings.
> Several months ago I was approached by an immortal who
> told me, "The Dao cannot be bound by rules and regulations.
> The teachings should be given to any student who is worthy of
> receiving them, regardless of age, sex, or social status. Don't
> forget that the founder of your lineage, Lady Wei Huacun,
> received the Shangqing teachings from the immortal Wang Bo."
> (Wong, 2007, 114–118)

Over the centuries, a series of other Daoist lineages were founded by women. Around the year 900, a female priest named Zu Shu had visionary encounters with the Holy Mother of Numinous Radiance (Lingguang Shengmu), and founded a teaching lineage called the Way of Pure Subtlety. Her sect performed exorcisms called "thunder rites" and her priests were "thunder officials" (Despeux and Kohn, 2003,

17, 131–133). In the 1100s, a woman named Sun Buer (1119–1182) became the seventh master of the Complete Perfection (Quanzhen) sect of Daoism. After her marriage fell apart, she became a nun at Golden Lotus Hall, and received a title as "Serene One of Clarity and Tranquility." She attained full enlightenment in 1179, and founded a sub-sect called the Clarity and Tranquility (Qingjing Pai) branch. Later, the Complete Perfection sect had other sub-lineages inspired by women. One was the Morning Cloud (Yunxia Pai) lineage, which claimed to originate with He Xiangu, a legendary female member in the Eight Immortals of the Bamboo Grove. Another lineage, called "Purity and Tranquility," venerated the great female poet Cao Wenyi. Cao was famously honored by Emperor Huizong (r. 1101–1126), who gave her the title "Great Master of Literary Withdrawal into Clear Emptiness." Though most Daoist clerics were male, the female minority was always substantial. Down to the Qing dynasty (1644 to 1911), about a third of Complete Perfection sect clergy were women (Despeux and Kohn, 2003, 145–147, 18, 133–134, 157–158, 94–98).

A Tradition Flying Under the Radar

Beyond all the clerical institutions, women still prevailed in the realm of popular religion. Even the increasing segregation of the sexes under Qing-Manchu rule (1644–1911) pushed a rise in written teachings specifically for women. These texts (which were often penned or collated by male Daoists) included "Methods of Female Alchemy" (1801), "Essential Methods for the Female Golden Elixir" (1813), "The Precious Raft on Paired Cultivation of Women" (1834), or "Xi Wang Mu's Ten Precepts on the Proper Female Path" (1834) (Valussi, 2009, 141–143). Networks of women formed to compose or convey teachings, and these associations were basically invisible to outside observers. Maybe we get a picture of how these associations worked from a collection of women's writing, assembled in 1906 by He Longxiang. This was a series of 20 documents, all of them products of spirit writing séances conducted by women of a large extended family. The texts were reportedly received from several Daoist immortals, including Sun Buer and He Xiangu. The writings varied between one and 20 pages long. They explained how practices for women differed from those for men, and discussed which practices were most appropriate for virginal, mature, or post-menopausal women (Despeux and Kohn, 2003, 64–65, 207). Usually, such loose networks of women and their teachings flew under the radar of recorded history.

Over the past century, Daoism supposedly died out as the headlights of modernism banished superstition. For several decades Daoist institutions declined to almost nothing. But it seems unorganized religion just went underground, then sprouted again. The aunties and grannies resumed their trades of spirit writing, inner alchemy, meditation, Tai Chi, herbal medicine, astrology, geomancy, etc. These various practices drew attention from the curious, even in big cities. By now, many North Americans are more familiar with such "eastern-style" spiritual practices than they are with worship and prayer. The less organized Daoism gets, the more popular it seems to grow.

11: How Women Changed Buddhism in China and Tibet

When Buddhism first appeared in China, it seemed to be an all-male cult of Indian monks. At first, this Buddhism hardly spoke to China's family men, much less to its women. To most Chinese people, the early Buddhist missionaries seemed irrelevant. Popular religion in China was a family and community affair. Women did most of the work tending temples, statues, and ancestral shrines. They did most of the cooking for temple feasts or death anniversaries. Women were the most involved in divinations about health, marriage, or children. They were the main teachers of spiritual tradition to the next generation (Palmer, et al., 1995, 100). Basically, Han dynasty China was a civilization where family, progeny, sexuality, and community had central importance. All of this, the celibate male emissaries of Buddhism seemed to reject. As a Confucian critic named Zheng Yi later put it, "Let us look at Buddhism from its practice. In deserting his father and leaving his family, the Buddha severed all human relationships. Such a person should not be allowed in any community" (De Bary and Chan, 1960, vol. I, 478).

Making Buddhism Chinese

The Buddha reportedly affirmed that women were capable of reaching enlightenment. But most male monks presumed that all enlightened beings had to be male, since a soul had to evolve beyond a lowly female birth before it could possibly reach nirvana. This traditional Indian prejudice naturally found its counterpart in China. Even some Chinese women accepted it. So, in the year 550 CE, a seemingly high class woman named Tao Jung paid a scribe to carve her words of penance on a temple colophon: "Results are not born of thin air: pay heed to causes and results will follow. This explains how the Buddhist disciple and nun Tao Jung—because her conduct in her previous life was not correct—came to be born in her present form, a woman, vile and unclean" (Ebrey, 1981, 53–54). Some Buddhist scriptures denounced this sort of pious prejudice, and claimed that all sentient beings have equal potential. But Min Jiayin observes, "Unfortunately, when Buddhist scriptures were translated into Chinese, the passages containing the doctrine of equality were left out" (Min, 1995, 596–597).

The early world-denying version of Buddhism encountered a major difficulty in China: it had to compete with popular Daoism. And Daoist cults generally appealed to the whole family, partly because they featured a pantheon of goddesses, teachers, and spirit mediums. Besides, farming villagers were seldom interested in "renouncing the world." They were more prone to worship deities of nature than to wish for salvation from the earthly realm. The Indian monastic practice of begging for alms was so repugnant to Chinese values, that the practice basically died out among China's Buddhists (Hawkins, 2004, 240–241). To compete successfully in China, Buddhism had to change. And it did change, with almost amazing flexibility. One of the first clues we have of this, is an image of the Queen Mother of the West, found on a clay brick from the late Han dynasty. She is seated on the ground, in a pose resembling the Buddha. She faces the viewer directly, and wears robes like those of a Buddhist monk. Perhaps the artist sensed an affinity between the Chinese and Indian images. Both were lords from the West (the direction of death), and both were guides to eternal bliss (Cahill, 1993, 27).

The competition of Daoism and Buddhism was mainly a positive contest for popular appeal. But unfortunately it was also a contest of appeal to the rulers. Over several centuries, leaders or lobbyists for each religion tried to gain official backing from the government. The Buddhists sucked up to sympathetic royals, faking evidence that Emperor Sui Yangdi (569–618) and Empress Wu Zetian (690–705) were incarnations of the Buddha. Sure enough, Empress Wu justified her seizure of power by circulating the *Great Cloud Sutra*, which predicted the reincarnation of the Buddha Maitreya as a female ruler

(Muramatsu, 1960, 254; Ebrey, 1996, 116). Meanwhile, certain Daoist worthies tried to get the government to ban Buddhist institutions, and during the 440s, 570s, and 840s, they pretty much succeeded. It didn't help when Buddhist leaders got revenge in the 1200s. They secured patronage from the hated Mongol conquerors, who let a Tibetan cleric turn the former Song emperors' palace into a Buddhist temple. Things could get almost as nasty as in Western religions.

Fortunately, competition can also produce good fruits. And in seeking to shed their own liabilities while stealing the Daoists' advantages, the native Chinese Buddhists made a series of brilliant moves. In Zhan (Chan, or Zen) Buddhism, a series of Chinese teachers shed the Indian context of world-renunciation, and recast enlightenment as an awakening to life's wonder in the present moment (Ching, 1993, 126–127). The Zhan monks also worked rather than begged for their food. Similarly, the Sanjie Jiao sect renounced monastic living, downplayed reverence for texts, and taught that all life was filled with the Buddha nature. Rather than cutting off relations with society and nature, these Buddhists sought a better quality of relationship. The founder of Pure Land Buddhism made it sound quintessentially Chinese: "Those who rejoice in the Way of the Buddha invariably first serve their parents and obey their lords" (Ebrey, 1996, 97). World-renunciation and monasticism still appealed to some people. But the sects which spread most widely promoted practices that family people could do in their daily lives, like chanting mantras (Hawkins, 2004, 249, 256–257). And then came the important innovation of creating Buddhist goddesses—most importantly Guanyin (Kuan Yin), the goddess of universal compassion (Palmer, et al., 1995, 17–21). Basically, Chinese Buddhists melded Buddhism with Daoism, the way Zen melded with Shinto in Japan. The result was an Oriental Buddhism, which was "anti-worldly" only in its aversion to the "worldly ambition" of warlords. The emaciated yogi-like Buddhas of Indian imagery began morphing into fat, laughing Buddhas, akin to the Daoist Eight Immortals.

The Female World Savior

According to historians, the name Guanyin is a translation from "Avalokitesvara," who is a male bodhisattva described in the *Lotus Sutra*. Avalokitesvara could take any form to assist those who suffer. His name meant "The Lord Who Hears the Cries of the World" (Palmer, et al., 1995, 4–5). But in China, Avalokitesvara (translated Kuan Shih Yin, or Guanyin) became female. It had to be a calculated response to popular demand.

In the Madonna-like image of Guanyin, the values of all Chinese religions could be honored at once. The Buddhist concern to relieve suffering through insight, the Daoist esteem for women's spirituality, and the Confucian regard for social justice, all found expression in one beautiful female figure. This was an image the Chinese could relate to. She appears in a white gown, which is the color of death, the West, and rebirth. Usually she holds either a scroll (the *Lotus Sutra*) or a lotus flower, symbolizing the flowering of mind and soul. Sometimes she is depicted with 1,000 arms, and the peacock's 100 eyes are her eyes, the better to respond to all suffering in the world. Reportedly, Guanyin answers prayers for children, and the children she gives come wrapped in placentas white as snow. She is portrayed riding a lion-like creature called a *hou*, which in older myths was the mount of the earth's guardian queen (Palmer, et al., 1995, 38, 42). And her switch of sex, from male Avalokitesvara to the female Guanyin, illustrates the wisdom of earlier Sutras. As a Chinese composition called *The Precious Volume Amplifying the Diamond Sutra* argues, "Do not ask about degrees of enlightenment; stop differentiating between those who remain in the household life and those who leave it, do not adhere to [the difference between] clergy and laity. One needs only to understand that in the mind there is fundamentally neither male nor female. Why must one cling to outer form?" (Overmyer, 1985, 225).

Even the emperor (Huizong, in 1119) officially recognized Guanyin's sovereignty, appointing her as the goddess whose raft of salvation would bring all souls to safety. By the Ming dynasty (1368–1644) Buddhist temples across the country featured Guanyin as the primary focus of devotion. She eclipsed the Buddha, as Mary eclipsed Christ in cathedrals across Europe. As a recent visitor to Guanyin's holy island of Putuo Shan somewhat inaccurately explained, "in India, Buddha was a man. In China she's a woman" (Ward, 2004, 272). Great Daoist pilgrimage centers, such as White Cloud Temple or Mao Shan made shrines for her. Images of Guanyin appeared in millions of homes and village shrines. These images in the places of honor showed a simple picture of what the villagers valued most.

A Proliferation of Bodhisattvas and Dakinis

Naturally, one goddess was not enough for China's Buddhists. As usually happened in China, new immortal women rose to populate the Buddhist heavens, and their tales fit the patterns of goddesses who went before. The bodhisattva Xiang Nü, for example, was treated like a slave by her parents-in-law. They beat her for teaching piety to other servants, and punished her for protecting a rabbit they wanted to eat. They accused her of having illicit sex and threw her out, so she became a wandering holy woman. When her in-laws died they went to purgatory, but Xiang Nü prayed for them till their souls were released. In the end, they came to see her as their guide (Overmyer, 1985, 245–249).

Some of Buddhism's new goddesses served as the magnets for pilgrimage sites, the way *Anne of Green Gables* draws tourists to Canada's Prince Edward Island. So the legend of Princess Miaoshan was probably crafted from older legends during the winter of 1100 CE, by the abbot of Xiang Shan monastery in southern Henan. The abbot claimed that his monastery stood on the spot where Miaoshan lived, "over 4,000 years ago."

Miaoshan's parents ruled a kingdom, but they were usurpers, having seized the throne from the late King Xing Lin. As a karmic consequence, the new king and queen had no sons to inherit power, but only daughters, who would bring something else. When Miaoshan was conceived, her mother dreamed she had swallowed the moon. When the girl was born, the air was filled with perfume. The world burst into flowers. Miaoshan emerged from the womb bright and clean, trailing multi-hued clouds of glory. Everyone who saw it was convinced the girl was a goddess. But her parents wanted a boy, and ignored her.

In her youth, Miaoshan devoted herself to contemplation. She showed no interest in the court's prima donna lifestyle of socializing, dressing, and consuming. When it came time to marry her off, her parents arranged a match with a respected military man. Miaoshan, however, refused to marry a killer. To her flabbergasted father, she announced she would marry only if it would prevent "the three troubles of the world." And what were those?

She would only marry if it would help prevent the following sources of suffering: a) that age destroys people's beauty, b) that illness destroys their health, and c) that death separates loved ones.

At this totally impossible requirement, her parents exploded in rage. Miaoshan calmly explained, "My desire is to heal the world of all its ills ... of the fires of lust and the damp of old age; of all sickness. I wish to make all equal, regardless of riches and poverty. I want all things to be shared so that no one goes without or has more than they need. If I can marry a man who will help me with this, then I shall marry tomorrow."

Naturally, her parents screamed and threw her out. Like other Chinese holy women, Miaoshan went to live as a teacher on a mountain—near the place Xiang Shan monastery would later be built.

Years later, Miaoshan heard that her father had a terrible disease. Reportedly, there was only one cure—a medicine made from the eyes and arms of someone who gave them willingly. Without hesitation, Miaoshan gave her eyes and arms. The medicine was made, and a doctor brought it to her father. He was cured, and thanked the doctor.

The doctor said he should thank the one who sacrificed her own body.

On reaching the mountain where the donor was said to be, the king and queen saw a woman without eyes or arms, sitting in deep meditation. Only then did they realize it was their daughter, and comprehend the scope of her freedom from fear or desire (Palmer, et al., 1995, 63–70).

Tibet also introduced a host of Buddhist goddesses. And here also, female spiritual seekers had to cope with patriarchal traditions. The Tibetan princess Trompa Gyen reportedly complained to her guru,

> *Our minds seek virtue in the dharma,*
> *but girls are not free to follow it.*
> *Rather than risk a lawsuit, we stay with even bad spouses.*
> *Avoiding bad reputations, we are stuck in the swamp of cyclic*
> *existence ...*
> *Though we stay in strict isolated retreat, we encounter vile enemies.*
> *Though we do our dharma practices,*
> *bad conditions and obstacles interfere ...*
> *Next time let me obtain a male body,*
> *and become independent.*
> *So that I can exert myself in the dharma*
> *and obtain the fruit of Buddhahood.*

Trompa's guru said her problems were worse than that: "Having forsaken your own priorities, you serve another." Trompa was moving in with in-laws, slaving away to meet their demands, and getting no respect. The teacher admonished her: "A girl should value her own worth. Stand up for yourself Trompa Gyen!" (Simmer-Brown, 2002, 34–35).

In Tibet, as in China, male Buddhists lionized control of the major Buddhist institutions. The female saints generally operated as independent leaders of informal groups. But a series of great female teachers, including Yeshe Tsogyal (ca. 757 to 817 CE), played enormous roles in spreading Buddhism across Tibet. In one long teaching tour, Tsogyal first went to Kharak Gang, gathered 300 meditators, and brought seven of them to full enlightenment. Then she gathered 1,000 nuns in Jomo Nang, and 300 became accomplished teachers. Next she practiced at Sangak Ugpalung, gathering 1,000 monks and 1,300 nuns, and reportedly taught so effectively that every one of them achieved liberation. According to her medieval biographers, she was able to report of her life:

I, Tsogyal, while living at Chimphu, became a spring of teachings and instructions for the original disciples of the Guru [Padmasambhava], the new monks, my own disciples, and all who had faith in Guru Rinpoche—from Ngari, Mangyul, Purang, Mön, Tsang, Jar, Loro, Kongpo, the four provinces of Central Tibet, the four northern provinces, Dokham Gangdruk, from China, Jang, Hor, Menyak, and other lands. Thus my work for the sake of beings became as boundless as the sky, and the lineages of my disciples, the disciples of the Lady, have covered and filled the world. (Changchub and Nyingpo, 1999, 126–134, 151–152)

Both the Nyingma and Karma Kagyu schools of Tibetan Buddhism recognize Tsogyal as a fully enlightened Buddha. And besides Tsogyal, a host of other women, including Machig Lapdrön, Trashi Chidren, Gelongma Palmo, Chokyidronme, Dagmema, Ayu Khando, Thinley Wangmo, or Jetsün Lochen Rinpoche, also founded teaching lineages, mainly among women. In popular religion, these teachers became living goddesses, dakinis, or incarnations of the goddess Tara. As Guanyin surpassed the Buddha's popularity in China, so Tara became Tibet's sovereign deity (Day, 1990, 82). As Kees Bolle explains, "Tara ... is mightier than Buddhas and Bodhisattvas ... the mother who gives birth to all the Buddhas" (foreword to Beyer, 1973, 3).

For followers of this tradition, the essence of femininity was not earth, matter, desire, samsara, nurturance, or submissiveness—but the freedom of fearless, unlimited awareness, known as Prajanaparamita—the transcendant realization which is the mother of all Buddhas. As the Tibetan sage Milarepa explained, "Woman is essentially wisdom: source of spontaneous prajna [wise discernment] and subtle body. Never consider her inferior. Strive especially to see her as Vajravarahi [a guardian goddess]." And as Guru Padmasambhava saluted Yeshe Tsogyal,

> Yogini seasoned in the secret mantra!
> The ground of liberation
> is the human frame, this common human form—
> and here distinctions, male and female,
> have no consequence.
> And yet if bodhichitta [unlimited compassion] graces it,
> a woman's form indeed will be supreme! (Changchub and Nyingpo, 1999, 91)

Going a bit further, the *Hevajra-tantra* opened with the lines, "Thus I have heard: At one time the Lord dwelt in the vaginas of the vajra maidens who are the body, speech, and mind of all the Buddhas" (Simmer-Brown, 2002, 38, 182, 103). As the mantra "Om Mani Padme Hum" rather explicitly affirms, "Hail to the jewel in the lotus."

All this suggested a real respect for female powers and leaders. But over time, male teachers grew more predominant in monastic institutions. The practice of full ordination for women died out, and nuns were restricted to ordination as novices. As in Daoism, female teachers practiced mainly as independent yoginis, outside the ranks of priests or monastics. But in the view of many Tibetans, the independent path of yogins and yoginis seemed the highest, the most heroic, and the most direct path to enlightenment (Ray, 2000, 289–290).

"Right Sexuality" as a Spiritual Practice

Where the early Indian forms of Buddhism stressed renunciation of sex, Chinese and Tibetan Buddhism made a place for it in the spiritual path. The ancient tradition of opposite-sex teachers appeared, as with Yeshe Tsogyal and her guru Padmasambhava, or the sage Marpa with his enlightened wife Dagmema. The Nyingma school, which Padmasambhava and Tsogyal helped found, allowed marriage and families for monastics. It was a version of Buddhism where the Noble Path seemed to include "right sexuality." Yeshe Tsogyal spoke of spiritual love, in which "the Primordial Wisdom of Co-emergent Joy, whereby the defiled consciousness with its impure grasping and the habitual tendencies of the body, speech, and mind were purified in equal measure." As she explained in greater detail:

> *Now in my practice upon pleasure, which is Primordial Wisdom,*
> *essence of empowerment, I continually increased the rhythm*
> *of the Four Joys [the joys transcending ordinary pleasure]*
> *and never allowed it to diminish ... I was able to reverse the*
> *bodhichitta [energy of compassion] upward, and, by pressing*
> *down the vital energy and drawing up the lower energy, I held*
> *the pleasure in the "vase." I remained attentive to the bliss but*
> *did not crave it, and thus I practiced, laying aside all mentally*
> *fabricated concentration. Not for an instant did I give way to*
> *laziness. (Changchub and Nyingpo, 1999, 41–42)*

Teaching her female disciple Kalasiddhi, Tsogyal instructed: "Request the third initiation and train upon desire. For six months practice the Four Joys, or till the signs reveal themselves within your body. Blend and mingle energies of male and female. Rely upon the skillful merging of the winds, above, and below—male assisting female, female helping male. All should do according to this measure. Progress, persisting in the virtuosity of bliss" (Changchub and Nyingpo, 1999, 172–173).

The fact that such teaching from women found an honored place in Tibetan Buddhism shows remarkable openness in a mainly patriarchal tradition. Where mainstream Indian Buddhism had viewed the body as a hindrance to enlightenment, Tibet's Vajrayana Buddhism sought to harness the body's passions as tools for expanded awareness (Hawkins, 2004, 130). But "right sex" could also involve celibacy, which is also seen as a powerful tool for inner growth. And Tibet's monastics commonly deem celibacy as most appropriate for a student's needs. All Vajrayana practice is held to require close guidance from experienced teachers. And though all aspects of life can be treated as a focus of spiritual practice, the quality of sexual life receives no disproportionate emphasis.

In China, some famous teachings on spiritual sex (from a male perspective) were published in the 1600s, in a book called the *Carnal Prayer Mat*. The author (reportedly Li Yu) described a man seeking Buddhist enlightenment through basically Daoist sexual practices. The protagonist had to hide his activities in a moralistic Confucian society, but confided the most graphic details of his practice on paper. Eventually, he claimed that this practice led to an awakening. He discovered loving compassion for all of life, and came to view the universe as one. Then, having reached his goal of awakenment, the techniques by which he arrived became irrelevant (Kohn, 2009, 183). The whole notion that sexuality can be spiritual has popular appeal, as seen in the tenderly romantic novel of attachment and enlightenment, *The Dream of Red Mansions*. And then we have the 2011 Cantonese 3-D movie *Sex and Zen: Extreme Ecstasy*, which gets more sensational about it.

An Emerging Mythology of Compassion

The woman-friendly values of many Buddhists slowly changed the face of Chinese popular mythology. Older Daoist stories were revised to serve new goals, and respond to public sentiment. At Buddhist hands, the Queen Mother of the West became a compassionate mother of the world, rather than a fierce shaman-woman. Guandi (or Guan Gong), the Daoist god of war and martial arts, took on kindly qualities. After his heroic death in a war for the right, the Buddhists said he appealed for spiritual guidance to a heavenly Buddhist master. He quickly reached enlightenment, then joined other bodhisattvas like Guanyin in leading the world to peace. He even managed to read the whole corpus of Confucian writings, and was granted a posthumous doctorate as the god of literature.

Buddhists also changed the face of Hell. Of course the whole idea of Hell came to China with the Buddhists, as a kind of Purgatory for karmic debts (Ching, 1993, 216). But China's Buddhists added a kindly goddess to administer Hell's exit gate, and a loyal son to save his mother from the flames.

Usually, people imagine Hell as an intensification of whatever sort of suffering they hate most. So, Tibetans saw Hell as a place of freezing cold, and Chinese Hell became a bureaucratic nightmare of fiendishly oppressive government officials. There were nine administrative levels of China's Fengdu Hell. Each level was governed by a god specializing in specific tortures, such as slicing people to mincemeat or frying them in boiling oil. To this realm of horrors, the filial son Mulian traveled to save his mother's soul, and won her release. The deed was honored in the Hungry Ghost Festival, celebrated every fifteenth day of the seventh month, for the nurture of lost and suffering spirits.

Of course the tortures of Hell usually proceeded relentlessly, driven by the karmic law of consequence. But finally, when the chastened souls had paid their karmic debts to the last drop of blood or twist of the screw, they arrived at an exit chamber at the ninth level of Hell. There, they met the Buddhist goddess Meng Po, the underworld deity of amnesia. Meng Po, otherwise known as "Lady Dream," provided each soul with a cup of special tea, designed to mercifully erase the memory of Hell's agonies. Then, with their minds and karmic slates wiped clean, they passed through the gates of reincarnation for another chance to reach enlightenment. Only realized Buddhas were able to overcome the tea's effects, and recall their previous lives.

For approximately the past 500 years, the goddess Guanyin has been most popular deity in China. Having started as a patron of Buddhism, she now transcends the boundaries of at least five East Asian religions (Buddhism, Daoism, Confucianism, Cao Dai, and Shinto). In Japan and Korea she became "Kannon." Her image appears in most Daoist shrines, and on all the Daoist sacred mountains. When Portuguese monks arrived in the 1500s, they brought images of the Virgin Mary, which porcelain makers in Fujian immediately used as models for a classic white Madonna-figure of Guanyin (Palmer, et al., 2009, 33, 36). This goddess absorbed a host female religious heroes into one famous image, known across the globe by the literal meaning of her name—"She Who Hears the Cries of the World."

During the nineteenth-century movements against foot-binding and arranged marriage, many supportive Christian missionaries presumed that women's liberation was a Western concept, which stood opposed to Chinese tradition. But many Chinese leaders of these movements took their inspiration from extremely traditional quarters. In her late-nineteenth century essay "Opposition to Foot Binding," Zhang Mojun (Chang Mo-Chün) recalled arguing with her mother: "I have seen the gigantic stone sculpture of Kuan Yin [Guanyin] at the Yun-meng Temple in our district, more than twenty feet high, with natural feet and many hands. It is dignified and extraordinarily beautiful, full of vitality and power. Where in any of these can you see the so called three-inch golden lotuses [tiny bound feet]?" (Chang, 1992, 126).

Every image of Guanyin showed a strong, beautiful, unmarried woman, with obviously unbound feet. She was depicted as the greatest spiritual savior in the land. Her role was arguably the most important in the universe. In the late 1800s, she was a patron deity for women's groups against foot binding and arranged marriage (Shahan and

Weller, 1996, 20). Progressive Chinese claimed that great Western women such as Harriet Beecher Stowe or Florence Nightingale were bodhisattvas of compassion like Guanyin (Judge, 2008, 70). The West could offer no finer patron to the women's movement.

12: Confucianism as a Cult of "Mamas' Boys"

Confucianism is generally seen as China's bastion of patriarchal tradition, with a virtually Arabian array of sanctified controls on women. But before it was a state-backed cult of obedience to superiors, Confucianism was a protest movement against warlords, and a defense of ancient village values. In a sense, the first Confucian teachers were men standing up for their mothers' values. They were mama's boys—often in the best sense sense of the term.

Men Who Respected Their Mothers' Values

According to various traditions, Confucius and Mengzi (Mencius) both grew up in single-parent homes, raised by their mothers alone. The same applies to many leading Confucianists of later times, such as Kou Laigong (961–1023), Ouyang Xiu (1007–1072), the Cheng brothers, Cheng Ho and Cheng Yi (ca. 1030s to 1080s), Lü Xizhe (1039–1116), Gu Yanwu (1613–1682), or Wang Tingzhen (1757–1827). Less impressively, it applies to Generalisimo Chiang Kai-shek (or Jiang Jieshi, 1887–1975), who said that his widowed mother was "the personification of Confucian virtues." These men certainly gave due credit to their mothers, who were the tutors and pillars of their early lives (Judge, 2008, 132; Hu, 1992, 14). According to Tu Weiming, mothers were usually central in transmitting "Confucian" values of *jen*, or benevolence. A recent survey of biographies for major Confucian teachers since the 1300s shows a large majority were trained in childhood by their mothers rather than male teachers. Tu cites a woman in the 1600s who wished for her son: "I would like you to learn from the two fatherless gentlemen in ancient China: one was Confucius, whose father died when he was three, and the other was Mencius [Mengzi]" (Tu, 1992, 72).

It's commonly said that Confucianism is the Christianity of China. It started out as a movement of wandering teachers who were ridiculed and rejected by the warlord rulers. For a time the movement suffered serious persecution. But within several centuries Confucianism won impressive popular support, and the emperors co-opted it by making it an official imperial religion. With such patronage it became a religious arm of autocratic governments for almost 2,000 years. Then, like Christianity in the French or Russian revolutions, Confucianism was largely rejected in China's twentieth-century revolutions. Confucianism was then firmly labeled as a feudal ideology, designed for the oppression of common people and women. In recent decades most people considered it a discredited religion, consigned to the garbage dump of history. But after Confucianism was stripped of official patronage, its fate fell to the hands of ordinary people. In that case, maybe most modern children heard little about Confucius, save some stories from their mothers. And the mothers interpreted ancient traditions in their own ways.

The Past According to Confucius

Back in Confucius' time of the 500s BCE, North China was divided between several princely warlords, and Confucius reportedly wandered court to court, hoping some ruler would heed values from the past. While most Daoists avoided the warlords, Confucius hoped to reform them. Maybe his effort showed a need for approval from the powerful, or maybe it showed courage in the face of tyrants. Some observers ridiculed Confucius for running from one prince to the next, and urged him "to flee from this whole generation of men" (De Bary, 1991, 8). And in terms of any immediate results, his whole effort was futile. The rulers claimed his advice was totally unrealistic. Instead of helping them to maximize their wealth and power, Confucius urged them to "serve" the villagers like parents serving children. Of course that would mean either reducing taxes, or re-investing tax wealth in the villages. And successful rulers needed that income to win the arms race, control the land, and reap its fruits for themselves. To such men, Confucius argued that real power grew from observing ancient virtues of kindness and service. Maybe the words ascribed to him were really said by many people. But if he was only a symbol for many like him, that would make his legend even more authentic.

Where did this human relic of the Golden Age come from? Reportedly he was born in a family of courtiers to the Sung nobles. These were descendants of old Shang dynasty officials, who were defeated by the Zhou around 1050 BCE. The new Zhou rulers adopted the Shang courtiers as hirelings who specialized in divination, ancestral rites, calendar alignment, and record keeping. They were called *ju*, meaning "weak" and "yielding," since they depended on their new masters. Five hundred years later, many *ju* families still retained these roles, and this was the life Confucius was trained for. His father served the prince of Lu, but died when Confucius was young. His mother raised him alone, and he grew up disproportionately influenced by women. His family lived in poverty, and he identified with poor people. When he began courtier service, he found the palace culture of intrigue and flattery galling. His "superiors" tolerated him as a hanger-on (Mote, 1971, 29, 36–37). After some years he set out looking for a prince whose values he could support.

In his journeys and various jobs, Confucius reportedly went to the imperial Zhou archives and studied records of past dynasties. He made copious notes, then returned to Lu preaching about the Golden Age. Later he went to other states, each time studying their archives, and growing more convinced that the world must return to the ways of the ancients. He is widely credited with saving important sections of the royal files by copying them into updated Chinese before their archaic language was forgotten (Wu 1982, 38–39). The resulting "Confucian Classics" such as the *Classic of History*, the *Classic of Poetry*, the *Classic of Rites*, or the *Spring and Autumn Annals*, reflected tradition as known by the old Zhou noble clans. The heroes of these accounts were early warlords, but they claimed to follow earlier benevolent leaders. With a dash of pre-Confucian sentiment, the *Classic of Poetry* praised "the three mothers of Zhou" (Tai Ren,

Tai Si, and Tai Jiang) for inspiring the founders of the Zhou dynasty (Judge, 2008, 125). And as Mengzi pointed out, the *Classic of History* claimed that the rulers of yore treated their people "as if they were tending a new-born babe" (Mengzi III.A:5). By Confucius' time, the Zhou princes had either forgotten these old stories, or used them as justifications for the divine right of kings. But for Confucius, the sage-king stories showed that leadership in the past was utterly different.

When Confucius tried to revive the spirit of the pre-military age, he constantly referred to the web of relations, and the quality of relationships between people. Like a good mother's son, he emphasized that *jen* (human feeling) started with kindness and respect between family members. Contesting claims that duty to rulers came first, he said that a loyal son would avoid reporting his parent's crimes to the police (*Analects*, 13:18; Mote, 1971, 44–45). Virtue had to originate in kindness between family members. Only then could it grow outward to others. As Mengzi (Mencius) put it, "A benevolent man extends his love from those he loves to those he does not. A ruthless man extends his ruthlessness from those he does not love to those he loves" (Cotterell, 1981, 123). With mother-like optimism, the early Confucianists claimed that the capacity for compassion was inborn for every child. Anyone could feel this in their natural response to seeing a child in danger (Mengzi, 2A:6). This inborn capacity for compassion appeared as "buds" that could be nurtured, or stunted by abuse and neglect. But if nourished, the buds could flower to the full potential of the human spirit (Mote, 1971, 56–57). Being his mother's star pupil, Mengzi repeatedly emphasized that anyone can become a sage (6A:7; Li, 1992, 112).

This kind of logic doesn't sound so unusual for mothers. Maybe it seemed unusually good-hearted only when earnestly preached by their sons. Basically, Confucius taught that without mutual compassion, the web of human relationships would come undone. Calamity would befall first the family, then the whole village, and finally the kingdom. For most village elders and mothers, it was common sense.

But when Confucius urged such common sense on the warring princes, they found it irrelevant to their ambitions. Such moralistic objections interfered with their dreams of becoming masters over others. Unlike traditional leaders who led by example and had no powers of coercion over others, the Zhou lords tried to keep their subjects intimidated. In their view, a village man's obligations to his ruler took priority over obligations to his family. According to the *Zuo Zhuan* (*Tso Chuan*), "When a lord has issued his orders, nothing else matters" (Maspero, 1978, 82–84).

Since his appeals to rulers showed virtually no result, Confucius went and talked to ordinary people. Like a man "here by royal disappointment," he probably spent most of his life philosophizing with friends and local leaders. We have some personal information on several dozen of his students. Only two of the known ones came from aristocratic families. Most were commoners, and some were homeless. One of them, Yen Hui, "lived in a narrow alley, eating off a single bamboo plate and drinking out of a gourd" (Mote, 1971, 39–40; Maspero, 1978, 82). Such students were authors of the *Analects*, much as Muhammad's followers wrote down sayings of the Prophet after his death. The reports of Confucius suggest a conversational tone, with questions raised and tentative answers proposed: "To study and in due season to practice what one has learned—is this not a pleasure? To have friends that come from afar—is this not a delight? ... To be un-soured even if one is unrecognized—is this not noble?" (De Bary, 1991, 24). The discussion concerned how to live nobly. And in that art, Confucius obviously considered himself a student among students: "A sage it has not been mine to see. Could I just see a noble man, that would be enough." William de Bary says the *Analects* were much more about living well than ruling well (1991, 4–6).

As Confucius' students formed a social movement, they started to show hubris. Mengzi (Mencius) displayed open contempt for corrupt rulers, claiming to represent the people's conscience: "The people are the most important element; after them come the gods of the soil and of harvests; the prince is the least important ... When a ruler endangers the spirits of land and grain, he is removed and replaced." (7B:14, Tu 1992, 132). In saying this, Mengzi was building on Confucius' words as found in the *Analects* (XI:17). Concerning a ruler who taxed the poor without mercy, "The Master said 'He is no disciple of mine. You, my young friends, may attack him openly to the beating of drums'" Confucious, 1979, 108). In response to such effrontery, the Qin rulers moved to eliminate Confucianism. To make himself the center of all obligations, with "a position of sole supremacy," Qin Shihuang brushed aside the cobwebs of old-fashioned ethics, killed Confucian teachers, and burned their books. If Confucian morality came from the *literati* alone, that sort of persecution might have worked.

The transformation of Confucianism came after the peasant revolution against the Qin. The new Han rulers were more sympathetic to popular values, and saw political advantage in paying lip service to traditional virtue. After centuries of rejection and persecution, the surviving Confucian scholars proved eager to serve their new emperors.

Turning Confucius into a Dominator Prophet

Over the past 2,000 years, most Chinese rulers found that giving lip service to Confucius was a powerful way to control ethical judgment. If the rulers were willing to hire Confucian advisors, they could claim their decisions were taken with due consideration for sacred tradition. So, a compromise was struck. The warlords accepted Confucian scholars as their advisors, and the scholars were employed to do the emperor's bidding. And in exchange for employment or promotion, some scholars were willing to offer whatever kinds of advice their rulers wanted. Some displayed a tendency "to flock around the worst robber barons, vying with one another to become their counselors" (Needham and Wang, 1956, 102). In the process of offering advice that would sell, many Confucian ministers slowly altered their own values almost beyond recognition.

Confucianism first gained official status as a state religion during the reign of Emperor Wu (140–87 BCE). Wu appointed about 50 Confucian scholars to his bureaucracy, and declared himself a Confucian ruler. Within a century, the number of Confucian-trained officials rose to over 200. But these officials were appointees of the court, not representatives of the villagers (Gernet, 1996, 159; Huang, 1997, 63–64). And the kind of Confucianism that Emperor Wu accepted in his palace was far different from anything Mengzi or Confucius ever knew. Wu's version of Confucianism was more like Legalism (Miyakowa, 1960, 29).

It was actually a Legalist counselor of the Qin state, Han Feizi, who had first articulated a morality based on "the three bonds"—"the minister serving the ruler, the son serving the father, and the wife serving the husband" (Du Fangqin, 1995, 224). Supposedly, this dominator ideology was discredited when the Qin dynasty fell. But the Han dynasty scholar and consultant Dong Zhongshu (Tung Chung-shu, ca. 179–104 BCE) proposed a very similar doctrine, and called it Confucianism. Dong interpreted the *Book of Changes* (*Yi Jing*) to say, not that Yin and Yang must be kept in harmonious balance, but that "Yang is superior to Yin." With a similar accent on ranking, Dong drew his doctrine of "the Three Cardinal Guides"—"a ruler is a cardinal guide to a minister, a father is a cardinal guide to a son, and a husband a cardinal guide to a wife." This, Dong insisted, was the real point of Confucius' teachings. Emperor Wu was pleased with this interpretation. And as Qin Shihuang had banned all the hundred schools of philosophy save Legalism, so Emperor Wu proceeded to demote all doctrines save this very Legalistic Confucianism (Min, 1995, 566–567).

Dong Zhongshu's new version of Confucianism was more than a social policy; it also had an element of religious cosmology. Dong claimed the hierarchical social order was modeled on the hierarchical relationships of Heaven to Earth, and Yang to Yin. Society's chains of command were eternally fixed. Therefore the purpose of life was not self-cultivation, but performance of inborn duty. As Sun Xiao and Pan Shaoping explain, Dong gave the philosophy "a kind of theological touch ... For this reason, it is not an exaggeration to say that Dong Zhongshu ... was the founder of the teleological theory supporting the autocracy" (1995, 236). This quasi-religious mythology was embellished by later ruling houses. Future emperors inherited a cosmic role as descendants of legendary founding fathers. They served as pivots of Heaven and Earth. Their cult of divine monarchy resembled the cult of Japanese emperors.

Dong Zhongshu probably advocated this ruler-friendly version of Confucianism as a tactic to win the emperor's trust. Because after he gained office as a counselor, he made some effort to promote compassionate policies. He pushed the old Confucian proposal that all land be redistributed with equalized holdings for all farm families. Naturally the proposal hit roadblocks from court landowners. But Dong accepted a compromise, with the emperor decreeing certain limits on the size of estates (De Bary, 1991, 47). Probably this was the high point of Confucian influence on Emperor Wu.

In 81 BCE, the conflicts of Confucian scholars and quasi-Legalist bureaucrats came to a head in the famous Debate on Salt and Iron. The court ministers wanted to establish state monopolies on essential commodities like salt and iron, which they felt would guarantee strong revenues to build the state and army. The traditional Confucianists quoted Mengzi, claiming that most imperial functions should be left to the local people. The emperor, they argued, should be a basically symbolic leader. He should conduct rituals to inspire the people in devotion for ancient communal values. As for building the army, the Confucianists said it was a counterproductive waste of lives and money. With seemingly ridiculous idealism they told the emperor: "If you foster high standards in the temple and courtroom, you need only make a bold show and bring home your troops, for the king who practices benevolent government has no enemies anywhere. What need can he then have for expense funds?" (Ebrey, 1981, 24).

These old-fashioned Confucianists still expected leaders to give more than they took. Their arguments still represented village people's opinions. In popular culture, emperors who raised taxes for massive public works went down in history as bogeymen. Those who drafted large armies to expand the empire were depicted as ogres in village operas. If a ruler ordered people to serve him during the planting or harvest seasons, he was deemed both evil and an utter fool. The villagers and traditional Confucianists believed that a wise ruler would hardly touch the people, leaving them free to organize their affairs in peace (Lowe 1968, 64). As the yet-more populist Daoists explained in the *Huainanzi*,

The foundation of creating order
lies in making people content.
The foundation of making people content
lies in giving them sufficient use [of their time].
The foundation of giving them sufficient use
lies in not stealing their time.
The foundation of not stealing their time
lies in restricting the state's demands on them.
The foundation of restricting the state's demands on them
lies in limiting the desires [of the ruler]. (Roth, 1996, 141)

But these traditionalist Confucian protesters were arguing with an heir to the imperial throne as established by Qin Shihuangdi. And this fact showed where real power lay. The emperor's ministers pointed out that the wandering scholars were nobodies. They were supplicants to the court, some of them poor, with ragged clothes. Why should the emperor listen to people who had so little power, wealth, or respectability? With some compromises, the monopoly on salt and iron was applied. The villagers paid as new armies were raised and lost, fighting for empire in Korea or the wastelands of Central Asia.

Later, Confucian advisors won a concession from the emperors. They made knowledge of the Confucian classics a condition for employment in several branches of government service. After that, generation after generation of government officials were tested for knowledge of those books, before being hired to serve the authorities. The whole imperial administration was then cloaked in Confucian robes. The government could seem a Confucian priesthood, with the emperor as chief priest. The Confucian officials, however, were just employees. They depended for their jobs (and the welfare of their families), on successfully doing a despot's bidding, even if the emperor was a conquering warlord from Inner Asia.

The Battle for Confucianism's Soul

In the emerging dominator version of Confucianism, morality was about enforcing a chain of command between each class of human beings. In the semi-Confucian legal system, it was a far more serious crime for a son to abuse his father, than for a father to abuse his son. The same uneven standard applied to crimes between husbands and wives. Confucius was then proclaimed a prophet of patriarchy and the divine-right of kings. He was lifted entirely out of the context of the Golden Age, and used as a brand-name endorsement for tyranny.

Sometime between the late 700s and 1200s a new Confucian classic appeared, called the *Classic of Loyalty*. This book was attributed to the great Han dynasty Confucian scholar Ma Jung, but is now widely deemed a forgery. This classic emphasized loyalty to superiors (rather than compassion) as the primary virtue in life. It made loyalty to a ruler more important than loyalty to parents, spouses, or children. It re-defined loyalty as unconditional obedience rather than mutual concern. Many Daoists ridiculed medieval Confucianism as a cult of slavish obedience. And if the *Classic of Loyalty* was the new standard of orthodoxy, that criticism was right (Mote, 1960, 230). We may note however, that the Confucian cult of loyalty was usually more about loyalty to parents and children than to governors. And even

Confucian governors were so prone to obey their mothers, that many widowed empresses were virtual lords over their emperor sons (De Bary and Chan, 1960, vol. I, 169).

Of course many Confucianists rejected the new cult of blind obedience, and continued acting as representatives of popular morality. Especially under nomadic invaders such as the Mongols, many Confucian scholars refused to serve the rulers. Liu Yin (1249–1293), for example, wrote,

> *Those who uphold Dao frequently are led to follow a solitary course.*
> *This practice has existed since Zhou and Qin times.*
> *The solitary course of the recluse moreover merits approval:*
> *In a degenerate age, is it not meaningless to possess Confucian*
> *rank and office? (Wright, 1960, 15)*

For many people, views like that still represented the real Confucianism. As the old firebrand Confucian prophets like Mengzi used to say, "Those who counsel the great should view them with contempt ... What they have is nothing I would have ... Why should I stand in awe of princes?" (*Mengzi*, 7B:34) And to eliminate such remnants of early Confucianism, the first Ming Emperor (1368–1399) had the text of *Mengzi* purged of all comments against absolute monarchy. His officials lobotomized the ancient text to make it safe for tyrants. They corrected the Confucian record to weed out popular morality, and redefined orthodoxy as obedience to whatever the ruler desired. After that, the Ming and Qing dynasty emperors proclaimed themselves both guardians and definers of Confucian tradition. They sent out spokesmen to read official edicts in each village and teach the people morality.

Over the next several centuries, a minority of Confucian leaders still challenged abuse of power, and the consequences could be savage. When Emperor Ming Chengzu usurped the emperor's throne in 1402, the Confucian court historian, Fang Xiao-ru, refused to legitimate the seizure of power. For this insult, the emperor threatened to kill Fang, and exterminate all his male relatives to the "ninth agnate" (meaning four generations back to his great-great grandfathers, and four generations forward to the great-great grandsons, with all their siblings and cousins). When Fang refused to submit even at this, the emperor added a "tenth agnate," condemning all Feng's students and peers as well. And rather than endorse usurpation of power by military force, Feng accepted the death penalty for himself and 873 relatives or associates.

Later, the Confucian official Han Rui (1514–1587) publicly denounced two Ming emperors for corruption, and actually issued a memorial of impeachment against the Jiajing emperor in 1565. The emperor ordered Han killed, but died himself before the order was carried out. Han then emerged from prison a hero, so widely respected that the next emperor restored him as a minister. But once again, Han Rui presumed to defend the country from its ruler. He denounced the Longqing Emperor's court for corrupt land deals, and again was famously dismissed from office.

After the Manchu conquest of China in 1644, Lü Liuliang (1629–1683) tried to unify Confucian scholars against the invaders. He urged fellow bureaucrats to boycott service to the Manchus, because theft of power betrayed of the most basic Confucian values. Lü felt it would waste his breath and dignity to plead with the Manchu warlords. Instead, he organized an underground resistance, with a cause of eliminating all emperors. Lü argued that real Confucianism was opposed to all autocratic power. Of course many people found this argument shocking, since it contradicted everything they'd heard in the media.

If a ruler was corrupt and oppressive, Lü claimed that any bond to obey him was dissolved. He said Confucian advisors were no more bound to obey dictators than Confucius and Mengzi were bound to obey princes who rejected their advice. A Confucian leader was therefore a free agent, not a bound servant of the ruler: "Ruler and minister come together in agreement on what is right. If they can agree on what is right, they can form the relation of ruler/minister; if not, they should part, as is the case between friends … If they do not agree, there is no need for personal resentment or recrimination. If their commitment is not the same, their way cannot be carried out, and it is best to part" (De Bary, 1991, 64).

Lü's critical words and writings circulated for several decades before the Yongzheng emperor decided to erase them from public memory. In 1728, the censors destroyed Lü's writing, desecrated his grave, and punished his living descendents. It was part of an ongoing process of weeding China's crop of texts and scholars, for a Darwinian selection of the most servile. Any exhortations to civil disobedience for the sake of "higher" moral values were deleted from the record. This kind of censorship was not really efficient as in a modern state, but exemplary firings or killings of critical scholars kept most people quiet.

By the 1800s, the record was fairly clear: orthodox Confucianism stood for unconditional obedience to the three bonds, and a cult of the emperor. But still there was something suspicious about the official doctrine. In the classic *Doctrine of the Mean*, of which many uncensored copies remained, Confucius was recorded saying,

There are five relationships which concern all men, and three virtues by which they are fulfilled. The relationships of ruler and subject, father and son, husband and wife, older and younger brother, and of intercourse between friends—these five are the relationships which pertain to all men. Knowledge, humanity and courage—these are the virtues which apply to all men, and that by which they are practiced is one. (The Mean, XX; De Bary and Chan, 1960. vol. I, 120)

The sage here seemed to recommend one set of moral standards for all. No separate list of virtues appears for each class of humans, such as "obedience" for inferiors and women only, or "strength" for superiors only. After nearly 2,000 years of censorship, it was still impossible to control what people remembered. Most people still had the notion that Confucius taught mutual respect. They had to wonder how his cult became a force for contempt. As novelist Annie Wang put it, "A country of courtesy, that's how the Chinese describe China, but Chinese life is full of disrespect and humiliation" (2002, 291).

In the late 1800s, a number of would-be reformers made a last-ditch effort to rescue Confucius from fundamentalism. Kang Yuwei (K'ang Yu-wei, 1858–1927) made a serious bid to reinterpret Confucius as a progressive reformer. Building on a tradition of modern-style textual analysis, Kang claimed that the "original" Confucian teaching emphasized mutual care between equals, not unilateral control by superiors. In a series of hard-hitting articles such as "Study of the Classics Forged During the Xin [Hsin] Period," and "Study of Confucius' Institutional Reforms," Kang argued that passages defending social inequality were corruptions of the text, inserted by later editors (Chow, 1960, 289–290). The real Confucius had been a revolutionary prophet of equality, sort of like Jesus Christ. The real Confucian teaching would lead naturally to democracy, women's liberation, and world brotherhood (Tan, 2008, 139).

In reply to such foolishness, fundamentalist officials insisted that the classics were inerrant. Real Confucianists could not pick and choose which aspects of the scriptural classics they liked. People had to either accept or reject the authority of China's founding fathers. China's people had to choose: either to uphold their sacred tradition as infallibly correct, or else betray their ancestral faith. In a rousing defense of the fundamentals, the orthodox scholar Zhang Zhidong issued a tract called "Exhortation to Learn" (1898). With angry, utterly inflexible conviction, he rejected revisionism, and condemned the moral pollution of "Western" ideas such as liberty, equality, and women's rights: "If we recognize the bond of subject to sovereign, the theory of the people's rights cannot stand. If we recognize the bond of son to father, then the theory that the father and son are amenable to the same punishments cannot stand ... If we recognize the bond of wife to husband, then the theory of equal rights for men and women cannot stand" (De Bary and Chan, 1960. vol. II, 84).

Zhang held this almost military-style ranking of people as the very essence of Chinese civilization. To defend it, he was ready to call on the armed forces: "In order to protect the race, we must first preserve the doctrine ... How is the doctrine to be maintained? It is to be maintained by strength, and strength lies in armies" (De Bary and Chan, 1960. vol. II, 83). But the army Zhang spoke of was the Manchu warlord army, which had conquered China in 1644 and held it by force ever since. Zhang's choice of fundamental loyalties was clear. He stood with the warlords, not the mama's boys.

In this argument over the soul of a nation, the hard-line fundamentalists won. They and their warlord masters had hijacked Confucianism so effectively, for so long, that their definition of "orthodoxy" prevailed in the public mind. Most people grew more convinced than ever that Confucius was indeed a dominator prophet. The next generation of young idealists tossed him out the window along with the Manchu rulers. That can happen to overly inflexible, legalistic religions.

For the next 75 years most Chinese people rejected Confucius as an enemy of their every aspiration. The Communists banned his works. The Red Guards broke into the Temple of Confucius in Qufu, erased the grave tablets of his parents, and burned the altars of his 72 most sagely followers. With spectacular hatred the Guards dragged his bronze images through the streets, dug up the graves of his descendants, and dumped their bones on the ground (Bordewich, 2004, 89).

Only in post-Maoist times did Confucius recover a following, as people looked with fresh eyes at the tradition's original face. Then, among a host of new media personalities, a female scholar named Yu Dan presented Confucianism as a populist, compassionate sort of

Chicken Soup for the Soul (Wasserstrom, 2010, 13–14). In 2006, her seven-day series on China Central Television was followed by the book, *Yu Dan's Notes on the Analects*, which sold maybe ten million copies. Next she wrote *Confucius from the Heart: Ancient Wisdom for Today's World*. Some critics said she was "castrating" Confucianism. But maybe the Confucianists should have started long ago to let the mothers teach directly, not just through their sons.

13: Family Values in the Warlord Age, and Now

The history of Chinese families traces an arc that broadly traces the fortunes of couples and children in Europe. On both subcontinents we start with primitive villagers, who knew no legally binding marriage, and whose arts or legends suggest reverence for women's powers. Then, both regions were repeatedly conquered by warlords from Inner Asia. In Europe's case this started with the Kurgan waves of the 4000s BCE. Later, the warlord tribes who overran Rome retained power as Europe's royal clans until the French Revolution, or down to World War I. In China the conquests started later (late 2000s BCE), but then warlords or invaders controlled much of the country till after World War II. On both subcontinents, the families of warlords became official role-models for the subject populations. In both places it was mainly women who questioned or rejected the family values of dominators.

For families in Neolithic China, it would be an anachronism to use the term "polyandry" (for women with multiple husbands). Because in the days "before people knew their fathers" there were no "legal" husbands. The term "polygamy" would also be misleading, because these people had no concept of "wife." While the primitive villagers remained independent, the relations they knew included lovers, mothers, the mothers' lovers, siblings, and other neighbors. Later, rising warlords of the Shang, Zhou, and other dynasties would teach the villagers "proper" family values. And these values of warlord families involved two double standards: one for men as opposed to women, and a second for rulers as opposed to subjects. The rulers' family values seemed to be eternal standards, reflecting universal reality. But their double standards actually took centuries to evolve, and centuries more to impose on ordinary families.

The Warlords' Families

Historically, polygamy for men was most common among tribes who lived on raiding. These include the Arab Bedouin, the Indo-Aryan conquerors of South Asia, the "barbarian" invaders of Europe, and the tribes that repeatedly conquered China. Liu Ruzhen lists several reasons why polygamy prevailed among the pastoralists northwest of China. First, their constant wars over scarce resources made for high losses of men, and a "surplus" of surviving women. Second, in traditional pastoral war, the maximum self-interest of each party was to eliminate the rival males, and absorb the rival females. The men who were most successful in this game could acquire dozens, or even hundreds of women. (1995, 327–328). The various raider clans had ongoing competitions to steal each other's women. And when the raider warlords died, they often took their female captives with them to the next world. It was theoretically possible for warrior women to join the raiding parties. But we don't hear of warlords letting their queens keep harems of captive men.

Where this sort of raiding economy was endemic, as across much of the old Middle East and North China, it grew dangerous for a woman to let her beauty be seen in public. So, by around 800 BCE in North China, the Zhou lords (as cited in the *Classic of Rites*) already demanded an almost Middle Eastern code of protective control: "Women must cover their faces when they go out" (X:12); "The wife's words should not travel beyond her own apartment" (I: 24) (De Bary and Chan, 1960, vol. I, 154–155). In regions subject to warlord raids, towns and even villages had walls with night watchmen. The locals commonly assumed that any woman who wandered the fields alone was asking to be seized, raped, and taken away.

To increase their raiding income, the warlord tribes began conquering nearby farming regions in the Yellow River basin. They demanded tribute from the villagers, but usually offered nothing in return. They did offer "protection," but this was a protection racket, where the farmers had to pay one warlord to protect them from the

231

next. After centuries of such rule, village families tended to adopt the manners of their rulers. But to start with, the villagers' family values were profoundly different. In primitive Chinese clans, the family names usually meant "descendant of woman X." Only in the warlord age were surnames increasingly based on the names of places—referring to the estates that warlords "gave" to male relatives or loyal officers (Ching, 1993, 25). The feudal lords then took women from the local clans, and had them take their husband's names, which generally meant "the lineage of men holding X estate." These lords competed to build biblical-style patrilineages for themselves, perhaps stretching back to the Yellow Emperor.

"Naturally," it was strictly forbidden for the warlords' numerous women to have any polyandrous relations with other men. There were jokes about women demanding an equal right to multiple partners, but it seems these stories just illustrated the need to control women. Princess Shanyin (during the 400s CE) reportedly complained to her husband: "Your majesty and I, though of different sex, are both descendants of the late emperor, but your majesty has several hundred beauties in the rear palace, while I have only one husband." The emperor thought about it, and presented her with 30 young men as lovers. But, as the story concludes, she still wasn't satisfied (Sun and Pan, 1995, 265).

If at first polyandry seemed natural to village women, then strong countermeasures were required to prevent it. In most cases the warlords' women were strictly isolated from the subject population, and placed under armed guard. Eventually, the guards had to be eunuchs. As for the ruler's polygamy, that served to ensure he had sufficient sons to inherit and defend his kingdom. And the double standard of restricting his women served to eliminate claims to inheritance from half-sons. So, extra wives for the emperors are recorded from at least the Shang dynasty (ca, 1700–1050 BCE). King Wuding is recorded having 64 women, 30 of them with a rank of *Fu*, meaning "king's consort" (Du Jinpeng, 1995, 133). To control the conflicting claims of these women and their children, the Zhou princes evolved their important legal distinction between wives (whose children could inherit estates), and concubines (whose children could not) (Du Fangqin, 1995, 176). As the *Discussions at the White Tiger Pavilion* explained, "The rites forbid the betrothal of a woman as concubine. This means she cannot be raised [to the position of wife] (Mann, 2002, 101).

In warlord administrations, the top dogs and their officials wrote the rules for families, and sometimes enforced them. Rulers tended to keep their family customs, while the subjects slowly modified theirs. And the compromise position for commoners was monogamous marriage. It could be argued that monogamy was neither patriarchal nor matriarchal, but a partnership with equal rights and restrictions for all. At least Confucius made that argument, citing classic texts as evidence that this was the way of the ancients: "The beginning of the way of a gentleman can be traced to the alliance between a wife and her husband." Or, "What the emperor is to the empress, the sun is to the moon, and yin to yang" (Zhang, 1995, 418–419). The *Classic of Rites* said that the marriage ceremony involved a couple sipping wine from cups made from halves of the same melon. After this, "They now formed one body, were of equal rank, and pledged to mutual affection" (Mann, 2002, 98). This, the early Confucianists suggested, should be the single standard for both rulers and subjects.

By all indications, Confucius was utterly unsuccessful in persuading the warring princes to give up their extra women. No doubt the princes pointed out that the Yellow Emperor was reportedly polygamous, siring 25 sons, only two of them by his principal wife (Wu, 1982, 60). The princes probably accused Confucius of being a weakling who had no interest in women (Du Fangqin, 1995, 219–220). But whether or not Confucius had anything to do with it, the monogamous standard took hold across North China. Polygamy was legally banned starting in the Spring and Autumn period (722–481

BCE), but this was a law for commoners only. For rulers, polygamy was deemed not only legal, but indispensible. Monogamous marriage was for subject people. But marriage itself was still just a personal agreement between lovers or families. Only later, through a recorded series of legal reforms, did marriage become a lifelong obligation enforced by the state.

Teaching the Villagers Proper Family Values

In popular folklore, the "Double Seven Festival" (seventh day of the seventh lunar month) is a women's feast day. It commemorates the divine daughter of the stove god, who came to earth out of love for a cowherd boy—like the Radha in every woman and her cowboy Krishna. This myth has many versions, which often feature conflict between daughter and father. For example, Jade Girl, the daughter of the Jade Emperor, came to earth because she admired the beautiful Wuyi mountains. There, she met and loved a local boy named Da Wang. But her overbearing father ordered her back to heaven, and threatened to turn her to stone if she disobeyed. Jade Girl refused, preferring to be a stone than be separated from her lover. The Jade Emperor mercilessly turned the couple into a rock formation. Then he tried to hack them apart, turning them into a famous pair of facing cliffs, which still wore the flowers and golden haze they gave each other as wedding presents (Gerant, 1995, 109–115).

In another myth, the Jade Emperor's daughter was Zhi Nu, a divine weaver of heavenly garments. She wove the clothes of deities, plus gossamer clouds and constellations across the skies. One day, however, she ran away to earth and fell in love with a cowherd boy. The Jade Emperor ordered her to leave her man and get back to heaven. When she refused, he exercised his fatherly prerogative, turning the two lovers into stars on opposite sides of the sky. Zhi Nu became Vega in the constellation Lyra, and her cowboy became Altair in the constellation Aquila. There, in remote isolation, Zhi Nu slaved away at her weaving, keeping her master pacified. But once a year, flocks of magpies swarmed into the sky, formed a bridge between the two constellations, and allowed the couple to be briefly united.

That's the villagers' fairy tale version of family morality.

In the real world, warlord rulers claimed responsibility for correcting their "backward" subjects, especially in matters of sexuality. And to these ruling polygamists, matrilocal families were uncivilized, while sexual freedom for women was utterly barbaric. A manly warlord used his daughters as bargaining chips for alliances with other dominant families, while training his boys to take over the kingdom. That was the root of arranged patrilocal marriage, and that was a system warlords could respect. Letting women choose their own lovers, or having men marry into the women's families, would undermine everything a warlord fought for. In the interests of morality, the conquerors imposed their own family values on their subjects. Starting with the first warlord kingdoms in North China, they suppressed matrilocal families and made polyandry for women a crime. The rulers denied recognition to any sexual relationship other than patriarchal marriage, with the male given legal guardianship over the woman. Where family property used to be jointly owned, the rulers issued laws to bolster male control. As the Qing dynasty laws harped on a familiar theme, "Within a family, all lands and grains are to be managed by the [male] master; all properties and money are to be controlled by the master" (Zhang, 1995, 419, 429). With that, monogamous, patrilocal marriage slowly became the standard for the vast majority. But it took a lot of social engineering to get there.

As the empire expanded to absorb China's southern provinces, the rulers sent officials to govern and civilize the southern barbarians. Around 200 CE, a governor called Jen Yen arrived to oversee the district of Lo Yüeh, which now overlaps Vietnam. Jen found the southerners still had no proper concept of patrilineage. To his dismay, the women took lovers and bore children without regard for the father-son relationship. But in a report to his superiors, Jen claimed success in changing the people's ways. He instructed them in correct relations, then assembled 2,000 people to be married as monogamous couples, all in one ceremony. After that, Jen said the fathers recognized their own children for the first time. From Hainan Island around 26 CE, we have another self-congratulatory report from governor Wei Sa. Due to his own efforts, local shamanism was overcome, the people had submitted to marriage rites, and schools of Confucian virtue were established. The whole local culture reportedly converted to the rulers' ways within a year. Elsewhere, progress was not so miraculous. For several centuries to come, governors appointed to South China repeatedly ordered native tribes to cover their naked bodies and get properly married. (Miyakawa, 1960, 30–31, 34). But the officials' work approached completion as they registered lands for taxation under the names of male family heads, appointed headmen for each village, and made those men accountable for securing local obedience.

Clearly these policies made an impact on the friendships of local people, especially with the passage of many generations. But even a thousand years later, during the Song dynasty (960–1279 CE), Marco Polo reported that women in Hangzhou (Hangchow) were so unrestricted in their affections that they commonly had both husbands and four or five other lovers (Gernet, 1962, 164). It seems that spouses had little recognized right to delimit each other's friendships. During the Yuan Mongol dynasty (1279–1368), the rulers were still trying to restrict men from marrying into matrilocal families. A Mongol law advised, "Wealthy families with only one son who can afford weddings are not permitted to send their sons into their brides' homes" (Liu, 1995, 350).

To help teach family values as known in the imperial court, the Han dynasty female scholar Ban Zhao (ca. 45–120 CE) wrote an essay called *Admonitions for Women*. This text laid down the "three obediences and four virtues" appropriate for females, such as waiting upon their husbands as commoners serve the emperor. Ban's voice was authoritative because she was co-author of the official *History of the Han Dynasty*, an accomplished poet, and a lecturer at the royal library (Tao, 2004, xxii). Her book became a classic for literate women till the dying days of the Manchu dynasty (around 1900). And over all those centuries, it was usually the best-educated women who were most indoctrinated in male supremacy. Of course, their husband's jobs could depend on it. Around the year 630 (CE) a county magistrate named Ruan Song was fired from office because his wife was insubordinate to him. Ruan's supervisors reasoned: "The wife is hard while the husband is gentle. If a wife cannot be controlled, how can he manage the common people?" (Guo, 1995, 306–307).

Drama was another tool for educating the public. But the dramas sponsored by powerful families or government officials needed to overcome the influence of plays produced by local villagers. The villagers' productions reveled in tales of forbidden love, heroic bandits, or supernatural adventures. The higher class productions countered this with tales of filial sons, dutiful wives, or chaste widows, whose ideal was "not to show their feet while walking, nor show their teeth while smiling" (Issei, 1985, 152; Huang, 2004, 31). The gentry-sponsored comedies offered instructional ridicule of the uncivilized. One play called "The Shrew" (appearing around 1000 CE) concerns an outrageously insubordinate young woman, who manages to demolish her marriage within days of the wedding. When her new husband tells her to behave properly, she shoots back, "What do I care about silly rules ... With a sudden laying about of my fist, I'll send you sprawling all over the room." The groom's sister whispers to the mother-in-law, "Why don't you keep her under control? How very unseemly it would be if she carried on like this unchecked! People would only laugh at us" (Ebrey, 1981, 90–91). But the Shrew rushes heedlessly to her tragicomic ruin. Clearly, it was the duty of family heads to keep their women under control, or the results would be shameful indeed.

The Warlord Women

Of course women of the imperial courts were not just innocent pawns in the hands of male warlords. These women had game plans of their own. Concerning the Warring States period (475–221 BCE), Du Fangqin writes that life in the noble houses was a stormy sea of "buffeting waves whipped up by the quest for power." In that situation, many women "wanted to be patronized and supported, and exchanged their moral qualities, dignity, and freedom for patronage and support" (1995, 217). But seeking security this way had heavy costs. As the warlords' power and wealth expanded, the princes generally acquired extra women the way Imelda Marcos acquired shoes. Some women were bought, some given as gifts, seized in war, or exchanged for diplomatic alliances. The women of these growing harems were assigned ranks—sometimes up to 14 levels of privilege or demerit. And among these numerous women, the jockeying for advantage could be absolutely murderous. For a rather legendary example from Warring States times, the king of Qi gave a beautiful concubine to King Huai of Chu. Huai's jealous wife, Queen Zheng Xiu, told the concubine, "The King loves you greatly, but he dislikes your nose. If you cover your nose when you see him, you will continue to win his love." The concubine followed Queen Zheng's advice. But when King Huai asked "Why does she cover her nose when she sees me?" the Queen replied, "She often says you have a stench about you." At which Huai yelled, "Off with her nose!"

The outhouse goddess Qi Gu got her start as a divinity in a similar way. She was a mistress of Liu Bang, the first emperor of the Han dynasty around 200 BCE. And Liu Bang's principal wife, Empress Lu, absolutely hated her. As soon as Liu Bang died, Empress Lu stripped Qi Gu of her mistress title, ordered her limbs chopped off, and had her thrown down the latrine. Naturally, such a horrible fate evoked sympathy from all quarters, and Qi Gu was soon elevated to goddess-hood. Like other outhouse goddesses, she appears to people in the toilet, bringing them insights, or conveying whole texts from the other world. With dozens or hundreds of women in the rulers' harems, the competing women were not the only ones with "woman problems." The emperors themselves sometimes appeared in court with scratches on their faces or blackened eyes from their wives' jealous attacks. To deal with this, the court legalists actually made jealousy a crime—for women only (Lin, 1992, 40).

A few leading court women were actually warlords in their own right. These were noblewomen of nomadic tribes which established dynasties like the Wei and Jin (between 220 and 420), the Sui (589–618), the Tang (618–906), the Liao (907–1125), the Jin (1125–1234), the Yuan Mongols (1279–1368), and the Qing (Manchu) dynasty (1644–1911). The women who helped found these dynasties could be expert on horseback, frightfully skilled with a bow and arrow, and stunningly proud. Their personal strength and authority could be shocking to Chinese city dwellers. For example, the first empress of the Sui dynasty (589–618) came from the Toba tribe. Her name was Tuku, and she grew up in a world of murderous intrigue, where various court factions conspired to eliminate each other. Tuku emerged triumphant, but what sort of feminine virtues did she represent? As Arthur F. Wright describes her, "She was in some respects a typical northern woman of the period: harsh, puritanical, a fanatical monogamist, a sharp and economical household manager: she was also meddlesome, vindictive, and insanely jealous" (Wright, 1960, 49–50).

So long as these warlord women were living in the northwest wilderness, they were self-reliant managers of nomadic camps, and often full members of their tribes' ruling councils. But when they came to the capital cities of China, they came as members of a conquering elite. Rather than riding the open steppes, they lived in guarded palaces, protected from the surrounding subject population. A paradox then arose which eludes many discussions of women's "status." On one hand, the warlord's women could be full partners in dominating others. But if women could join in the quest for superiority, then that competition tended to apply between themselves and their husbands.

Though competition for dominance wasn't really functional for couples or parents, by the Warring States period it was widely accepted as the law of life, even for lovers. In any relation between a warlord and another person, somebody had to come out on top. Classical thinkers like Xunzi (Hsün-tzu, ca. 312–230 BCE) explained it was simply a matter of order: "The father is the master of the family. One master means rule, two masters means chaos. From time immemorial it has never been witnessed that a family can last long when two masters are competing for dominance" (Zhang, 1995, 428). Likewise, the *Yi Jing* advised, "If Yin is the dominator in a family, then a man becomes an outsider ... Therefore Yang will become weak and Yin will be strong ... If you meet a woman who is physically stronger than you, do not accept her" (Sun and Pan, 1995, 252). Such attitudes could grow into a cultural force of evolution, with a counter-natural agenda for selective breeding of the most submissive women.

To control and protect their treasure troves of women, the emperors increasingly employed eunuchs. In that case, the emperor was literally the only one in the palace with a penis. Then the eunuchs became another source of "inner court" intrigue. And meanwhile, the hundreds or thousands of palace women had to scheme for the one man's favor by any means available. It's likely that this ruthless search for cosmetic advantage led to the invention of foot binding, since smaller feet seemed more ultra-feminine (Li, 1992, 75). Naturally, the court women launched elaborate schemes to place their own sons on the throne. Their schemes could involve slandering other mothers, poisoning them, killing each other's children, or even killing the king. As the Legalist philosopher Han Feizi (200s BCE) explained, "A man of fifty has not lost his interest in women, but a woman begins to lose her looks before thirty. When a woman whose looks are deteriorating serves a man who still loves sex, she will be despised and her son is not likely to be made heir. This is the reason queens, consorts, and concubines plot the death of the ruler" (Ebrey, 1996, 51–52).

Perhaps it was all due to Mamo, a legendary demoness who loved to sow hatred and chaos. Anyway, it grew commonplace to blame all political problems on scheming women, whose selfishness seemed worse than that of male warlords. As the *Book of Songs* explained,

> *Clever men build cities;*
> *clever women topple them.*
> *Beautiful these clever women may be,*
> *but they are owls and kites.*
> *Women have long tongues*
> *that lead to ruin.*
> *Disorder does not come down from heaven;*
> *it is produced by women. (Ebrey, 1996, 34)*

If women would only accept their places, so this story went, such strife would cease. They should also accept that when an emperor died, the new one required a whole new harem. After the Qin dynasty, women were seldom killed with their lords. But at least they were consigned to permanent chaste widowhood. Dead warlords were supposed to own their women forever.

The history of imperial despotism contains one episode of formal rule by a female emperor, namely Wu Zetian (Wu Tse-t'ien), from 690 to 705 CE. And some modern historians say that Empress Wu tried to reduce inequality between the sexes. She had the Daoist *Dao De Jing (Tao Te Ching)* added to the reading list for imperial university students, possibly because Daoism was popular among women. She also secured a ruling that the deaths of mothers should be honored with a three-year mourning period in all cases. Previously, such mourning periods for mothers were observed only if the father had already died. Empress Wu also patronized Buddhist teachers, and Buddhism was more popular among women than men. But Wu proved as ruthless as any man in eliminating rivals for power, even if they were her relatives. This was normal for male rulers, but for an empress it seemed hypocritical. In the view of later male administrators, Wu was guilty of preaching compassion while practicing vicious power politics. As the Later Jin dynasty historian Liu Xu explained, "Her willingness to crush her own flesh and blood showed how great her viciousness and vile nature was, although this is nothing more than what evil individuals and jealous women might do" (wikipedia.org/wiki/Wu_Ze_Tian). It all seemed to serve as a warning on the perils of letting hens supplant roosters. Only with the rise of the modern women's movement did Empress Wu get some fairly favorable press. In the 1960s, Mao Zedong's wife, Jiang Qing, tried to make Wu a positive example to the nation—partly as propaganda for Jiang's own political ambitions. Later, modern TV dramas portrayed Empress Wu as a strong-willed fairy-tale princess.

The Evolution of Family Law Under Barbarian Rulers

Many religions, such as Islam and Confucianism, make "family law" the core of sacred tradition. And chief spokesmen of these religions often argue that their family laws are eternal and universal. But actually their rules evolved over time, and in the case of Chinese family law, this record is quite well documented. In general, it's a record that leads inexorably downhill for women's rights, from Zhou times until the twentieth century.

In pre-dynastic times, women could initiate divorce. No authority beyond the family held a wife subject to an abusive husband, and no law prevented her from marrying again. It was the first conquerors of all China (in the Qin dynasty, 221–207 BCE) who first criminalized remarriage after divorce—for women only (De Bary and Chan, 1960, vol. II, 89). Later, the originally nomadic Sui dynasty (589–618 CE) decreed that women above a certain rank could never remarry if their husbands died. This, of course, protected the patrilineal inheritance of great estates. By Tang and Song times (600s to 1200s) it was a crime for wives to strike their husbands, but not for husbands to strike wives. The penalty for the wife was a year of penal servitude; a concubine got a year and a half. By the Ming and Qing dynasties

(1300s to 1911), women who struck their husbands got either 100 blows with a heavy bamboo, or death by strangulation. Also, since women were placed under their husbands' legal control, the women shared punishment for their husbands' crimes. The Qin laws (200s BCE) required the death penalty for wives, concubines, and children of male criminals (Sun and Pan, 1995, 253). And this sort of "collective punishment" remained common over most of Chinese history.

These laws governing family relations evolved step by step over centuries, growing ever more restrictive dynasty by dynasty. And the records show which rulers did the most to control women. Usually, things were worst when warlords from the pastoral northwest tribes ruled the country (Zhang, 1995, 421, 433–434, 449).

The Yuan dynasty Mongols (1279–1368) were the first rulers to allow men to sell their wives into slavery as punishment for adultery. They also permitted husbands to kill their wives for "resisting arrest," if caught in adultery. The Yuan law said that any children born of an adulterous love affair must be given to the male offender, while the woman could be sold by her husband—to anyone except her lover (Zhang, 1995, 436). Meanwhile, the Yuan removed all legal limits on the numbers of wives and concubines men could have (Liu, 1995, 337). It was basically a matter of recognizing reality, because when the Mongols conquered a region, they took whatever women caught their eyes. Genghis Khan personally took over 500 women for himself, and had 40 buried with him in his grave.

Concerning property rights, married women in ancient times retained ownership of their own property if divorced. But the Mongol conquerors imposed a new law for divorced women: "Her dowry and other properties are to be left at the disposal of her former husband. She is not allowed to take them with her." And since women themselves were property, the Mongol code ruled that if women ran away from their husbands, the government would deal them 100 blows with a heavy bamboo. After that, the husbands could sell them into slavery. If a wife ran away and married another man, she had to be strangled (Zhang, 1995, 430, 420).

The Sung dynasty (960–1279) was a period when China stood under growing attack from northern warlords. And as the area under native Chinese control shrank, nationalist feeling grew militant. To make the country stronger, patriotic moralists stressed duty and obedience as the soul of Confucian civilization. In this spirit, Ouyang Xiu (1007–1072) insisted, "The wife follows her husband, and to the end of her days will not remarry. The servitor serves his ruler, and will die in preference to serving another. This is the great standard of human ethics" (Mote, 1960, 230–231). Official Confucianism began to resemble Japanese *bushido*, especially for women. A scholar named Cheng Hao popularized the idea that a Confucian widow could never remarry, even if she starved alone. And many felt that this *fatwa* of Cheng Hao's marked a turning point toward moral renewal. As the scholar Fang Bao explained, "Henceforth, men began to regard women's loss of chastity as a shame, and they hated and despised them for it, and this is why women are self-disciplined and exert themselves" (Guo, 1995, 285–286). Later, the Ming dynasty *Ordinances on the Family* thoughtfully added that widows who remarried would lose their estates, and any man who married a widow would also lose his estate—to her late-husband's male relatives (Zhang, 1995, 432). So eternally was a woman supposed to be owned by her master, and so firmly was she blocked from any other option.

Perhaps we see a culmination of all these trends in the records of Daoyi village, in southern Manchuria under the Manchu (Qing) dynasty, during the 1700s. The death certificates from those years show a high death rate for children. Roughly half the children in Daoyi were dead before age 20. But the death rate for girls was substantially higher than for boys. By the time each generation came of marriageable age, there were quite a few more men than women. And this imbalance was then made worse, because the most powerful men commonly took several wives and concubines. As a result, almost every woman was either married or widowed by age 30, while around 20% of the men never had a wife. We can imagine the pressure and ferocious jealousy surrounding the women in this situation (Spence, 1999, 95–96). We also know how gangs of "surplus" men often become loose cannonballs in society. Such men might join the army, to vent their aggression on outside enemies. Other unattached men might band together as a force for patriarchal-style religion. But if such semi-honorable options failed, the surplus men could easily turn to banditry, and prey on the local population for both income and sex. At that time (in the 1700s) the Manchurians were conquerors of all China, partly because of their surplus military-age manpower. Perhaps no more literal example could be found of a community suffering from imbalance between yin and yang. To many Chinese observers, this imbalance was obvious. While the Manchu emperors insisted that their own family values were one with Confucian orthodoxy, the Confucian scholar Qian Dayi asked, "Haven't the sages gone too far in suppressing women? Formulating principles on the relations between men and women serves not only to protect husbands but also wives" (Zhao Shiyu, 1995, 393).

In an overview study of ancient Chinese law, Zhang Zhijang concludes that for over 2,000 years, "women's subordination to men became ever more entrenched." Also, "the legal codes of the Yuan [Mongol] and the Qing [Manchu] dynasties ... contributed most to this development" (1995, 449). Over time, migrants from these ruling tribes were gradually absorbed by Chinese society, but not without imposing their own cultural influence. The invader tribes enforced their principles of unconditional loyalty to the strongest leader. They let combat decide who was strongest, and believed this represented Heaven's will. They treated women as property, or as booty of battle. And their noble houses served as role models for Chinese families. If ordinary families behaved differently, the invader rulers generally assumed it was a problem to be corrected. As the patriarch-scholar Chen Hongmou complained during the Manchu dynasty, "A woman's proper ritual place is sequestered in the inner apartments. When at rest, she should lower the screen; when abroad, she must cover her face in order to remove herself from any suspicion or doubt, and prevent herself from coming under observation. But instead we find young women accustomed to wandering about, all made up, heads bare and faces exposed, and feeling no shame whatever!" (Mann, 2002, 110).

All this force of law and instruction had its effect. As people learned to copy their rulers, women increasingly held their husbands accountable for being the master. It grew accepted that men who married into their wives' matrilocal households had to be somehow inferior (Wolf, 1970, 59). Couples increasingly bought the idea that it was shameful and weak for men to show open affection toward their wives. It grew ordinary to make brides prove their virginity by displaying blood-stained sheets after their wedding nights. The legend of Boji, a high-class woman who died in a house fire rather than come out before strangers, grew "popular." But this kind of indoctrination was never quite accomplished. Even today, some remote communities still practice matrilocal marriage and polyandry. In the 1980s, sociologist Cai Hua spoke with old women in Yunnan Province who used to sleep with visiting Tibetan traders. One woman explained, "Each time the Tibetan merchants came back to Yongning, we were happy, and we would meet them with chickens and with hay for their horses. They also brought food. They gave us clothing and shoes. When they left they gave us some money ... They were nice to us and we liked them." What most Chinese people had long since learned to view as prostitution, these women still saw as a special friendship (Cai, 2001, 225).

The process of standardizing local morals continued down to recent decades. In 1950, the Communist government ruled that most families of the ethnic Na and Naxi communities in Yunnan were in violation of the Republic's matrimonial law. They still lived in matrilocal families, and the women still practiced polyandrous relationships. Hoping to modernize the locals, the government issued incentives to break up matrilineal families: "In the region in which the inhabitants follow the matrilineal system, the distribution of land will occur according to the residences of the men. If a man wants to set up a home by himself, the land will be distributed to him, instead of being distributed to his maternal family." That was in 1956. The government officials couldn't understand why not even one Na man came forward to take this offer (Cai, 2001, 385–386).

With the Great Leap Forward in 1958, Party officials in Yongning determined to promote "the superiority ... of socialist monogamy as compared with the *açia* [or visitation] system in the various stages of the evolution of matrimonial forms." Local Communist cadres were encouraged to set a positive example by regularizing their own relationships in somewhat festive marriage ceremonies.

In the Cultural Revolution of the 1960s, the attack on the "four olds" involved direct force. The production brigade in Wenquan lined up 73 pairs of known lovers for mandatory marriage ceremonies. Of these, 46 couples defended their freedom by filing for divorce within a few months. Only a few of the rest stayed married for more than a few years. Another push in 1971 had similar results.

Finally, in 1974, the Yunnan Provincial governor announced "We must resolutely reform the backward matrimonial system of the Naxi in Yongning." The People's Commune ordered all couples under 50 years old to get married. All mothers were required to declare the fathers of their children, and marry them. Otherwise their grain rations would be cut. Again the government imposed marriages on people, and most of them promptly filed for divorce.

Finally after 1976, public tolerance for such intervention faded away. The government tried to refuse grain rations to children born out of wedlock, but that policy was legally struck down in 1981. Most Na and Naxi resumed their traditional ways. Of course social change of all kinds challenged the viability of matrilocal farms. But like gay rights activists, the locals secured a ruling for their Autonomous District: "The Moso [or Na] have the right to follow their traditions if they so desire" (Cao, 2001, 385–398, 403–404).

Rival Traditions of Parenting

While the *Analects* of Confucius (which are attributed to the teacher himself) tended to stress mutual care between family members, the *Classic of Rites* recorded different priorities of the Zhou princes. These early rulers stressed duty unto death for subordinates, and made the authority of parents both unconditional and life-long. As the old princely saying went, "One has to die if his father wants him to, and the minister has to perish if his ruler wants him to." The *Classic of Rites* seemed to demand this logic of ordinary parents: "When one's parents are angry and not pleased and beat him until he bleeds, he does not complain but instead arouses in himself feelings of reverence and filial piety." The rulers enforced such sentiments, ruling that children who struck their parents back could be killed. As in ancient Rome, fathers could legally kill their children for showing disrespect. Even when the children got married, the *Classic of Rites* said that satisfaction of the parents was still primary: "If a man is very fond of his wife, but his parents do not like her, she should be divorced" (De Bary and Chan, 1960, vol. II, 155–156).

Compared to this totalitarian standard of parenting, we get a different glimpse of tradition in Jan Myrdal's *Report from a Chinese Village* (Liu Ling village, Shaanxi, during the early 1960s). A schoolmaster there explained, "Farmers don't really bring their children up at all. They simply do not have time to attend to their children. So, when the children do go to school, they are quite undisciplined. They are also quite unaccustomed to keeping fixed hours. At home, you see, they have been allowed to come and go as they like." This sounded like a complaint about village parenting skills. But concerning classroom discipline, the teacher said, "All forms of physical punishment are forbidden. For a teacher to raise his hand against a pupil is a crime, no matter what the circumstances under which it is done. We discuss problems with the parents. In extreme cases we can expel a pupil. But that is only on paper. We have never had to expel anyone" (Myrdal, 1965, 314, 295).

Apparently, the kids of Liu Ling ran around with little supervision. To urban westerners it might seem careless and irresponsible. But the villagers assumed that all adults would act like aunts or uncles towards all the children, so the kids would be watched wherever they ran. If they got into mischief, the nearest adult might warn them of discipline by a legendary bogeyman (Gernet, 1962, 153). In general, it seems the prevailing attitude was more neighborly and less authoritarian than in traditional Europe.

Of course each family has its own sort of parent-child relations. And endless accounts from literate people show Chinese parents treating daughters as far less valuable than boys. In vast numbers of homes the whole calculus of patrilocal marriage came into play, by which everything invested in a girl would only be lost when she married and moved away. Of course many married daughters only moved to another part of the village, and they often helped their parents all their lives. But wherever full-blown patriarchal tradition took hold, the inequality of sons and daughters was often overwhelming. A Confucian official named Fu Xian (217–278 CE) wrote a poem of pity for girls in higher class families like his own:

> Bitter indeed it is to be born a woman.
> It is difficult to imagine anything so low! ...
> A girl is raised without joy or love.
> No one in her family really cares for her.
> Grown up, she has to hide in the inner rooms,
> cover her head, be afraid to look others in the face.
> And no one sheds a tear when she is married off,
> All ties with her own kin are abruptly severed ...
> Her husband's love is aloof as the Milky Way,
> yet she must follow him like a sunflower in the sun.
> Their hearts are soon as far apart as fire and water.
> She is blamed for all and everything that goes wrong.
> (Despeux and Kohn, 2003, 3)

In families of the ruling clans, only boys could be warriors, officials, or inheritors of family estates. Supposedly boys were also more valuable as farmers, but that is doubtful. For ordinary working families, women were often the hardest workers on the farm. Only being married out to other families could possibly render them less beneficial. Even on the job market, girls were often more employable than boys, taking readily available work as embroiderers, cooks, concubines, zither players, actresses, prostitutes, chess players, servants, or shop keepers (Gernet, 1962, 148). In visiting modern working families, Marjory Wolf found that "in general, the treatment of a girl is not dramatically different from that of her brothers." But as she grows up, "an adult daughter will be nearly irrelevant to her father" (1970, 45). Maybe the daughters were more relevant to their mothers, and the women's family values were often different.

Usually, relations between parents and children shifted strongly with the age of the child. For infants and toddlers, the timeless attitude of mothers prevailed, and Chinese fathers were also famous for indulgent affection toward young children of both sexes. But later, "education for the real world" tended to set in. According to the parents' sense of social reality, it might seem obvious that "you cannot be your son's friend and correct his behavior." Both fathers and mothers might stop expressing love for a child, lest it undermine their authority (Wolf, 1970, 41, 44). The parents could easily adopt the traditional rulers' standard, and judge family relations by the degree of obedience, not the degree of cooperation.

For upper class children in recent centuries, education for girls and boys diverged dramatically with age. Upper class boys went off to school at around age ten, and the girls stayed home. Instead of going out to learn, the girls received new restrictions on going outside, lest their budding bodies draw attention, and widening experience hamper their adjustment to social isolation. Where upper class boys were "capped" as men at about 20, girls had a hair-pinning ritual at around 15. After that, the parameters of girls lives shrank further

(Mann, 2002, 96). That was the "standard," but for ordinary village families life was quite different. In poor families, the girls were trained for work outside the house. Almost all daughters learned to run a farm, a business, or a craft. In many areas of South China, all the adolescent girls in a village joined "girl's houses" where they spent their spare time weaving, singing, learning women's traditions, and forming bonds to last a lifetime (Watson, 1994, 39).

Since learning to write Chinese was so time-consuming, literacy was a luxury available mainly for upper class boys. And since literacy was the mark of civilization, women seemed to automatically rank among the uncivilized (Louie, 2008, 16–17). If women learned to write, they usually had to teach themselves. And we even have cases of women inventing their own writing systems, like the "dakini scripts" of Tibetan women. In the Jianyong region of Hunan, women used an ancient script in their embroidery, which was only known to women. They said this script was invented by Yaoji, the youngest daughter of the Queen Mother of the West, who found that earth women were good at needlework, but illiterate. Yaoji brought them "women's writing" from heaven. Of course millions of women taught themselves the mainstream Chinese script, if only to become their son's drill masters in the Confucian classics. But as for using literacy skills themselves, there were clearly no jobs a girl might prepare for in the Confucian bureaucratic system.

As is common with clerical elites, the male government officials managed to officially exclude female competition for their jobs. But probably most people never accepted this as either natural or helpful. Many novels of the Qing period (1643–1911) featured heroines dressed as men, who take top honors in the official exams and assume high office. One such novel was *Born Again*, written in the late 1700s by two women, Chen Duansheng and Liang Deshen. In 1828, Li Ruzhen published a novel where 100 brilliant women take the official exams and become bureaucrats under Empress Wu (ca. 700 CE). In their adventures, some of them visit the "Woman's Kingdom," where all conventions of Confucian society are upended. The men powder their faces, bind their feet, or pluck out their beards, to compete for attention from the ruling women. Men's work is attending domestic chores and waiting on the women's pleasure (Lin, 1992, 51–54). In another popular novel, *Flowering Brush*, by Qiu Xinru, a female degree holder is turfed out of office when her gender is discovered. The heroine cries, "Father gave me the talent. Why didn't he give me the right sex? Now a promising career has been completely dashed after all the painstaking efforts I've gone through. What a waste of talent!" (Li, 1992, 108–109). These stories seemed to be "anti-traditional," but also appealed to a deeper sort of tradition.

During the 1600s, a Confucian scholar named Zhang Xuecheng wrote an essay claiming that the ancient traditions of education were far more equal. He said that women's studies in early times were focused on learning specific professions, such as becoming shamans, historians, artisans, or soothsayers. Only in more recent dynasties did education for high class women collapse into generalized training for females as a gender, such as learning womanly conduct, speech, appearance, and female-specific virtues (Mann, 2002, 103–104). In the distant past, Zhang argued, vast numbers of girls grew up to be religious or business professionals. But maybe this was true all along. For example, even in the highly patriarchal Song dynasty, a directory for Hangzhou city (from around 1200 CE) listed numerous businesses that were obviously owned by women. These included the Five Sister's Fish Custard shop, Granny Cao's Meat Pie, Ma Wang's Tea Shop, Aunt Weng's Wine Shop, Granny Li's Custard with Mixed Vegetables, and Ugly Granny's Herbal Medicine Store (Gou, 1995, 301). It seems Zhang Xuecheng was a bookish historian, who noticed the non-patriarchal customs in old documents, but didn't seem to notice that women's vocational training was still happening in most farming or business families. Among working people, girls had always learned a trade. It was a tradition leading to the modern female entrepreneurs of Shanghai, Hangzhou, Taiwan, or Hong Kong.

Around 1911, as the imperial court stopped being the official role model for China's families, the popular demand for girls' training returned like water from behind a leaking dam. A group of female students calling themselves the "Humanitarian Association" ridiculed China's backwardness in women's education: "While in Europe and America children learn their habits from their mothers, in China, the mother's level of knowledge is even lower than that of her children" (Judge, 2008, 123). To reject this seemed patriotic. Of course millions of families still placed all their investment on boys. Millions of girls slaved in sweatshops to help pay school fees for their male relatives. And the discrepancy in investment for girl's education declined only slowly. By the year 2000, the percentage of female students at junior level colleges was 41%, in master's degree programs 36.3 %, and in doctoral programs only 26.6% (Ma, 2004, 118–119). But the ancient ideal of real meritocracy was coming, especially for all the families with one female child.

A Legacy of Strong Women

In the big picture of history, China is an often-conquered land, where the conquerors usually treated local people as war booty or tax mules. The result is a heritage of trauma. Among the higher classes, especially in North China, women came under a local form of purdah. They were not to mix with commoner men, or do the work of low-born subjects. In time, these women's roles grew so delimited that they were commonly foot-bound, to enhance sex appeal even at the expense of every other human function. Somehow, it grew widely accepted that foot binding was "Confucian," though Theodore De Bary suggests it had nothing more to do with Confucianism "than whale-bone corsets or spike-heeled shoes had to do with Christianity" (De Bary, 1991, 104). And to many Chinese women, the whole-force-backed system was an obvious deception. So, in the last years of the Qing-Manchu dynasty, the fiery young martyr Qiu Jin gave her "Address to Two Hundred Million Fellow Countrywomen": "When men said we were useless, we became useless: when they said we were incapable, we stopped questioning them even when our entire female sex had reached slave status. At the same time we were insecure ... so we did everything to please men. When we heard that they liked small feet, we immediately bound them just to please them" (Ebrey, 1981, 248).

But if the female dependants of warlords or landlords were commonly submissive, the millions of village women must be counted among the toughest survivors on earth. I've already mentioned Mao Zedong's 1925 report from rural Hunan, which said the authority of husbands over wives had always been weak. These village women worked the fields like men, and held roughly equal power in family decisions. They even had "considerable sexual freedom" (Spence, 1999, 376). Within a generation, peasants like these across China would support a general trashing of dynastic marriage laws. After that, a northern village woman named Li Yiuhua advised Jan Myrdal, "We had a slogan: 'Free Their Feet!' Now their feet are free and ... Marriage is now free too. It's only those directly concerned who have any say in it. That's a good thing. Women are hard workers. Do you see that the women down there have baskets beside them as they weed, but the men don't? That's because the women aren't only weeding, they are also collecting grass for the family's pig" (Myrdal, 1965, 10).

With the Communist marriage law of 1950 came a brief explosion of divorces, as people cast off unhappy arranged marriages. The government banned bigamy, forcing men to choose between their wives and concubines. Most people stopped calling women by their husband's surnames (Zhang, 2008, 61–62). For a few years, revolutionary fervor meant new freedom for women. Then the priority of stability revived, and divorce became shameful again. The saying of old-fashioned women prevailed, "Marry a rooster, follow a rooster; marry a dog, follow a dog."

At least freedom in marriage and divorce was now legal. And government control of the housing market meant that couples could get places to live through the civic authorities, not their family patriarchs. In most families both the husband and wife had full-time jobs, so sharing of parenting work got a bit more equal. All this tended to boost the independence and authority of women, even young women. As a man in Huhhot, Inner Mongolia explained, "In the past the mother-in-law was fearsome; now the wife is fearsome" (Jankowiak, 2002, 376–377, 370). Still, a certain official support for patrilocal marriage remained. Government-issued housing was almost always registered in a man's name. In a divorce, the husband kept his family property, and the woman often walked away with nothing. (Chen, 2004, 167–168). Divorced women had to find a temporary place, then wait a decade or more for the next government housing allocation. They might be told, "It's easy for a woman. Just find another man with a flat and you'll have everything you need" (Xinran, 2002, 216).

The collapse of arranged marriages also came at the cost of a rising marriage market. Where women could choose, masses of them wished to leave the villages. Men with land in isolated places often felt they could only lure a bride with cash incentives. As Jan Wong asked a farmer east of Beijing, "Anybody here bought a wife lately?" "Loads," he answered. "Otherwise, nobody could find a wife. The women in our village all want to marry someone in the city" (1996, 327). At least this was "dowry" in which the man paid the woman, instead of the other way around as in India.

After 1979, the state's one-child policy both helped and hurt women at the same time. With all the old expectation that boys were more profitable than girls, the rate of female abortion soon rose to almost Shang dynasty proportions. The government put up big posters advising "Daughters Also Count as Descendants," or "Having a Son or a Daughter is Exactly the Same," but probably most people thought this was an official lie (Hessler, 2010, 52). By 1999, the Chinese Academy of Social Sciences reported a male/female population ratio of 120 males for every 100 females. To deter violations of the one-child policy, China banned birth control to unmarried women, required them to have abortions if found to be pregnant, and banned anesthetic during the operation, in order to ensure the experience was discouragingly hellish (Wong, 1999, 305, 302; Ward, 2004, 267). Government officials made control of unauthorized pregnancy into an extortion racket.

Next, the shift to a market economy hit women first. As unprofitable state corporations shed their costs, there were 260,000 workers laid off in Tianjin city alone, in just the first six months of 1996. Of these, 70% were middle-aged women (Evans, 2008, 353). Wan Qingshu reported, "The mechanisms of competition have led to a philosophy based on 'the survival of the fittest,' in which women begin at a historical disadvantage, still holding a weaker share of the national resources" (Wang, 2004, 101). Though a woman's value was no longer deliberately depressed by the rulers' laws, it was still tossed to the commercial and marriage markets for hard-nosed assessment. And the results could be absolutely horrifying.

Most women were no longer "protected," either by the family or the state. But it seems they commonly adjusted to freedom better than most men. In adapting to the new economy, the number of women leading new businesses was disproportionate. And as China's for-profit economy gained momentum, the mass migration of village women to urban factories began. Huge cities holding almost nothing but factories (with dormitories) arose. The total migration rose past a hundred million, making this the greatest movement of human population in world history. And clearly, the population of these boomtowns was mainly female (Chang, 2008, 12). More girls went out into the world to find their fortunes, and the boys more often stayed home on the farm. In the factory boomtowns, many thousands of migrant women flaunted their sex appeal as "personal secretaries" to rising businessmen. Millions more became pillars of support to their parents, families, and home communities. Many were just teenage girls, but they already overshadowed their fathers in ability, income, and prestige.

I'd like to point out a book by Lijia Zhang, called *Socialism Is Great!: A Worker's Memoir of the New China*. It's a journal of Zhang's discoveries, covering the first decade of her working life. It starts as she's forced to quit school and take a factory job in 1980, and ends as the police question her for leading a 1989 democracy march. Through it all, Zhang is honest, smart, and funny, with a drive for life like a heat-seeking rocket. She's on a quest for learning, skills, cash, potential. She teaches herself English, partly out of ambition, partly for the candor and beauty to be found in the worlds of English lit. While mastering engineering skills at a Nanjing rocket factory, she gets stronger and more beautiful all the time. Her love life grows more courageous. Her honesty gets stunning.

In *Factory Girls*, Leslie T. Chang follows the lives of several young women around the industrial mega-city of Dongguan. This is a journey through satanic mills, full of uncertainty and "eating bitterness." But the women are always scheming, jumping jobs, taking night classes, moving out. A 17-year old educational consultant named Tian Peiyan addresses a secretarial skills class: "In a factory of one thousand or ten thousand people, to have the boss discover you is very hard. You must discover yourself. You must develop yourself. To jump out of the factory you must study ... You are here because you don't want to be an ordinary worker with a dull life. If you are waiting for your company to lift you up, you will grow old waiting." The schemes and scams are legion, but the aspiration is great. A young saleswoman called Wu Chunming addresses recruits to her cosmetics network: "My friends, do we want to follow the road of our mothers and fathers? No! Give yourselves a round of applause!" (2008, 174, 66).

Probably most women had never been dependent. Most had always been realistic and hard-headed. But now their hard-headed independence grew more blatant. A university student told radio show host Xinran, "Never think of a man as a tree whose shade you can rest in ... There is no real love. The couples who appear loving stay together for personal gain, whether for money, power, or influence"

(Xinran, 2002, 48). Rejecting all dependence or subordination, millions of *nu qiang ren* (superwomen) became company managers and tiger moms at the same time.

In terms of future prospects, the market appreciation for women was bound to rise. Because if market demand came from freely chosen popular dreams, what else would people value more than good women? Certainly the village men shelling out their life savings to attract a bride weren't taking women for granted. And for just one sign of popular demand for greater equality, the cities of Nanting and Zhuzhou recently started a child care program in which a father's and mother's employers each cover half the woman's salary while she's on maternity leave (Jiang, 2004, 217).

Frightening as the ride might be, China was probably swirling into a new configuration of family values in the wake of the warlord age. And maybe the Confucian scholar Kang Yuwei (1858–1927) wasn't so wacko after all, when he predicted a return of the most ancient values of real partnership in his *Book of Great Equality*: "The European and American custom of taking the husband's surname will be entirely prohibited and changed ... In getting married, women will be entirely independent, and will themselves choose their mates ... We will not have the old terms of husband and wife. For, since men and women will be entirely equal and independent, their love contracts will be like treaties of peace between two states" (Bauer, 1976, 315).

14: Goddess Religions of the Modern and Planetary Age

As in most culture wars, the "the woman question" was close to central in China's modern revolutions. When angry masses of people threw aside the Manchu monarchy and the Confucian state, they demolished the most powerful structures for controlling women. But after 1911, more revolutionary wars raged for nearly 40 years. And in those battles, conflict over women's status took several dramatic turns. On one hand, the political factions which promised women the most usually won. When landlords accused the Communists of plotting to share men's wives, most people ended up supporting the Communist call for freedom in marriage and divorce. But most women felt it wasn't their way to push directly for their own advantage. They generally ended up serving "greater" causes, for the general good of most everybody else.

Avenging Angels and Iron Girls of the Revolution

The Republican and Communist revolutions featured scores of heroic women, whose fame often rivaled any heroine of the French Revolution, be it Maryanne or the goddess of liberty. For example, Qiu Jin (1875–1907) was a lightning-rod leader of the anti-Manchu revolt, who died in the cause at age 31. She had married a government official, but rejected him for his loyalty to the Manchu rulers. In 1903 she went to study in Japan, then returned to found a women's magazine and a school for girls. We've already seen a bit of her essay, "Address to Two Hundred Million Fellow Countrywomen." But she went beyond denouncing oppression of females, and argued that women must be the saviors of Chinese civilization: "We all know the nation is about to perish and men are incapable of saving it. Can we still think of relying on them?" (Judge, 2008, 220).

While serving as principal at her "School of Great Unity," Qiu Jin organized a Zhejiang province branch of the rebel United League.

Her cell of revolutionaries plotted to kill the governor, then overthrow the Qing dynasty. But a co-conspirator was caught, and tortured into confessions. Then the police came after Qiu Jin. The rulers assumed it was business as usual to chop off this woman's head. They thought it would keep China's people intimidated instead of galvanizing them for revolt.

After the 1911 revolution, the Nationalist government "immortalized" Qiu with a shrine-like grave beside West Lake in Hangzhou. Later, the People's Republic dedicated a museum to her in Shaoxing City. Millions of people read her fiery essays and poems, like this:

> *It's our own fault our country is in turmoil*
> *That I must wander homeless everywhere*
> *My blood boiling, afraid to look around me*
> *My gut as cold as frostbitten spring blossoms*
> *I'd spend everything for a fine sword*
> *And boldly swap my finery for wine*
> *My boiling blood raging in fury*
> *Threatening to become an encompassing blue wave (cited in Xu, 2009)*

During the 1911 revolt, a 19-year-old woman named Wu Shuqing organized a "women's revolutionary army" of several hundred volunteers, who outfought units of the Manchu army near Hankou. Other units in the Republican wars included the Guangdong Women's Northern Expedition Army, the Shanghai Women's People's Army, and the Northern Expeditionary Women's Dare-to-Die Corps (Lu, 2004, 60).

When the May Fourth Movement swept China in 1919, a 15-year-old girl named Deng Yingchao repeatedly drew rallies of over 100,000 people, electrifying the city of Tianjin with her condemnations of colonial powers, and demands for women's rights. Later she joined the Communist rebels, married Zhou Enlai, and survived the Long March. After the Communist Revolution she served as a chairman of the All-China Democratic Women's Federation. By 1956, this Federation had 76,000,000 members (compared to only 11,000,000 in the Communist Party), which probably makes the Women's Federation the largest organization of local people in world history (Lee, 2004, 74; French, 1985, 243).

Other heroines of the revolutionary decades were not political, or leaders, but simply women who drew attention to the cruelty of traditional ways. Some of these women weren't even real people. The girl featured in Xia Yan's 1936 news report "Indentured Worker" was possibly a montage of several real girls. But this brutally realistic account of one day in the life of a textile factory worker raised nationwide concern about the course of progress. Then there was *The Goddess*, a 1934 film starring Ruan Lingyu. This was the story of a single mother, devoted to giving her son a good education. In the best Confucian mother's tradition, she felt sure that her son, if properly trained, had the capacity to make a real difference in the world. But the expense of school fees forced her into prostitution, and the spider web of society's double-binds for women. A year after this film was released, the actress Ruan Lingyu herself committed suicide—on International Women's Day. Her estranged husband had refused to grant her a divorce. When she found another man, her ex-husband reviled her morality in the press and sued her for her money. In the past this would be normal. Now, probably the vast majority of young people sympathized with the woman.

We could go on listing goddess figures, real or not, who made a national impact on the course of a social revolution. But with the Japanese invasion by 1937, all other causes grew subordinate to the great anti-imperialist war. This theater of World War II is little publicized in the West, but it was as brutal as the Nazi invasion of Russia. About 20 million Chinese people died, and the emotional impact shaped generations of survivors. During those years of horror, patriotic women served the troops, not any cause of their own. War called for self-sacrifice, not self-actualization. In that harsh light, the pre-war cause of women's rights seemed selfish.

In general, war tends to maximize fanaticism. And even after the war and the revolution, the wartime generation retained a mentality suited to combat. For war heroes like Mao Zedong, the great ideal of patriotic self-sacrifice led to a puritanical point of zero tolerance for self-interest. In that case, no degree of self-sacrifice was ever enough (Madsen, 1984, 149, 236). The self existed only to serve something else, which was supposedly more important. Many thought it was glorious. One new woman of the revolution, a Mrs. You who worked as an oil exploration surveyer, explained:

> The idea of women's liberation in those days was very masculinized. I wanted to be able to do anything boys could do. In the propaganda team I wanted to dress up to play the boys' roles ... There are other stories of Chinese women too, Hua Mulan following the army, Qiu Jin in the 1911 revolution, and Communist women like Song Qingling and Deng Yingchao. Those women influenced me a lot—in those days we were all imitating heroes. (Xinran, 2008, 111–112)

We'll skip the exploits of "iron girl shock teams" or female Red Guards, who seemed bent on erasing femininity for the sake of socialist selflessness. These women's cruelty to those less "virtuous" could be equal to that of any male fanatic. But even at the height of the Cultural Revolution, women often had their own interpretations of official values. Dr. Li Qunying found that other staff at her hospital refused to treat a man accused as a counter-revolutionary. She gave him medicine and a three-day sick leave from work. The Red Guards caught her, tore the sick-leave to shreds, and accused Dr. Li of sympathy for subversives. She said "I was practicing the 'revolutionary humanitarianism' that Chairman Mao advocated, and they couldn't argue with that" (Li, 2000, 165).

For the first 25 years after the revolution, "equality" of the sexes basically meant that women could work, dress, and act like men of the People's Liberation Army, with an equal duty to sacrifice themselves for the country. Some saw it as glorious, and free-spirited women faced a stream of abuse for seeking anything else. In Annie Wang's novel *Lili*, a group of rebellious teenage girls are ordered to emulate Liu Hulan, a Communist girl who died in the revolutionary war at age 15: "Look at Liu Hulan, she was so young, yet she had the courage to die for her beliefs. What revolutionary consciousness she has at only fifteen! Don't you feel ashamed of yourselves? Look at yourselves, a bunch of female hooligans, a pack of scumbags! Our Party gives you enough to eat and keep you warm, but you still can't keep your pants on!" (Wang, 2002, 4).

At least on paper, the legal rights of men and women were leveled. And despite all the rhetoric of heroic self-sacrifice, the good of women and the good of the country were not such different things. Most poor women (the "burden or bitterness sufferers") had always dreamed of "crawling over the threshold of the state" to get a government job. And the government-allocated employment system eventually assigned salaried work to a large majority (sometimes over 90%) of at least the urban women (Chau, 2006, 29; Jiang, 2004, 208–209). Naturally, even this boon tended to become a sacrifice for the nation. The jobs assigned to husbands and wives were commonly in different regions. Millions of separated couples compared themselves to the Weaving Girl and Cowherd Boy, sentenced to different ends of the sky by the Jade Emperor (Li, 2000, 128). Still, most of the women who served as leaders, workers, soldiers, or heroes of the people, struck some sort of balance between self-sacrifice and self-interest. The artist Pan Jiajun captured a certain beauty of it in the 1971 propaganda poster "I Am Seagull," where a young telephone linewoman calls in a successful repair, giving her code name with a smile in the pouring rain.

Later of course, most accomplishments of building the nation or liberalizing the economy were attributed to a few big men. And most women didn't care if headmen got the credit, so long as they could take steps in the right direction. If "development" and "nation-building" were a new religion, women had their part in it, like the part they had in older religions. But as in the past, there was a women's version of liberation. As Lu Xiaojiang (founder of China's first non-government institute of women's studies in 1985) explained, the Chinese language developed two different terms for "feminism." One was *nüguan zhuyi*, or the doctrine of equal rights, etc. The other was *nüxing zhuyi*, meaning "feminology." And this concerned freeing women from cooptation by the state, to honor their own sensibilities and find their own paths (Judge, 2008, 237–238).

If modern women advanced in some ways, what happened to women's religions? Many women ditched all religions from previous generations, to embrace a new one. And true converts to modernist socialism accepted that all older religions had been instruments of oppression. Of course the revolutionary ideals of social equality, economic fairness, partnership of the sexes, etc., bore a striking resemblance to dreams of the Golden Age. But those ideals were now officially designated as *anti*-religious.

Battle Lines of Modern Religious Life

When the Canadian doctor Norman Bethune came to help the Communist army against the Japanese, he hoped to fight for a new age of equality and brotherhood. And somehow, this dream seemed radically atheistic at the time. Both Bethune and Mao Zedong were contemptuous of religion as they knew it. But while joking informally, they both compared themselves to religious idealists of the past. In Christian tradition, the early monks and nuns pooled their property and shared all things in common. And this seemed commendably pious if they did it on isolated monastic estates. But it seemed to be a war against God when the communist movement tried to foist that dream on the whole surrounding society. Likewise, the motto of the French Revolution, "Liberty, Equality, Fraternity" was widely seen as a rejection of everything Christianity ever stood for—though some would say those ideals were close to the heart of real Christianity. So modern idealists, from Voltaire to Marx, and Norman Bethune to John Lennon, deemed themselves enemies of religion. And they rejected religion because it failed to live up to its own ideals.

In China, it was roughly the same. Back in 1884, when Mao Zedong was a schoolboy, the dissident Confucian scholar Kang Yuwei wrote an essay which Mao admired. It was a commentary on the *Classic of Rites*, which expressed the old religious sort of popular idealism:

When both the "ruler" and the "state" will have been abolished, all men will be obliged to obtain their sustenance from what is publically owned and no longer rely on their private property ... Once private property has become useless, why should anyone continue to employ force and deception and thus infringe on honesty and justice? ... When such evil individuals disappear, so will the evil thoughts that go along with such acts. Inside and outside will be the same, a boundary between them will no longer exist. For that reason, the outer gates will no longer be locked, weapons and arms will be unknown. (Bauer, 1976, 303)

Such dreams were inverted opposites to warlord-dominated society. And like countless rebels of the past, the modern ones hoped that an ideal world was just a revolution away. The new Golden Age could be seized by an act of will. And though the modern rebels felt they were original thinkers, their sentiments echoed the ancient themes of popular religion.

Like religious associations of the past, the atheistic Communists used traveling drama troupes to spread their word. In 1945 they produced a play called *The White Haired Girl*, about a village girl who is raped by her landlord. She becomes pregnant, and flees to the mountains to have her baby. Feeling permanently shamed, she survives on what she can scavenge in the forest. Her hardships are so great that her hair turns white. Villagers who catch sight of her think she is a spirit, or a forest immortal. Then one day the revolution prevails, and the landlord falls from power. The White Haired Girl dares return to her village, and openly accuses her abuser before the people.

Many early Communists felt that women's values were crucial to changing the world. For example, Li Dazhao (1888–1927), a co-founder of the Communist Party, wrote an essay describing the change of heart needed for the future. We may notice this was written in 1918, during World War I:

> *Most of the preceding discussions about natural evolution centered about the survival of the fittest and [advocated that] the weak are the prey of the strong ... Now we know that these discussions were greatly mistaken [because] biological progress does not arise from struggle but from mutual aid. If humanity wishes ... to exist and if it wishes happiness and prosperity, then it must have mutual friendship and ought not to rely upon force for mutual extermination ... This spirit of mutual aid, this ethic, this social ability, is able to cause human progress ... It is a naturally produced authority. Its mysterious nature is similar to the mystery of sex, the mystery of mother love ... (Bauer, 1976, 378–379)*

In all these ways, the Communist movement built on old religious dreams. At first, Mao hoped to follow in the footsteps of Kang Yuwei, and wanted to separate the good from the bad in Chinese culture. In a 1940 speech "On New Democracy" he argued, "To throw away ... [our culture's] feudal dross, and to absorb its democratic essence ... We must separate all the rotten things of the ancient feudal ruling class from the fine ancient popular culture that is more or less democratic and revolutionary in character" (De Bary and Chan, 1960, vol. II, 228). So there was good and bad in traditional culture.

But which parts of tradition were the bad parts?

Some argued that popular religion was counterproductive because it relied on useless means for gaining a better life. As a Communist Youth League secretary argued, "These words from the *Internationale* say it well: 'We have never had a savior, nor do we rely on gods' ... we alone must pursue that happier life. There is no reason why we should place our fate into the hands of gods and ghosts!" (MacInnis, 1989, 444–445). If the religious hope for divine help made people passive, then faith was a block to building the future. But some religious people were activists, and the early revolutionaries needed all the allies they could get. Therefore Mao argued, "Communists may form an ... anti-feudal united front ... with certain idealists and even with religious followers, but we can never approve of their religious idealism or religious doctrines" (Ching, 1990, 125). Like most politicians, Mao needed to choose his allies and enemies carefully. He needed to build winning coalitions, and target opponents he could beat.

Many rebels hoped to form an idealists' alliance with popular religion. But the old-style warlords, landlords, and patriarchs claimed that religion was on their side. They said that Chinese religion stood for tradition as they defined it, and they defined it as submission to the existing powerholders. If that was right, then religion was the revolution's enemy. And increasingly, rebels like Chen Duxiu (1879–1942) accepted the powerholders' claims. These new idealists came to believe that popular religion had never been an expression of ordinary people's hopes. It was just a set of servile superstitions imposed by the overlords, which would deny all freedom and block all progress.

Probably most revolutionaries claimed to promote the good and suppress the regressive. But the kinds of religion they labeled "regressive" were usually the popular "primitive superstitions" of village people. Even before the Republican revolution of 1911, Dr. Sun Yat-sen (Sun Yixian) designated popular religion as his enemy: "The revolutionary army undertakes to overthrow the Manchu tyranny, to eradicate the corruption of officialdom, to eliminate depraved customs, to exterminate the system of slave girls, to wipe out the scourge of opium, superstitious beliefs, and geomancy ... and so forth" (De Bary and Chan, 1960, vol. II, 117–118). The new Republican government tried to restore Confucian values while suppressing "silly village superstitions." So in 1931, Chiang Kai-shek's government banned "martial arts and magic spirit" movies. Over 200 of these films had been made since 1927, but the government didn't approve of romanticizing rebel outlaws, or claiming they had support from gods and goddesses. Later, the Communists extended this ban on superstitious films, which lasted till Jet Li made *The Shaolin Temple* in 1982 (Berry, 2008, 300–302).

While the Nationalists tried to affirm Confucianism but oppose popular religion, the Communists increasingly labeled all religion as a force for oppression. In Mao's opinion, there were four systems of authority to be thrown off: the state's political authority, the extended family clan authority, the male authority over women, and the "theocratic authority" of gods and spirits. By the mid-1920s, Mao was happy to report a growing rejection of religion by ordinary villagers: "Theocratic authority begins to totter everywhere as the peasant associations have taken over the temples of the gods as their offices. Everywhere they advocate the appropriation of temple properties to maintain peasant schools and to defray association expenses, calling this 'public revenue from superstition.' Forbidding superstition and smashing idols has become quite the vogue in Liling." Still, Mao cautioned overly enthusiastic Communists from trespassing on the villagers' choices: "The idols were set up by the peasants themselves, and in time they will pull them down with their own hands ... The idols should be removed by the peasants themselves ... it is wrong for anyone else to do these things for them" (De Bary and Chan, 1960, vol. II, 210–213).

But by 1944, Mao was growing more willing to do it himself.

He complained that in the region around Yanan, "Out of the 1.5 million people in the Shan-Gan-Ning Border Region, there are still more than one million illiterates and two thousand spirit mediums; superstitious thinking is still affecting all of the masses." In that part of Shaanxi, people even evoked the spirit of the Canadian doctor Norman Bethune. In prayers for healing, they lit cigarettes and called on his name. And though Bethune was a hero of the revolution, the Party deemed this another case of superstition to be suppressed (Chau, 2006, 44, 47).

Still, the Communists tried to avoid alienating all religious people. They promised to respect the main institutionalized religions, except for Confucianism. As Ren Jiyu described the usual Communist policy, "We must differentiate between religion and feudal superstition. Religious activities, such as those of Buddhism, Islam, Christianity, and Daoism, are legal ... [But] Feudal superstition is different, and such activities as dancing in a trance, witchcraft, and fortune telling are illegal. Our policy is to protect religious belief, but not feudal superstition" (MacInnis, 1989, 400–401).

The War on Superstition

After the 1949 revolution, the villagers divided the land more equally, and for a few years reaped bigger crops. They rebuilt war-torn villages, and renovated local temples across the country. The time when villagers would reject their folk religions seemed long overdue. So long as the civil war had continued, the Communist cadres behaved like preachers of a new popular religion. But after the revolution succeeded, Communism became a new state creed. It then developed the familiar attributes of a state-backed faith: doctrines, scriptures, preachers, rituals, martyrs, saviors, police-backed inquisitions. The Communists tolerated other institutional religions, so long as these made no challenge to Communism's official status. But in the field of unorganized popular religion, the Communists wanted a monopoly. Like most rulers since Shang times, they were less concerned to control patriarchal religion than to restrict the shamanic popular religions of village people and women.

The period of forced suppression for popular religion lasted just over a decade, from 1963 to 1976. In 1963 the government banned temple festivals and "superstitious merchandise" such as paper spirit money or incense. Then the Party leaders simply tore up the 1954 constitution's protection of organized religions. In 1966 they authorized demolition of all village temples, be they Daoist, Buddhist, or devoted to local deities—unless the buildings were converted to useful facilities like storehouses or schools (Chau, 2006, 47). And not content to remove these structures, the Party reps held "struggle sessions" to root out old sentiments from people's minds. The Red Guard crusaders seemed bent on eliminating devotion to anything "less" than the state. By their logic, family loyalties should be subsumed in commitment to communal production brigades. Lineage associations, temple societies, or traditional marketing networks should be treated as disloyal special interest groups (Zarrow, 2008, 38). Of course China's people were already famous for putting community interests before individual desires. If they insisted on certain rights, they usually meant rights for their group. As for personal self-interest, a traditional morality like that of clan mothers had always encouraged selfless giving—and giving, and giving, usually till the individual dropped. But that wasn't good enough for the Red Guards with their patriotic attacks on other people's selfishness.

Eventually, most people got sick of so much self-righteous abuse. As the Cultural Revolution's war against all "olds" alienated a growing majority of people, most local officials grew reluctant to further offend their friends. They got tired of trying to stamp out things that most people wanted to do. After the Gang of Four fell from power, most government officials stood aside as villagers across the nation broke up their production communes, re-divided their land into family plots, and started reopening their temples. Some Westerners claimed it was a great spiritual victory over godlessness. But basically, it was a just a matter of letting people get on with their lives as before (Chau, 2006, 240–241, 13). Across China, the old religious specialists hung out their shingles for customers. So in 1983, sociologist Gong Jianlong found a sorceress making good money, and asked "Why are Superstitious Activities on the Rise Again?":

Devout believers in ghosts and deities are not only limited to old folks and women; a sizeable number consists of young people. For instance, among a total 461 members of Qingsan Brigade in Cailu Commune, over 95 percent are believers ... There is an old sorceress, Zhang so-and-so, in Jiangzhen Communue, self proclaimed as being able to "call immortal celestial beings," "to capture demons," "to cure the terminally ill," who set up in her home four incense tables; every day a continuous flow of people go to her for "fortune telling" and healing, making her front door and courtyard like a marketplace. (MacInnis, 1989, 388)

Officially, there was no real change of policy. The Eleventh Party Congress in 1979 still sought to define the cultural enemy: "By superstition we generally mean activities conducted by shamans and sorcerers, such as magic medicine, magic water, divination, fortune telling, avoiding disasters, praying for rain, praying for pregnancy, exorcizing demons, telling fortunes by physiognomy, locating house or tomb sites by geomancy, and so forth." The Congress still threatened to punish witchcraft: "Sorcerers, witches, and those who spread rumors or swindle people ... are to be imprisoned, held in custody, or kept under surveillance for up to two years" (MacInnis, 1989, 30–34). But actually, most local officials just stopped trying to enforce the policy. There was a growing "zone of indifference" toward religious practice. Only in a few high profile cases did Party reps. complain, trying to draw some legal limit on superstition. As the *Guangzhou* news reported in March of 1986:

Wu Quan County standing committee vice-chairman Liang
Rurong and others participated in such a large-scale
superstitious feudal activity, the so-called ancestral sacrifice,
that it was shocking ... Such traditions of the masses as the
Qingming grave sweeping, the commemoration of ancestors, and
the encouragement of descendants are humanly sensible and
beyond reproach. But the graveside offering known as "southern
snake goes to sea" is completely beyond the limits of normal
activity, and thus is typical of feudal superstitious behavior. It
mobilized over 12,000 participants, dispatched over 140 motor
vehicles, slaughtered over 160 pigs, and made a noisy hubbub. It
both wasted human, material, and financial resources, adversely
affecting production, and incited a feudal, clannish mood among
the masses, endangering the social order. (MacInnis, 1989, 407)

Women's Religion Resumes with a Bang, as Usual

In villages of Shaanxi Province, there are basically two kinds of
spirit mediums. The *wushen* invoke possession by "proper deities"
such as the Black Dragon King of Longwanggou village, or the
goddess Guanyin. The *shenguan*, on the other hand, get possessed by
ghosts, ancestral spirits, or people who've become immortals. People
go to both sorts of spirit mediums for support, guidance, or fun. The
mediums often operate out of village temples, and a popular spirit
medium can draw good business to a temple. The temples are also
centers for community life, where weddings and funerals, prayers
and offerings, social occasions, village meetings, and annual festivals
can happen.

The annual festivals generally last several days, and are held to
celebrate the "birthday" of a local deity. These festivals are usually
the high point of social life for a village. They often involve drama
productions, concerts, speeches, processions, trade fairs, and a huge
hubbub of social action. All this is good for business. The construction

crews, community organizers, musicians, actors, spirit mediums, fortune tellers, sculptors, merchants, caterers, geomancers, healers, and assorted wise women, all get some of the action (Chau, 2006, 52–55, 2–3). The money changing hands gets circulated rather than lost.

Once the government officials stopped trying to suppress all these things, local Party leaders were often the first to help reorganize village temple committees. Putting on their Chamber of Commerce caps, they became boosters for local culture. So, between the late 1980s and late '90s, villages across the northern third of Shaanxi Province built or renovated about 10,000 temples (Chau, 2006, 12–13, 2–3). In the Puxian region of Fujian, Kenneth Dean surveyed around 600 villages, finding 1,639 active temples, containing statues of over 1,200 different deities (2003, 35–36). Out in Tibet, the Chinese Religious Affairs Bureau and the Tourism Bureau started collaborating to generate tourism. By 1986 they claimed that 1,300 Tibetan lamaseries had been reopened (compared to perhaps 6,000 closed since 1959) (MacInnis, 1989, 184–185). A Tibetan woman working as an official guide told Jan Wong, "The same people who destroyed the monasteries are walking around today with their prayer wheels, talking about independence" (1999, 170).

All this reopening or rebuilding temples proved good for employment. Local Party leaders got new roles for themselves, managing profitable community assets. Since socialist propaganda workers were no longer paid to tour the villages extolling the old revolution, these actors, choreographers, opera singers, or musicians turned to their traditional clients, and worked the temple festival circuit (Chau, 2006, 54–55, 248). As government jobs in communes and factories declined, women pushed their skills in new directions. Many "took a role" as local shamanesses.

Some of the religious revival was real pent-up demand for tradition. The San Yuan Daoist temple in Guangdong had been turned into a plastics factory during the Cultural Revolution. On reopening in July 1982, it faced a crush of 110,000 participants for the Lantern Festival, which is roughly equivalent to Valentine's Day (MacInnes, 1989, 217–218). Perhaps the first statue of a deity raised in post-Mao China was a huge figure of the goddess Guanyin, erected in the forecourt of a maternity hospital in Guangdong. In Guiping County of Guangxi, worshipers of Guanyin rebuilt her temple and held her birthday festival in 1985. The whole surrounding hill was covered with people, who burned their incense and littered spirit money all over the grounds (Weller, 1994, 217). For Guanyin's 1988 birthday, Donald MacInnis went to the Nanputuo Temple in Xiamen, Fujian and described the scene: "Thousands of people were working their way through the temple complex day and night, whole families, old people, young people, an almost equal number of men and women. Most of them were offering incense before the various sacred images and burning spirit money in big bronze kettles; others were simply curious visitors." On the second day, the abbot said attendance was a bit down from the previous year due to increased entrance fees, but around 30,000 people had paid (1989, 135).

Beyond local festivals, both religious leaders and government tourism officials encouraged a rise of pilgrimages to sacred mountains and renowned temples. Starting in the 1990s, the Republic of China Association of Spirit Mediums (in Taiwan) helped organize annual pilgrimages to the goddess Mazu's "ancestral" temple at Meizhou Island on the Fujian coast. Since there were an estimated 100 million devotees of Mazu in the world, this pilgrimage had serious potential. In 2010, the Dajia Jenn Lann Temple in Taiwan organized a pilgrimage through 20 townships, to accompany the goddess on her round of blessing various temples. Representatives from temples on the mainland came as well, looking to expand their own pilgrimage business. A Taiwanese organizer named Tsai Ming-hsien complained to the BBC that mainland temple leaders saw no distinction between profit and devotion: "They're reviving the temples to make money. They're running temples like enterprises, not based on faith. They hold the festivals like a carnival, for tourism. They're always

asking us how to make it run so that it makes money" (http://news.
bbc.co.uk/2/hi/asia-pacific/8629453.stm). Sure enough, the Daoist
Yuanfu Wanninggong Temple near Nanjing attracted about 650,000
visitors in 1997, raking in near 10,000,000 RMB (Lai, 2003, 112).
It could seem terribly greedy. Many new temples were little more
than tacky museums or tourist-trap theme parks. Still, if the temple
associations got rich, they commonly sponsored scholarship funds,
schools, forestation projects, and local charities of all types. Or they
raised monuments, like the 20-meter-high marble statue of Mazu on
Coloane Island.

As in modern Japan, China saw a series of "new religions,"
mostly promoted by women. In Taiwan after WWII, "The Compassion
Society" combined worship of three traditional goddesses: Guanyin,
Wusheng Laomu (Laozi's Mom), and the Queen Mother of the West.
The devotees wear blue-green uniforms, hold rites, enter trance
states to contact the goddesses, and do ecstatic dancing, or "jumping."
As Robert Weller explains, "Any member of the cult is liable to
experience jumping, that is, direct possession by the cult gods." The
Compassion Society also practices healing arts and community service
work (Weller, 1994, 77; Despeux and Kohn, 2003, 45). Another new
organization is the Compassion Relief Merit Society (Ciji gongdehui),
founded by the Buddhist nun, Zhengyan. It operates something like
the Sisters of Charity, and may be the largest civil organization in
Taiwan. In Zhiwuying village of Hebei Province, a certain Ms. Wu
recently claimed to be an incarnation of the Silkworm Mother (Cangu
Nainai), an ancient goddess who has healed people since her first
coming 10,000 years ago (Fan, 2003, 54–57).

And then there are the large organizations teaching various
versions of qigong, either as a practice for health and vitality, or as
a religious quest. The Communist Party adopted qigong in the 1950s
as a health and fitness program. But since many people took it as a
Daoist or Buddhist religious practice, the Cultural Revolution tried
to ban it. Then in the 1970s qigong made a comeback. Several huge

movements emerged, with practitioners appearing in most every park. Most qigong leaders were men, but one notable female master was Zhang Xiangyu, a former actress with the Qinghai Performance Troupe, who claimed powers to heal and receive visions. Despite the 1989 martial law restrictions on public meetings, Zhang held gatherings of thousands, night after night. She was arrested, and Party newspapers accused her of deception and witchcraft. One follower protested, "The reason they locked her up was because she was a woman and she did not have enough powerful clients to back her up when she started to make a lot of money" (Chen, 2002, 325–326).

The most popular schools of qigong practice include Tantric Qigong (Zangmigong), which is based on Tibetan Buddhist practice, Central Qigong (Zhonggong), which has a more Chinese Buddhist context, and the Dharma Wheel Practice (Falungong), which was officially banned in 1999. The Falungong scared the government by filling sports stadiums with devotees, teaching that its qigong practice could lead to superhuman powers plus a new social order, imposing cult-like restrictions on its members, and then staging mass protests over police restrictions on its leaders (Kohn, 2009, 201, 189–190; Overmyer, 2008, 179). As in the past, the government made certain arbitrary distinctions between religions that aimed to support the rulers, and those that hoped to replace them. Being torn over what was acceptable, the officials attempted to distinguish "scientific qigong" from "superstitious qigong." And if the government banned the Falungong brand of qigong, people in the parks did *taijiquan* (Tai Chi) instead.

Another trend was a rise of home-grown Christian groups, often run as house churches with female leaders. Some local shamanesses diversified their services by channeling the power of Jesus, which seemed to give them a more international appeal (Ching, 1990, 134). Again, the government officials didn't agree where to draw the line. In the year 2000, according to Agence France-Presse, some overly legalistic officials in the Wenzhou region destroyed around 1,200 temples and churches for not being "registered properly" (Dean, 2003, 39).

But there's one class of semi-religious practitioners the government never suppressed—the several hundred thousand traditional healers. Rather than declaring these people superstitious quacks, the government tried to work with them, to bridge the gap between hospitals and villages. The result was an inexpensive network of "bare-foot doctors" with widely varying abilities. These healers mixed elements of modern allopathic medicine with acupuncture, herbal treatment, breathing and stretching exercises, diet control, and massage. Doctors with formal degrees commonly dismissed them as village tricksters. But the World Health Organization studied the system and outlined its merits in the 1978 study *The Promotion and Development of Traditional Medicine* (Ching and Küng, 1989, 165). No doubt the local healers are ineffective in many emergencies. But this is a basically home-grown movement of popular self-help. Its value is mainly preventative, and its influence is one reason why China has an average life expectancy in the 70s—despite having per capita income lower than a hundred other nations (Smil, 1993, 88). In recent decades, various methods of Chinese traditional healing grew popular across the globe. You can probably get books like Xiaolan Zhao's *Ancient Healing for Modern Women: Traditional Chinese Medicine for All Phases of a Woman's Life*, Bronwyn Whitlocke's *Chinese Medicine for Women*, or Livia Kohn's *Chinese Healing Exercises* in the local library.

As in the past, most of the people pursuing new or ancient religions were women. A man called Old Chen psychoanalyzed them this way: "Chinese women have religious faith, but they seem able to believe in several religions at the same time. Women who believe in the spiritual and physical exercises of qigong are always changing the type of qigong they practice and the Master they follow; their gods come and go too. You can't blame them: the hardships of life make them long for a way out" (Xinran, 2002, 88).

In general, religion is booming, but not in a seriously organized way. It's an open market for any sort of religion, or mix of several religions, offering almost any route to almost any goal. Robert Weller walked through Taipei with an eye for shrines:

A walk down the street (nearly any street) quickly confirms the statistical impression. Major temples are booming, and old Earth God shrines have been rebuilt in high style everywhere. In the large cities, every few blocks seem to offer a sign advertising a new shrine, usually in someone's apartment. The owners often do not register legally, and the government has found these shrines very difficult to control, in spite of increasingly loud complaints by neighbors kept awake by the divine racket. (1994, 116)

Modern Daoism has gone mainstream, sometimes with upscale market appeal. The temple boards of directors increasingly operate hotels for pilgrims. The Chinese Daoist College in Hunan graduated its first class of 48 Daoist female clerics in 2007. Wang Yier, the chief editor for the *Journal of Chinese Daoism* says over half the Daoists living in temples around China are female, and these total over 10,000 women (Wang, 2009, 164–173). In North America, Daoist masters like Mantak Chia began attracting the kind of attention teachers of yoga or Buddhism started received a generation earlier. Posh Daoist spas like the Intertwined Dragon Temple in Chongqing now offer retreat facilities for the rich, with meditation and lecture halls, massage parlors, qigong and martial arts classes, hot tubs, herbal medical treatment, acupuncture, and dining halls. They also hold seminars on the arts of longevity as known to the Yellow Emperor, 5,000 years ago (Kohn, 2009, 195). Let the buyer beware, and know the program by its fruits.

In this fairly hot religious market, many people just pray for winning lottery ticket numbers. Many seekers seek benefit only for their own family. Things can get hypocritical. People used to honor local deities for the sake of community welfare, as in holding rites for rain. But now most people seek either personal gain or personal growth. The initiative is mainly under the seeker's control. The popularity of any practice or deity is a sum of many personal choices. And though most temples are devoted to male deities, any guesstimate of total temples and devotees must put goddesses like Guanyin, Mazu, Wusheng Laomu, or the Lady Linshui (Chen Jinggu) close to the top of the heap.

Will the Greatest Women's Counterculture on Earth Please Stand Up

As in any culture, people are constantly deciding which traditions to keep, and which to forget. The simplistic Cultural Revolution answer was to just dump everything old. But most people want a more careful selection of what's helpful or oppressive. And many feel that the traditions of village wise women are a lot more helpful that those of dominator warlords. Of course warlord-style power still has its admirers. As Julia Ching warned after the 1989 Tiananmen Square massacre, "In my opinion, Chinese history has been moving toward more rather than less concentration of power in the hands of the few." Others such as Bo Yang (in *The Ugly Chinaman and the Crisis of Chinese Culture*) blamed the people as much as the rulers for China's top-down system, accusing his countrymen of being petty, mean, filthy, muddleheaded, cruel, childish, racist, belligerent, pusillanimous, backward, duplicitous, paranoid, and sadistic (Parfitt, 2011, 225). And many women would agree. But when people choose which values they prefer for themselves, most will probably go for values of partnership and equality. As dissident leader Ren Wanding predicted, "The democracy movement of 1989 is the mid-wife for a new party ... Perhaps the infant girl democracy may be killed in its cradle, but she will definitely be born again in the next storm" (Ching, 1990, 98–99). Many Westerners assumed that the "goddess of liberty" erected by students in Tiananmen Square was a copy of the American statue of liberty. But many Chinese people saw it as a socialist-realism-style sculpture of a female people's hero, or an image of the goddess Guanyin (Weller, 1994, 195).

As in the past, a whole side of China's evolving civilization is made by women, for women. Women's traditions from a time before patriarchy are alive and growing. And as China exerts rising influence across the world, its counterculture of women's values may bring a better balance, both in China and elsewhere. Women's traditions of bodily and spiritual health, harmony with nature, peace of mind, compassion, and freedom of spirit are something the world needs. After working for decades in hyper-developing Taiwan, a Jesuit father named Louis Guthheinz reflected that the driving passions of the modern world—of empires, maximized growth, "this ultimate wanting to control everything" was so yang. And the whole world needed more balance with yin (Ching and Küng, 1989, 269–270). Western practitioners of Daoism like Michael Winn felt they were doing something about that:

> *Neidan [or Inner Alchemy] opens the door to understanding exactly how the human soul, like the brain, is binary in nature. We are divided into yin-yang aspects at many different levels of the body and psyche, polarities often in conflict. The purpose of internal alchemy is to speed up the integration of the warring halves of our soul as part of human evolution. (2009, 199)*

In Micheal Saso's opinion, the blend of popular Chinese religions offered a balanced message to the world: "The person who is filled with respect and benevolence for others and compassion for all living things, and who lives in close harmony with nature, lives long and is filled with inner peace and blessing" (Saso, 1995, 1). Or, as Livia Kohn explains of the Daoist Eight Immortals, "Accepting life and death as a single flow, they take neither seriously and make the best of all they meet. Their happy attitude, their playful way of being, is characteristic of the popular image of the immortal today" (Kohn,

1993, 281). At least that's one version of Chinese tradition, which many Westerners find increasingly attractive.

My sentimental favorite example of positive influence is from Macau, where the Portuguese government offered the city a farewell present in 1997. It erected a 20-meter-high statue of Guanyin overlooking the harbor. But the artist, Cristina Leiria, clearly melded the goddesses of China and Portugal into one figure. It was both the Virgin Mary and Guanyin at the same time, symbolizing a fusion of the best and most beautiful from both the East and the West (Palmer, et al., 2009, xi–xx). Here, I suspect, is an early sign of a coming planetary religion, in which no tradition, authority, or sex prevails, but all things beautiful and good share the world's admiration.

A Fragmentary Glossary of Goddesses and Divine Couples

Abkai Hehe. Sky Mother of the Manchu people, who gave birth to the universe and the first shamaness, then saved all creatures from the flood.

Ba (Pa). The goddess of drought.

Bana-jiermu. Earth Mother of the Manchus, who oversees many other goddesses of sun, moon, cloud, rock, hot spring, or sea soul.

Baogu (Bao Gu). A legendary healer and master of medicinal plants, who reportedly lived in the 300s CE.

Bixia Yuanjun (Pi-Hsia Yuan Chin). The goddess of dawn, childbirth, and destiny, who brings health and good fortune to the newborn, and protection to mothers.

Busangga and Yasangga. The divine couple which created the world according to Dai tradition.

Cai Xun Zhen (Ts'ai Hsün-chen). A girl who defied her parents, ran away from home, and became a deified Daoist immortal.

Can Nu (Cannu, or Cangu Nainai). The Silkworm Mother, protector of silkworm culture, mothers, families, and healing. A magic horse skin whisked her to heaven, after which she returned as a silkworm and lived in a mulberry tree. Worshiped on the third day of the third month.

Cao Wenyi. Sage-patroness of the Purity and Tranquility lineage of Quanzhen Daoism (fl. 1119 to 1125). A famous poet, who was given the title "Great Master of Literary Withdrawal into Clear Emptiness."

Chang'e. (Chang O, Heng-o). Stole the elixir of immortality and floated to the moon. In another adventure she came to earth, delivered a magic potion which killed a cruel emperor, and re-ascended to the moon.

Chang Rong. A forest immortal who ate only raspberry roots.

Chang Xi (Chang-hsi). A consort of Di Jun (Black Bird) who gave birth to the twelve moons.

Chen Jinggu (Lady Linshui). A deified shamaness from the coast of Fujian, who founded a line of female adepts for healing, exorcising spirits, calling souls, conducting seasonal rites, making rain, aiding childbirth, and fighting enemies of the people.

Chien Ti. A goddess who was impregnated by the sky god Di Jun when she swallowed an egg while bathing. She then gave birth to Yin Hsieh, founder of the Shang Dynasty.

Chokyidronme. A Tibetan Buddhist master of the 1400s, recognized as the embodiment of the meditation deity Vajravarahi. Also known as Samding Dorje Pagmo, she began a line of female tulkus, or reincarnate lamas, which continues to the present.

Chuang Mu (Ch'uang Mu, or Ch'ang Mu). The goddess of the bedroom and of sexual delights.

Cinnabar Mother of Highest Prime. The imperial lady who resides in the third star of the Big Dipper constellation, who governs time and the six yin powers.

Dagmema. The enlightened wife of Tibetan sage Marpa.

Dakinis. Enlightened goddesses of Tibet, whose name means "sky dancers."

Dechen Karmo. Mother of all the Buddhas.

Dongling, Holy Mother. Daoist saint who attained great powers, but was accused of lechery and witchcraft by her jealous husband. She was jailed, but vanished to freedom, leaving only her slippers behind.

Dragon Girl. A girl who saved Xiamen Island from the Serpent King.

Ekadzati. A female wisdom protector of the Tantric teachings.

Ehuang. A consort of the sky god Di Jun, who gave birth to the Tribe of Three-Bodied People. She was also wife of the primordial emperor Shun.

Feng Bo Bo (Feng Po-Po). A goddess of winds, storms, and moisture.

Five Shards Constellation. The unmoving spot around which the stars revolved, also called the "womb point" from which the universe was born.

Fufei. A daughter of the snake emperors Fu Xi and Nü Wa. She was lured into the water by the river's admiring spirit, where she became the goddess of the Luo River.

Gong Detian (Gong De Tian, or Kung-Te-Tien). The goddess of Luck, who has a magic pearl which grants wishes.

Guanyin (Kuan Yin). The goddess of universal compassion, a Buddhist bodhisattva, known as "She Who Hears the Cries of the World."

Gyen, Trompa. A Tibetan princess who became a great Buddhist teacher.

Hengshan Goddess. The deity of Hengshan peak in Hunan, also known as the "Primal Mistress of the Purple Barrens."

He Xiangu (He Xian Gu, He-Hsien-Ku, or Ho-Hsien-Ku). One of the eight Daoist immortals, a woman who discovered the potion of immortality. Alleged founder of the Morning Cloud (Yunxia Pai) lineage of the Complete Perfection (Quanzhen) sect of Daoism.

Hou. A lion-like creature which in older myths was the mount of the earth's guardian queen.

Hu Tu (Hou-T'u). Female deity of the earth, like Gaia. She was the ruler of magic and fertility, to whom the Emperor offered sacrifices on a square marble altar in the Forbidden City each summer solstice. Sometimes said to be male.

Jade Maiden. The first woman, who the first man, Peng Gu, discovered wandering the cosmos. The first couple then generated the lineage of divine ancestors.

Jade Maiden of Highest Mystery. A divine representative of the sun who engages in sexual relations with selected adepts.

Jade Maiden of Profound Wonder. The mother of Laozi, who gave birth to the sage by immaculate conception, taught him the Dao, and ascended bodily into heaven as a realized immortal.

Jasper Lady. A woman of power who gave Emperor Yu magic help to control the floods.

Jiang Yuan (Chiang Yuan). Recorded in Zhou-era legend as mother of Hou Ji (Hou Chi, or Lord Millet), founder of the Zhou clan, after being impregnated by stepping on the footprint of Di Jun (Black Bird).

Jiao, Refined Master (Chiao). A female Daoist master of Tang times, who initiated and loved male students.

Jiu Xian Nai (Chiu Hsian Nai). A South China shamaness with cult following.

Jun Di (Chun Ti). The Daoist goddess of light, who has three heads, one of which is a pig. Her chariot is also pulled by pigs, which are the seven stars of the Great Bear constellation.

Jin Hua, Lady (Lady Chin Hua). A divine protector of the people.

Lan Cai-He (Lan Ts'ai-Ho). One of the Eight Immortals, either an effeminate male dressed as a woman, or a very eccentric woman with a male voice, who carried a flute, a basket of fruit, and ruled over music.

Lao Jun (Lao Chün). A holy mother of creation.

Lavatory Ladies. Goddesses of the outhouse, namely Qi Gu and Zi Gu.

Li Teng Kong (Li T'eng-k'ung). A girl who defied her parents, ran away from home, and became a realized Daoist immortal.

Lie Zu (Luozu, Lei-Zi, Lei-Tsu, Lei-Tzu, Hsi-Ling-Shih) Wife of the Yellow Emperor, who discovered silk, cultivated silkworms and mulberry trees, and invented the loom.

Lingguang Shengmu (the Holy Mother of Numinous Radiance). A goddess who appeared to the Daoist priestess Zu Shu, which led her to establish a Daoist lineage called the Way of Pure Subtlety.

Li Ye. A famous Daoist court priestess, Tang dynasty (618–906 CE).

Long Mu (Lung Mu). A South Chinese holy woman who protected people from the forces of evil.

Lo Shen. Goddess of rivers and ruler of water magic.

Luo River goddess. See Fufei.

Luozu. A wife of the Yellow Emperor. She initiated silk production.

Magu. An ancient female immortal, also called "the Hemp Lady." Revered by the Complete Perfection sect of Daoism. Portrayed wearing a tiger-head pouch, a sword, and a head dress symbolizing the freedom of heaven, with wild hair and bird-like fangs.

Ma Ku. Goddess of springtime, honored in Spring rites.

Mamo. A wrathful Tibetan dakini who eats flesh.

Ma Xian Ku (Ma Hsian Ku). A holy shamaness who protected her people.

Mat Chinoi. The serpent Goddess who was mother of the Chinese people.

Mazu (Ma Tsu, or Tien Hou—the Queen of Heaven). A girl from Fujian who traveled in spirit while asleep to save sailors at sea. She protested against an arranged marriage by starving herself to death, and continued saving sailors in the spirit.

Meng Jiang Nu (Meng Jiangnu). A woman whose husband was conscripted to build the Great Wall, and journied there to help him in winter. She found he had died, and wept till the wall built over his body collapsed.

Meng Po Niang (Mong-Po, Lady-Meng, Meng-P'o, Meng-Po-Niang-Niang, Mi-Hung-Tang). The goddess who lives just inside hell's exit door, who gives the potion of forgetfulness to each soul departing for a new reincarnation.

Miaoshan. And incarnation of Guanyin, who refused orders to marry, was cast out of her family, yet later gave her eyes and arms for medicine to cure her father of a disease.

Milotou. Primordial goddess in Yao tradition, who gave birth to all creatures.

Momu. An extraordinarily ugly woman with a hunched back and club-feet, who impressed the legendary Emperor Huangdi by healing a girl who was bitten by a poisonous snake. Momu was invited to oversee the divine palace, and her administration was ever proficient, partly because her ugliness drove away evil spirits. To this day villagers keep pictures of her, to ward off evil.

Mulan. A legendary woman who disguised herself as a man to serve in her father's place in the army, and helped defeat the barbarian enemy.

Nü Ji. Immortal lady who attained power through sexual practices.

Nü Wa (Nü Kwa). Snake goddess, who with the male snake god Fu Xi, created the world. She then saved the world from flood and collapse by repairing the sky.

Pan Jinlian (P'an-Chin-Lien). The goddess of sex and prostitutes.

Prajanaparamita. The Great Mother, who is transcendent realization of emptiness—the realization which is the "mother" of Buddhahood.

Qi Gu (C'hi-Ku, or Tsi Ku). The goddess of the outhouse. When women want to know the future, they go to the outhouse and ask Qi Gu.

Qi Xiang Nai (Ch'i Hsiang Nai). A divine woman from South China who protected people from evil.

Qi Xiao Yao (Ch'I Hsiao-yao). A girl who rejected her father's "rules for women," left her husband, was widely suspected of being possessed by an evil spirit, but achieved her goal of becoming a Daoist immortal.

Qiu Jin (Ch'iu Chin). A fiery feminist revolutionary who was martyred by the Manchu authorities in 1907.

Sao Cing Niang (Sao-Ts'ing Niang). The goddess of clouds, whose mercy ends drought.

Shangyuan Furen. The Lady of Highest Prime, a source of revelations to the Highest Clarity sect of Daoism.

Sien Zang (Sien Tsang) Wife of the divine farmer Shennong. She wove the clouds that clothe the heavens.

Shin Mu. The mother of perfect intelligence. China's holy virgin.

Songzi Niangniang. The Lady Who Brings Children. In charge of conception, pregnancy, delivery, child welfare.

Suiren. A primordial teacher of indeterminate sex, who invented fire-making with wooden drills.

Sun Buer (Sun Pu-erh). A Daoist Master of the 1100s CE, seventh master of Complete Perfection (Quanzhen) sect of Daoism. Credited with many magical feats and wondrous teachings. Founded Qingjing Pai sub-ineage (Lineage of Clarity and Stillness).

Sunu. A woman who helped the Yellow Emperor stimulate the crops by inventing and playing her twenty-five string qin instrument, to orchestrate the growing seasons.

Taimu, Lady. An ancestress of Fujian legend, who led her followers to open the land, and became the earliest forebear of the Min people.

Taimu goddess. Primary mother of the Yue nationality, who moved to a cave on Mt. Lanshan, attained immortality, and rode to heaven on a nine-colored dragon horse.

Taishan Goddess. The bringer of fertility and rain, patroness of Mount Tai, sister of the Jade Emperor, also called "old Mother, " "Old Grandmother of Tai," "the Heavenly Immortal," "Green Jade Mother," or "Goddess of the Azure Clouds."

Tara. Tibetan goddess of unconditional awareness and compassion. Best known as either Green Tara or White Tara. White Tara is also known as "Tara of the Seven Eyes"—with eyes on her hands, feet, and forehead, to symbolize her all-seeing mercy.

Tenma goddesses. Twelve spirits of Tibet's mountain ranges, who protect the people and religion of Tibet.

Tian Mu (T'ien-Mu). The goddess of lightning. Her husband, the dragon Lei Gong, supplies the thunder.

Ti Ying. A woman who dared challenge the Han emperor (in 167 BCE) with an appeal for mercy on prisoners, and won a ban on the worst kinds of torture.

Tuoyalaha. Famous ancient shamaness of the Jurchen people, who stole fire from the fire god in a time of endless night, carried it in her mouth, and saved her people from freezing in the dark.

Tou Mou. Goddess of the polestar, who serves as the record-keeping scribe of the Immortals, patroness of writing, and judge of all people.

Tru'ng Thac and **Thu'ng Nhi**. Two sisters who led a Vietnamese rebellion against Chinese rule in Han times, and were later deified.

Tsogyal, Yeshe. A female Buddhist saint and a co-founder of the Nyingma school of Tibetan Buddhism, (ca. 757 to 817 CE).

Vajravarahi. A Tibetan female guardian spirit, who defends practitioners of meditation from distractions. Usually portrayed with a pig's head protruding from her crown.

Wei Huacun (Wei Hua-ts'un). An enlightened Daoist female master. After her death, she appeared to Yang Xi (Yang Hsi), and gave him the first texts of Shangqing

Daoism. She is also a mountain goddess residing on the eminence of Lojiang in Fujian.

Wolado Mama. The cosmological star-planting goddess of the Manchu, who wears white wings and carries a bag of stars to create the constellations.

Wu. Female shamans.

Wusheng Laomu. The Eternal Mother, the mother of Laozi.

Xi. Male shamans.

Xiang (Hsiang) **River Goddesses**. Two goddesses of the Xiang River, named Ehuang and Nüying, whose tears for the dead emperor Shun reportedly made the water patterns in bamboo.

Xiang Nü (Hsiang Nü). A Buddhist female saint who overcame abuse by her in-laws and saved them all.

Xiao River goddess. One of many river goddesses in the Yangzi basin.

Xi He (Hsi Ho). Empress and wife of the Yellow Emperor, Huangdi. She reportedly gave birth to the ten suns. Later she drove the sun as a chariot, though later myths changed the sex of the chariot driver.

Xi Shi (Hsi-Shih). A goddess of Cosmetics and Perfumes, who was so beautiful that when the evil Prince Wu beheld her, he fell into a stupor, which allowed the righteous exiled King Yue to regain the throne.

Xi Wang Mu (Hsi Wang-mu). The Queen Mother of the West, great shamaness of the world pillar, gatekeeper of death, birth, healing, and immortality; also called The Primordial Ruler.

Xie Xiran. A Tang period Shangqing Daoist adept.

Xin Qi Niang (Hsin Ch'i Niang). A sainted South Chinese mother.

Yang. The patroness of shamans, one of the ten immortal sorcerers on Wu-shan, the Mount of Sorcerers.

Yangze River Goddess. A goddess evolked by southern shamenesses, as recorded in the Nine Hymns (Chiu Ko) of early 200s BCE.

Yao Chi (the Jasper Lady). A goddess who guided emperor Yü in controlling the primordial flood. She could shape-shift to any creature's form.

Yao Chi Jinmu (Yao-chih chin-mu). Golden Mother of the Jasper Pool, the Keeper of Paradise.

Yaoji. A patron goddess of Wushan, or Shamaness Mountain. Also, a daughter of the Queen Mother of the West, who brought women's writing to the embroidering women of Jianyong.

Yasangga and **Busangga**. The divine couple which created the world according to Dai tradition.

Yin and Yang. The two primordial male and female principles by which all the universe was created.

Yinjiang. The first shamanness, created by the Sky Mother Abkai Hehe, according to the Nian Manchu people.

Youchao. A primordial teacher of unknown sex, who taught people to built tree houses.

Yu Jiang (also called Maonü). A famous "hairy lady of the forest," who reportedly escaped her role as concubine for Prince Ying of the Qin state, and understandably fled to the wilds. They found her there hundreds of years later, living naked and free on a diet of pine needles and pure qi energy.

Yu Xuanji. A famous Daoist court priestess of the Tang dynasty.

Youying, Lady. Otherwise known as Lady Right Bloom of the Palace of Cloud Forest, a mountain goddess who was reportedly a daughter of the Queen Mother of the West.

Zhepama and **Zhemima**. The goddess and god who jointly created the world according to Achang tradition.

Zhi Nu (Chih Nu, Zhinu). A goddess of spinners, weavers and clouds. She wove both silk garments and clouds for the Lord of Heaven, but fell in love with a cowherd boy, who stole her clothes as she bathed. Her father, the Jade Emperor separated the lovers in constellations at opposite side of the sky. The lovers could unite only once a year, when magpies created a bridge across the Milky Way.

Zheng Wei (Cheng Wei). A Han dynasty saint who was abused by her army officer husband, feigned madness, and vanished into a new life as an independent holy woman.

Zi Gu (Tzu-Ku, Tzu-Ku-Shen). A goddess of toilets, who was murdered for jealousy while in the latrine. She haunted latrines thereafter, and became the patroness of spirit writing from beyond.

Ziwei Furen. The Lady of the Purple Tenuity, a source of revelations to the Highest Clarity sect of Daoism.

Zu Shu. A Daoist priestess who had visionary encounters with the Holy Mother of Numinous Radiance (Lingguang Shengmu), and founded a teaching lineage called the Way of Pure Subtlety.

Sources

Baptandier, Brigitte. 1996. "The Lady Linshui: How a Woman Became a Goddess." In Meir Shahan and Robert P. Weller, editors. *Unruly Gods: Divinity and Society in China*. Honolulu, HI: University of Hawaii Press.

Barber, Elizabeth Wayland. 1994. *Women's Work: The First 2000 Years, Women, Cloth, and Society in Early Times*. New York: W.W. Norton & Company.

Barnard, Noel. 1983. "Recent Archaeological Evidence Relating to the Origin of Chinese Characters." In David Keightley, editor. *The Origin of Chinese Civilization*. Berkeley, CA: University of California Press.

Barraclough, Geoffrey, editor. 1989. *The Times Atlas of World History*. Third Edition. London: Stone, Norman, Time Books Ltd.

Bauer, Wolfgang. 1976. *China and the Search for Happiness*. Michael Shaw, translator. New York: Seabury Press.

Bernhardt, Kathryn. 1992. *Rents, Taxes and Peasant Rebellion: The Lower Yangze Region, 1840–1950*. Stanford, CA: Stanford University Press.

Berry, Chris. 2008. "Cinema: From Foreign Import to Global Brand." In Louie, Kam, editor. *The Cambridge Companion to Modern Chinese Culture*. Cambridge: Cambridge University Press.

Beyer, Stephen. 1973. *The Cult of Tara: Magic and Ritual in Tibet*. Berkeley, CA: University of California Press.

Bielenstein, Hans. 1953. *The Restoration of the Han Dynasty*. Goteborg: Elanders, Boktryckeri, Aktiebolag.

Birrell, Anne, 1988. *Popular Songs and Ballads of Han China*. London: Unwin Hyman.

Birrell, Anne. 1993. *Chinese Mythology: An Introduction*. Baltimore and London: Johns Hopkins University Press.

Blumenberg, Bennett and Leslie Blumenburg. 2006. *Early Myth and the Goddess in Ancient China*. Ancient History and Religion Timeline Project. Blumenberg Associates LLC. http://ancienthistory.ahrtp.com

Bokenkamp, Stephen. 1996. "Declarations of the Perfected," and "The Purification Ritual of the Luminous Perfected." In Donald S. Lopez, Jr., editor. *Religions of China in Practice*. Princeton, NJ: Princeton University Press.

Bol, Peter K. 1992. "'This Culture of Ours': Intellectual Transitions in T'ang and Sung China." In Tu Weiming, Milan Hejtmanek, Alan Wachman, editors. *The Confucian World Observed: A Contemporary Discussion of Confucian Humanism in East Asia*. Honolulu: Institute of Culture and Communication, The East–West Center.

Bordewich, Fergus M. 2004. "Master Kung." In Sean O'Reilly, James O'Reilly, and Larry Habegger, editors. *Travelers' Tales, China: True Stories*. San Francisco:

Travelers' Tales.

Brown, Liam D'Arcy. 2003. *Green Dragon, Sombre Warrior: Travels to China's Extremes*. London: John Murray.

Brownell, Susan and Jeffrey N. Wasserstrom, editors. 2002. *Chinese Femininities / Chinese Masculinities: A Reader*. Berkeley, CA: University of California Press.

Cahill, Suzanne E. 1986. "Performers and Female Taoist Adepts: Hsi Wang Mu as the Patron Deity of Women in Medieval China." *Journal of the American Oriental Society*. 106, 155–168.

Cahill, Suzanne E. 1993. *Transcendence & Divine Passion: The Queen Mother of the West in Medieval China*. Stanford, CA: Stanford University Press.

Cai Hua. 2001. *A Society Without Fathers or Husbands: The Na of China*. Asti Hustvedt, translator. New York: Zone Books.

Cai Junshang. 1995. "Myth and Reality: The Projection of Gender Relations in Prehistoric China." In The Chinese Partnership Research Group, Min Jiayin, editor. *The Chalice & the Blade in Chinese Culture: Gender Relations and Social Models*. Beijing: China Social Sciences Publishing House.

Cai Zhuozhi and Lu Yangguang. 1994. *100 Celebrated Chinese Women*. Singapore: Asiapac Books.

Campbell, Joseph. 1986. *Oriental Mythology: The Masks of God*, New York: Penguin Books.

Chan, Alan K. L. 1990. "Goddesses of Chinese Religion." In Larry W. Hurtado, editor. *Goddesses in Religions and Modern Debate*. Atlanta, GA: Scholars Press.

Changchub, Gywala and Nyingpo, Namkai, 1999. The Padmakara Translation Group. *Lady of the Lotus Born: The Life and Enlightenment of Yeshe Tsogyal*. Boston: Shambhala.

Chang, Kwang-chih. 1980. *Shang Civilization*. New Haven, CT: Yale University Press.

Chang, Leslie T. 2008. *Factory Girls: From Village to City in a Changing China*. New York: Spiegel & Grau.

Chang Mo-chün. 1992. "Opposition to Footbinding." In Li Yu-ning, editor. *Chinese Women Through Chinese Eyes*. Armonk, NY: M.E. Sharpe, Inc.

Chau, Adam Yuet. 2006. *Miraculous Response: Doing Popular Religion in Contemporary China*. Stanford, CA: Stanford University Press.

Chen Mingxia. 2004. "The Marriage Law and the Rights of Chinese Women in Marriage and the Family." In Tao Jie, Zheng Bijan, and Shirley Mow, editors. *Holding Up Half the Sky: Chinese Women Past, Present, and Future*. New York: The Feminist Press.

Chen, Nancy N. 2002. "Embodying Qi and Masculinities in Post-Mao China." In Susan Brownell and Jeffrey N. Wasserstrom, editors. *Chinese Femininities / Chinese Masculinities: A Reader*. Berkeley, CA: University of California Press.

Ch'en Heng-che. 1992. "Influences of Foreign Cultures on the Chinese Woman," in Li Yu-ning, editor. *Chinese Women Through Chinese Eyes*. Armonk, NY: M.E.

Sharpe, Inc.

Cheng Te-k'un. 1959. *Archaeology in China, vol. 1., Prehistoric China*. Cambridge: W. Heffer & Sons Ltd.

Cheung Kwong-yue. 1983. "Recent Archaeological Evidence Relating to the Origin of Chinese Characters." In David Keightley, editor, Bernard Noel, translator. *The Origin of Chinese Civilization*. Berkeley, CA: University of California Press.

China Speakers Bureau. 2009. A *Changing China*. Amherst, MA: Trombly International.

Ching, Julia. 1977. *Confucianism and Christianity*. Tokyo: Kodansha.

Ching, Julia. 1990. *Probing China's Soul: Religion, Politics, and Protest in the People's Republic*. San Francisco: Harper & Row Publishers.

Ching, Julia. 1993. *Chinese Religions*, London: MacMillan Press.

Ching, Julia and R.W.L. Guisso, editors. 1991. *Sages and Filial Sons: Mythology and Archaeology in Ancient China*. Hong Kong: The Chinese University Press.

Ching, Julia and Hans Küng. 1989. *Christianity and Chinese Religions*. New York, London: Doubleday.

Chou, Hung-hsiang. 1979, "Chinese Oracle Bones." In *Scientific American*. 240: 135–149.

Chow, Tse-tsung, 1960. "The Anti-Confucian Movement in Early Republican China." In Arthur F. Wright, editor. *The Confucian Persuasion*. Stanford, CA: Stanford University Press.

Chung, K. C. 1983. "Sendai Archaeology and the Formation of States in Ancient China." In David Keightley, editor. *The Origin of Chinese Civilization*, Berkeley, CA: University of California Press.

Clarke, David. 2008. "Revolutions in Vision: Chinese Art and the Experience of Modernity." In Kam Louie, editor. *The Cambridge Companion to Modern Chinese Culture*. Cambridge: Cambridge University Press.

Cleary, Thomas. 1989. I*mmortal Sisters: Secrets of Taoist Women*. Boston and Shaftsbury: Shambhala Publishing.

Cohn, Samuel K., Jr. 2006. *Lust for Liberty The Politics of Social Revolt in Medieval Europe, 1200 – 1425*, Cambridge, MA: Harvard University Press.

Confucius, *The Analects*. 1987 (c. 1979). Translated with Introduction by D.C. Lau. Harmondsworth, UK: Penguin Books.

Cotterell, Arthur, 1981. *The First Emperor of China*. London: MacMillan London Ltd.

Davis, Deborah. 1989. "My Mother's House." In Perry Link, Richard Mansen, Paul G. Pinkowicz, editors. *Unofficial China*. Boulder, CO: Westview Press.

Day, Terence P. 1990. "The Twenty-one Taras: Features of a Goddess Pantheon in Mahayana Buddhism." In Larry W. Hurtado, editor. *Goddesses in Religion and Modern Debate*. Atlanta, GA: Scholars Press.

Dean, Kenneth. 2003. "Local Communal Religion in Contemporary South-east China." In Daniel L.Overmyer, editor. *Religion in China Today*. Cambridge: Cambridge University Press.

De Bary, William Theodore, 1991. *The Trouble With Confucianism*. Cambridge, MA: Harvard University Press.

De Bary, William Theodore, Wing-tsit Chan, Burton Watson, editors. 1960. *Sources of Chinese Tradition*, volumes I and II. New York: Columbia University Press.

Debaine-Francfort, Corinne. 1999. *The Search for Ancient China*. Discoveries® series. New York: Harry N. Adams, Inc., Publishers.

Despeux, Catherine, and Livia Kohn. 2003. *Women in Daoism*. Cambridge, MA: Three Pines Press.

Dorsey, James Michael. 2004. "Emperor Qin's Army." In Sean O'Reilly, James O'Reilly, Larry Habegger, editors. *Travelers' Tales, China: True Stories*. San Francisco: Travelers' Tales.

Duara, Prasenjit. 2008. "Historical Consciousness and National Identity." In Kam Louie, editor. *The Cambridge Companion to Modern Chinese Culture*. Cambridge: Cambridge University Press.

Du Fangqin, 1995. "The Rise and Fall of the Zhou Rites: A Rational Foundation for the Gender Relationship Model." In The Chinese Partnership Research Group, Min Jiayin, editor. *The Chalice & the Blade in Chinese Culture: Gender Relations and Social Models*, Beijing: China Social Sciences Publishing House.

Du Jinpeng, 1995. "The Social Relationship of Men and Women in the Xia-Shang Era." In The Chinese Partnership Research Group, Min Jiayin, editor. *The Chalice & the Blade in Chinese Cultur: Gender Relations and Social Models*. Beijing: China Social Sciences Publishing House.

Durant, Will. 1956. *Our Oriental Heritage*. New York: Simon & Schuster.

Ebrey, Patricia Buckley, editor. 1981. *Chinese Civilization and Society: A Sourcebook*. New York: The Free Press.

Ebrey, Patricia Buckley. 1996. *The Cambridge Illustrated History of China*. Cambridge: Cambridge University Press.

Eisler, Riane. *The Chalice & the Blade: Our History, Our Future*. San Francisco: HarperOne.

Engels, Fiedrich, 1987. *Marx and Engels, Collected Works*. Laurence and Wishart, London.

Eno, Robert. 1996. "Dieties and Ancestors in Early Oracle Inscriptions." In Donald S. Jr., editor. *Religions of China in Practice*. Princeton, NJ: Princeton University Press.

Evans, Harriet. 2002. "Past, Perfect, or Imperfect: Changing Images of the Ideal Wife." In Susan Brownell and Jeffrey N. Wasserstrom, editors. *Chinese Femininities / Chinese Masculinities: A Reader*. Berkeley, CA: University of California Press.

Fagan, Brian. 2008. *The Great Warming: Climate Change and the Rise and Fall of Civilizations*. New York: Bloomsberg Press.

Fan Lizhu. 2003. "The Cult of the Silkworm Mother as a Core of Local Community Religion in a North China Village: Field Study in Zhiwuying, Baoding, Hubei."

In Daniel L. Overmyer, editor. *Religion in China Today*. Cambridge: Cambridge University Press.

Fan Wu. 2006. *February Flowers*. Toronto: Doubleday Canada.

FitzGerald, C.P. 1972. *The Southern Expansion of the Chinese People*. Canberra: Australian National University Press.

Fogg, Wayne H. 1983. "Swidden Cultivation of Foxtail Millet by Taiwan Aborigines: A Cultural Analogue of the Domestication of Setaria italica in China." In David Keightley, editor. *Origins of Chinese Civilization*. Berkeley, CA: University of California Press.

Freedman, Maurice. 1970. "Ritual Aspects of Chinese Kinship and Marriage," In Maurice Freedman, editor. *Family and Kinship in Chinese Society*. Stanford CA: Stanford University Press.

French, Marilyn. 1985. *Beyond Power: On Women, Men, and Morals*. New York: Ballantine Books.

Fried, Morton H. 1983. "Tribe to State or State to Tribe in Ancient China?" In David K. Keightley, editor. *The Origins of Chinese Civilization*. Berkeley: University of California Press.

Gardner, David K. 1996. "Zhu Xi on Spirit Beings." In Donald S. Lopez, Jr., editor. *Religions of China in Practice*. Princeton, NJ: Princeton University Press.

Gernant, Karen. 1995. *Imagining Women: Fujian Folk Tales*. New York: Interlink Books.

Gernet, Jacques, 1962. *Daily Life in China on the Eve of the Mongol Conquest, 1250–1279*. H. M. Wright, translator. Stanford, CA: Stanford University Press.

Gernet, Jacques. 1996. *A History of Chinese Civilization*, 2nd edition. J.R. Foster, and Charles Hartman, translators. Cambridge: Cambridge University Press.

Gou Shiyu, 1995. "A Fixed State of Affairs and the Mispositioned Status: Gender Relations in the Sui, Tang, Five Dynasties, and Song Dynasty." In The Chinese Partnership Research Group, Min Jiayin, editor. *The Chalice & the Blade in Chinese Culture: Gender Relations and Social Models*. Beijing: China Social Sciences Publishing House.

Gregory, Peter N. 1996. "Buddhism of the Cultured Elite." in Donald S. Lopez, Jr., editor. *Religions of China in Practice*. Princeton, NJ: Princeton University Press.

Griffith, Samuel. B., translator and editor. 1963. Sun Tzu. *The Art of War*. Oxford: Oxford University Press.

Harrison, James P. 1969. *The Communists and Chinese Peasant Rebellions: A Study in Re-writing History*. New York: Atheneum.

Hawkins, Bradley K. 2004. *Asian Religions: An Illustrated Introduction*. London: Pearson Longman.

Hayes, James. 1985. "Specialists and Written Materials in the Village World," in David Johnson, Andrew J. Nathan, Evelyn S. Rawski, editors. *Popular Culture in Late Imperial China*. Berkeley: University of California.

Hessler, Peter. 2006. *Oracle Bones: A Journey Through Time in China*. New York: HarperCollins.

Hessler, Peter. 2010. *Country Driving: A Journey Through China from Farm to Factory*. New York: HarperCollinsPublishers.

Ho, Ping-ti. 1975. *The Cradle of the East*. Hong Kong: The Chinese University of Hong Kong.

Hsü, James C. H. 1991. "Unwanted Children and Parents: Archaeology, Epigraphy and the Myth of Filial Piety." In Julia Ching and R.W.L. Guisso, editors. *Sages and Filial Sons: Mythology and Archaeology in Ancient China*, Hong Kong: The Chinese University Press.

Huang, Ray. 1997. *China: A MacroHistory*. Armonk, NY: M.E. Sharpe, Inc.

Huang Yang. 2004. "Chinese Women's Status as Seen Through Peking Opera." In Tao Jie, Zheng Bijun and Shirley Mow, editors. *Holding Up Half the Sky: Chinese Women Past, Present, and Future*. New York: The Feminist Press.

Hu Shih. 1992. "Woman's Place in Chinese History." In Li Yu-ning, editor. *Chinese Women Through Chinese Eyes*. Armonk, NY: M.E. Sharpe, Inc.

Huber, Louisa G. Fitzgerald. 1983. "The Relationship of the Painted Pottery and Lung-shan Cultures." In David Keightley, editor. *The Origin of Chinese Civilization*. Berkeley, CA: University of California Press.

Hui Lin Li. 1983. "The Domestication of Plants in China: Ecogeographical Considerations." In Keightley, David, editor. *The Origin of Chinese Civilization*. Berkeley, CA: University of California Press.

Hurtado, Larry W., editor. 1990. *Goddesses in Religions and Modern Debate*. Atlanta, GA: Scholars Press.

Hymes, Robert. 1996. "Personal Relations and Bureaucratic Hierarchy in Chinese Religion: Evidence from the Song Dynasty." In Meir Shahan and Robert P. Weller, editors. *Divinity and Society in China*. Honolulu, HI: University of Hawaii Press.

Ingram, Shirley C. and Rebecca S. Y. Ng. 1995 (c. 1983). *Cantonese Culture: Aspects of Life in Modern Hong Kong and Southeast Asia*. Hong Kong: Asia 2000.

Issei, Tanaka. 1985. "The Social and Historical Context of Ming-Ch'ing Local Drama." In David Johnson, Andrew J. Nathan, and Evelyn S.Rawski, editors. *Popular Culture in Late Imperial China*. Berkeley: University of California Press.

Jagchid, Sechid and Paul Hyer. 1979. *Mongolia's Culture and Society*. Boulder, CO: Westview Press.

Jiang Yongping. 2004. "Employment and Chinese Urban Women Under Two Systems." In Tao Jie, Zheng Bijan and Shirley Mow, editors. *Holding Up Half the Sky: Chinese Women Past, Present, and Future*. New York: The Feminist Press.

Jankowiak, William. 2002. "Proper Men and Proper Women: Parental Affection in the Chinese Family." In Susan Brownell and Jeffrey N. Wasserstrom, editors. *Chinese Femininities / Chinese Masculinities: A Reader*. Berkeley, CA: University of California Press.

Jankowiak, William. 2008. "Ethnicity and Chinese Identity: Ethnographic Insight and Political Positioning." In Kam Louie, editor, *The Cambridge Companion to Modern Chinese Culture*. Cambridge: Cambridge University Press.

Jiao Tianlong. 1995. "Gender Relations in Prehistoric Chinese Society: Archaeological Discoveries." In The Chinese Partnership Research Group, Min Jiayin, editor. *The Chalice & the Blade in Chinese Culture: Gender Relations and Social Models*. Beijing: China Social Sciences Publishing House.

Judge, Joan. 2008. *The Precious Raft of History: The Past, the West, and the Woman Question in China*. Stanford, CA: Stanford University Press.

Katz, Paul R. 1996. "Enlightened Alchemist or Immoral Immortal? The Growth of Lü Dongbin's Cult in Late Imperial China." In Meir Shahan and Robert P. Weller, editors. *Unruly Gods: Divinity and Society in China*. Honolulu, HI: University of Hawaii Press.

Keightley, David. 1983. "Preface," and "The Late Shang State: When?, Where?, What?" In David N. Keightley, editor. *The Origins of Chinese Civilization*. Berkeley, CA: University of California Press.

Kinsley, David. 1989. *The Goddesses Mirror: Visions of the Divine from East to West*. Albany NY: State University of New York Press.

Kleeman, Terry F. 1996. "The Lives and Teachings of the Divine Lord Zitong." In Donald S. Lopez, Jr., editor. *Religions of China in Practice*. Princeton, NJ: Princeton University Press.

Kohn, Livia. 1993. *The Taoist Experience: An Anthology*. Albany, NY: State University of New York Press.

Kohn, Livia. 1996. "Laozi: Ancient Philosopher, Master of Imortality and God." In Donald S., Jr., editor. *Religions of China in Practice*. Princeton, NJ: Princeton University Press.

Kohn, Livia. 2009. *Introducing Daoism*. New York: Routledge.

Kohn, Livia and Robin R. Wang, editors. 2009. *Internal Alchemy: Self, Society, and the Quest for Immortality*. Magdalena, NM: Three Pines Press.

Kruger, Rayne. 2004. *All Under Heaven: A Complete History of China*. Etobicoke, ON: John Wiley & Sons Ltd.

LaFargue, Michael. 1992. *The Tao of the Tao Te Ching: A Translation and Commentary*. Albany NY: State University of New York.

Lai Chi-Tim. 2003. "Daoism in China Today, 1980–2002." In Daniel L. Overmyer, editor. *Religion in China Today*. Cambridge: Cambridge University Press.

Laughlin, Charles. 2008. "The Revolutionary Tradition in Modern Chinese Literature." In Kam Louie, editor. *The Cambridge Companion to Modern Chinese Culture*. Cambridge: Cambridge University Press.

Lee, Lily Xiao Hong. 2004. "The Chinese Women's Movement Before and After the Long March." In Tao Jie, Zheng Bijan and Shirley Mow, editors. *Holding Up Half the Sky: Chinese Women Past, Present, and Future*. New York: The Feminist

Press.

Leo, Jessieca. 2011. *Sex in the Yellow Emperor's Basic Questions: Sex, Longevity, and Medicine in Early China*. Cambridge, MA: Three Pines Press

Levenson, Joseph R. 1960. "Ill Wind in the Well-Field: The Erosion of the Confucian Ground of Controversy." In Arthur F. Wright, editor, *The Confucian Persuasion*. Stanford, CA: Stanford University Press.

Li Hui-lin. 1983. "The Domestication of Plants in China: Ecographical Considerations." In David Keightley, editor. *The Origins of Chinese Civilization*. Berkeley, CA: University of California Press.

Li Jun. 1996. *Chinese Civilization in the Making: 1766–221 BCE*. London: MacMillan Press Ltd.

Link, Perry, Richard Mansen, Paul G. Pinkowicz, editors. 1989. *Unofficial China*. Boulder, CO: Westview Press.

Li Qunying and Louis Han. 2000. *The Doctor Who Was Followed by Ghosts: The Family Saga of a Chinese Woman Doctor*. Toronto: ECW Press.

Li Yu-ning. 1992. "Historical Roots of Changes in Women's Status in Modern China." In Li Yu-ning, editor. *Chinese Women Through Chinese Eyes*, pp. 108–109. Armonk, NY: M.E. Sharpe Inc.

Lin Yutang. 1935. *My Country, My People*. New York: Reynal & Hitchcock, Inc.

Lin Yutang, 1992. "Feminist Thought in Ancient China." In Li Yu-ning, editor. *Chinese Women Through Chinese Eyes*, pp. 51–54. Armonk, NY: M.E. Sharpe, Inc.

Liu Hong. 2001. *Startling Moon*. London: Headline Book Publishing.

Liu Ruzhen. 1995. "Women's Status and Gender Relations in the Liao, Jin, and Yuan Dynasties." In The Chinese Partnership Research Group, Min Jiayin, editor. *The Chalice & the Blade in Chinese Culture: Gender Relations and Social Models*. Beijing: China Social Sciences Publishing House.

Lopez, Donald S., editor. 1996. *Chinese Religions in Practice*. Princeton, NJ: Princeton University Press.

Lopez, Donald S. 1996. "Abridged Codes of Master Lu for the Daoist Community." In Donald S. Lopez, editor. *Religions of China in Practice*. Princeton, NJ: Princeton University Press.

Louie, Kam, editor. 2008. *The Cambridge Companion to Modern Chinese Culture*. Cambridge: Cambridge University Press.

Lowe, Michael, 1968. E*veryday Life in Early Imperial China*. London: B.T. Batsford Ltd.

Lu Meiyi. 2004. "The Awakening of Chinese Women and the Women's Movement in the Early Twentieth Century." In Tao Jie, Zheng Bijan, and Shirley Mow, editors. *Holding Up Half the Sky: Chinese Women Past, Present, and Future*. New York: The Feminist Press.

Ma Wanhua. 2004. "The Readjustment of China's Higher Education Structure and Women's Higher Education." In Tao Jie, Zheng Bijan, and Shirley Mow, editors.

Holding Up Half the Sky. New York: The Feminist Press.

MacFarquhar, Roderick. 1992. "The Problematique of the Confucian Value Orientation." In Tu Weiming, Milan Hejtmanek, and Alan Wachman, editors. *The Confucian World Observed: A Contemporary Discussion of Confucian Humanism in East Asia.* Honolulu, HI: Institute of Culture and Communication, The East–West Center.

MacInnis, Donald E. 1989. *Religion in China Today.* Maryknoll, NY: Orbis Books.

Mackerras, Colin. 2008. "Music and Performing Arts: Tradition, Reform and Political and Social Relevance." In Kam Louie, editor. *The Cambridge Companion to Modern Chinese Culture.* New York: Cambridge University Press.

Madsen, Richard. 1984. *Morality and Power in a Chinese Village.* Berkeley, CA: University of California Press.

Mair, Victor H. 1996. "The Book of Good Deeds: A Scripture of the Ne People." In Donald S. Lopez, Jr., editor. *Religions of China in Practice.* Princeton, NJ: Princeton University Press.

Mann, Susan. 2002. "Grooming a Daughter for Marriage: Brides and Wives in the Mid-Qing Period." In Susan Brownell, Susan and Jeffrey N. Wasserstrom, editors. *Chinese Femininities / Chinese Masculinities: A Reader.* Berkeley, CA: University of California Press.

Maspero, Henri, 1981. *Taoism and Chinese Religion.* Frank A. Kierman, translator. Amherst, MA: University of Massachusetts Press.

Maspero, Henri. 1978. *China in Antiquity*, Frank A. Kierman, translator. Amherst, MA: University of Massachusetts Press.

Meachum, William. 1983. "Origins and Development of the Yueh Coastal Neolithic: A Microcosm of Culture Change on the Mainland of East Asia." In David Keightley, editor. *The Origin of Chinese Civilization.* Berkeley, CA: University of California Press.

Milbraith, Lester W. 1989. *Envisioning a Sustainable Society: Learning Our Way Out.* Albany, NY: State University of New York Press.

Min Jiayin. 1995. "Introduction" and "Conclusion." In The Chinese Partnership Research Group, Min Jiayin, editor. *The Chalice & the Blade in Chinese Culture: Gender Relations and Social Models.* Beijing: China Social Sciences Publishing House.

Miyakawa, Hisayuki. 1960. "The Confucianization of China." In Arthur F.Wright, editor. *The Confucian Persuasion.* Stanford, CA: Stanford University Press.

Mote, Frederick M. 1960. "Confucian Eremitism in the Yüan Period." In Arthur F. Wright, editor. *The Confucian Persuasion.* Stanford, CA: Stanford University Press.

Mote, Frederick W. 1971. *Intellectual Foundations of China*, New York: Alfred A. Knopf, Inc.

Munsterberg, Hugo. 1986. *Symbolism in Ancient Chinese Art.* New York: Hacker Art

Books.

Muramatsu, Yuji. 1960. "Some Themes in Chinese Rebel Ideologies." In Arthur Wright, editor. *The Confucian Persuasion*. Stanford, CA: Stanford University Press.

Myrdal, Jan. 1965. *Report from a Chinese Village*. Michael, Maurice, translator. London: William Heinemann Ltd.

Naquin, Susan. 1985. "The Transmission of White Lotus Sectarianism in Late Imperial China." In David Johnson, Andrew J. Nathan, and Evelyn Rawski, editors. *Popular Culture in Late Imperial China*. Berkeley, CA: University of California Press.

Needham, Joseph and Wang Ling. 1956. *Science and Civilization in China*, vol., 2. London: Cambridge University Press.

Neinhauser, William H., Jr., editor. 1994. *The Grand Scribes Records, The Basic Annals of Pre-Han China*, by Sima Qien (Ssu-ma Chien). Tsai-fa Cheng, et al., translators. volumes I and II. Bloomington, IN: Indiana University Press.

Neskar, Ellen. 1996. "Shrines to Local Former Worthies." In Donald, S. Lopez, editor. *Religions of China in Practice*. Princeton, NJ: Princeton University Press.

Nickerson, Peter S. 1996. "Abridged Codes of the Master Lu for the Daoist Community." In Donald S. Lopez, Jr., editor. *Religions of China in Practice*. Princeton, NJ: Princeton University Press.

O'Connell, Robert. 1995. *The Ride of the Second Horseman: The Birth and Death of War*. Oxford: Oxford University Press.

O'Reilly, Sean, James O'Reilly, Larry Habegger, editors. 2004. *Travelers' Tales, China: True Stories*. San Francisco: Travelers' Tales.

Orzech, Charles. 1996. "Saving the Burning Mouth Hungry Ghost." In Donald S. Lopez, Jr., editor. *Religions of China in Practice*. Princeton, NJ: Princeton University Press.

Overmyer, Daniel L. 1985. "Values in Chinese Sectarian Literature: Ming and Ch'ing pao-chüan." In David Johnson, Andrew J. Nathan, and Evelyn S. Rawski, editors. *Popular Culture in Late Imperial China*. Berkeley, CA: University of California Press.

Overmyer, Daniel L., editor. 2003. *Religion in China Today*. Cambridge: Cambridge University Press.

Overmyer, Daniel L. 2008. "Chinese Religious Traditions from 1900 to 2005: An Overview." In Kam Louie, editor. *The Cambridge Companion to Modern Chinese Culture*. Cambridge: Cambridge University Press.

Ownby, David, 2002. "Approximation of Chinese Bandits: Perverse Rebels, Romanitic Heroes, or Frustrated Bachelors?" In Susan Brownell, and Jeffrey N. Wasserstrom, editors. *Chinese Femininities / Chinese Masculinities: A Reader*. Berkeley, CA: University of California Press.

Palmer, Martin, Jay Ramsay, and Man-Ho Kwok. 1995. *Kuan Yin: Myths and Prophecies of the Chinese Goddess of Compassion*. London and San Francisco:

Thorsous.

Palmer, Martin, Jay Ramsay, and Man-Ho Kwok. 2009. *The Kuan Yin Chronicles: The Myths and Prophecies of the Chinese Goddess of Compassion*. Charlottsville, VA: Hampton Roads Publishing Company, Inc.

Pan, Philip P. 2008. *Out of Mao's Shadow: The Struggle for the Soul of a New China*. New York: Simon & Schuster.

Parfitt, Troy. 2011. *Why China Will Never Rule the World: Travels in the Two Chinas*. Saint John, NB: Western Hemisphere Press.

Patai, Raphael. 1990 (c. 1967) *The Hebrew Goddess*, Third enlarged edition. Detroit: Wayne State University Press.

Pearson, Richard, and Shyh-charng Lo. 1983. "The Ch'ing-lien-kang Culture and the Chinese Neolitic." In David Keightley, editor. *The Origin of Chinese Civilization*. Berkeley, CA: University of California Press.

Ponting, Clive. 1991. *A Green History of the World: The Environment and the Collapse of Great Civilizations*. Harmondsworth, UK: Penguin Books.

Pulleyblank, E.G. 1983. "The Chinese and Their Neighbors in Prehistoric and Early Historic Times." In David Keightley, editor. *The Origin of Chinese Civilization*. Berkeley, CA: University of California Press.

Rainey, Lee. 1991. "The Queen Mother of the West: An Ancient Chinese Mother Goddess?" In Julia Ching and R.W.L. Guisso, editors. *Sages and Filial Sons*. Hong Kong: The Chinese University Press.

Ray, Reginald A. 2000. *Indestructible Truth: The Living Spirituality of Tibetan Buddhism*. Boston: Shambhala.

Rein, Shaun. 2009. "A Fast-Developing Consumer Society." In China Speakers Bureau. *A Changing China*. Amherst, MA: Trombly International.

Robinet, Isabelle. 1997. *Taoism: Growth of a Religion*. Phyllis Brooks, translator. Stanford, CA: Stanford University Press.

Roth, Harold D. 1996. "The Inner Cultivation Tradition of Early Taoism." In Donald S. Lopez, Jr., editor. *Religions of China in Practice*. Princeton, NJ: Princeton University Press.

Ruhlman, Robert. 1960. "Traditional Heroes in Chinese Popular Fiction." In Arthur F. Wright, editor. *The Confucian Persuasion*. Stanford, CA: Stanford University Press.

Sangren, P. Steven. 1996. "Myths, Gods, and Family Relations." In Meir Shahan and Robert P. Weller, editors. Unruly Gods: *Divinity and Society in China*. Honolulu, HI: University of Hawaii Press. 159.

Saso, Michael. 1995. *The Gold Pavilion: Taoist Ways to Peace, Healing and Long Life*. Boston: Charles E. Tuttle.

Saunders, Chas and Peter A. 1999–2010. www.godchecker.com., Godchecker, Inc.

Schafer, Edward H. 1980 (c. 1973). *The Divine Woman: Dragon Ladies and Rain Maidens in T'ang Literature*. Berkeley CA: North Point Press.

Schein, Louisa. 2002. "Gender and Internal Orientalism in China." In Susan Brownell and Jeffrey N. Wasserstrom, editors. *Chinese Femininities / Chinese Masculinities: A Reader*. Berkeley, CA: University of California Press.

Shahan, Meir. 1996. "Vernacular Fiction and the Transmission of God's Cults in Late Imperial China." In Meir Shahan and Robert P. Weller, editors. *Unruly Gods: Divinity and Society in China*. Honolulu, HI: University of Hawaii Press.

Shahan, Meir, and Robert P. Weller. 1996. "Introduction: Gods and Society in China." In Meir Shahan and Robert P. Weller, editors. *Unruly Gods: Divinity and Society in China*. Honolulu, HI: University of Hawaii Press.

Shiva, Vandana. 1988. *Staying Alive: Women, Ecology, and Development*. London: Zed Books.

Sima Qian. 1961. *Records of the Grand Historian of China: Han Dynasty*. Burton Watson, translator. New York: Columbia University Press.

Simmer-Brown, Judith. 2002. *Dakini's Warm Breath: The Feminine Principle in Tibetan Buddhism*. Boston: Shambhala.

Smil, Vaclav. 1993. *China's Environmental Crisis: An Inquiry into the Limits of National Development*. New York: M.E. Sharpe. Inc.

Snow, Edgar. 1938. *Red Star Over China*. New York: Random House.

Snyder, Gary. 1980. Foreword to *The Divine Woman: Dragon Ladies and Rain Maidens in T'ang Literature*, by Edward R. Schafer, Berkeley CA: North Point Press.

Sovatsky, Stuart. 2009. "On Being Moved: Kundalini and the Complete Maturation of the Spiritual Body." In Kohn, Livia and Robin R. Wang, editors. 2009. *Internal Alchemy: Self, Society, and the Quest for Immortality*. Magdalena, NM: Three Pines Press.

Spence, Jonathan D. 1996. *God's Chinese Son: The Taiping Heavenly Kingdom of Hong Xiuquan*. New York: W.W. Norton.

Spence, Jonathan D. 1999. *The Search for Modern China*. New York: W.W. Norton.

Sun Xiao and Pan Shaoping, 1995. "Order and Chaos: The Social Position of Men and Women in the Qin, Han, and Six Dynasties Period." In The Chinese Partnership Research Group, Min Jiayin, editor. *The Chalice & the Blade in Chinese Culture: Gender Relations and Social Models*. Beijing: China Social Sciences Publishing House.

Tan, Sor-hoon. 2008. "Modernizing Confucianism and 'New Confucianism.'" In Kam Louie, editor. *The Cambridge Companion to Modern Chinese Culture*. Cambridge: Cambridge University Press.

Tao Jie, Zheng Bijan, and Shirley Mow, editors. 2004. *Holding Up Half the Sky: Chinese Women Past, Present, and Future*. New York: The Feminist Press.

Teison, Stephen F. 1996. "The Spirits of Chinese Religion." In Donald S. Lopez, editor. *Religions of China in Practice*. Princeton, NJ: Princeton University Press.

Te Lin. 2001. *Chinese Myths*. London: Bookpoint Ltd.

Te-Tzu chang. 1983. "The Origins and Early Cultures of the Cereal Grains and

Legumes." In David Keightley, editor. *The Origin of Chinese Civilization*. Berkeley, CA: University of California Press.

Ting, V. K. 1931. "Professor Granet's La Civilisation Choise." *Chinese Social and Political Science Review*. xv., 267–269.

Thaxton, Ralph. 1982. "Mao Zedong, Red Miserables and the Moral Economy of Peasant Rebellion in Modern China." In Robert P. Weller and Scott E. Guggenheim, editors. *Power and Protest in the Countryside: Studies in Rural Unrest in Asia, Europe, and Latin America*. Durham, NC: Duke Press Policy Studies.

Treistman, Judith M. 1972. *The Prehistory of China: An Archaeological Exploration*. Garden City, NY: Doubleday & Co. Inc.

Tu Weiming. 1992. "Community and Culture." In Tu Weiming, Milan Hejtmanek, and Alan Wachman, editors. *The Confucian World Observed: A Contemporary Discussion of Confucian Humanism in East Asia*. Honolulu, HI: Institute of Culture and Communication, The East–West Center.

Valussi, Elena. 2009. "Female Alchemy: An Introduction." In Livia Kohn and Robin R. Wang, editors. *Internal Alchemy: Self, Society, and the Quest for Immortality*. Magdalena, NM: Three Pines Press.

Waley, Arthur. 1939. *Three Ways of Thought in Ancient China*, New York: The MacMillan Company.

Walker, Anthony R. 1996. "Calling on Souls and Dealing with Spirits: Three Laku Ritual Texts." In Donald S. Lopez, Jr., editor. *Religions of China in Practice*. Princeton, NJ: Princeton University Press.

Walls, James. 1980. *Land, Man and Sand: Desertification and Its Solution*. New York: MacMillan Publishing Co. Inc.

Wang, Annie. 2002. *Lili*. New York: Anchor Books.

Wang, Robin R. 2009. "To Become a Female Daoist Master." In Livia Kohn and Robin R. Wang, editors. *Internal Alchemy: Self, Society, and the Quest for Immortality*. Magdalena, NM: Three Pines Press.

Wang Che. 1981. "Precepts of the Perfict Truth Taoist Sect." In Patricia Ebrey, editor. *Chinese Civilization and Society, a Sourcebook*. New York: The Free Press.

Wang Qingshu. 2004. "The History and Current Status of Chinese Women's Participation in Politics." In Tao Jie, Zheng Bijan and Shirley Mow, editors. *Holding Up Half the Sky: Chinese Women Past, Present, and Future*. New York: The Feminist Press.

Ward, Barbara, E. 1985. "Regional Operas and Their Audiences: Evidence from Hong Kong." In David Johnson, Andrew J. Nathan, and Evelyn S Rawski, editors. *Popular Culture in Late Imperial China*. Berkeley, CA: University of California Press.

Ward, Tim. 2004. "Buddha's Sex Change." In Sean O'Reilly, James O'Reilly, Larry Habegger, editors. *Travelers' Tales, China: True Stories*. San Francisco: Travelers' Tales.

Wasserstrom. Jeffrey N. 2010. *China in the 21st Century: What Everyone Needs to Know*. Oxford: Oxford University Press.

Watson, Burton. 1963. *Mo Tzu: Basic Writings*. New York: Columbia University Press.

Watson, James L. 1985. "Standardization of the Gods: The Promotion of T'ien Hou ("Empress of Heaven") Along the South China Coast, 960–1960." In David Johnson, Andrew J. Nathan, and Evelyn S. Rawski, editors. *Popular Cultures in Late Imperial China*. Berkeley, CA: University of California Press.

Watson, Rubie S. 1994. "Girl's Houses and Working Women: Expressive Culture in the Pearl River Delta, 1900–1941." In Maria Jaschok and Suzanne Myers, editors. *Women and Chinese Patriarchy: Submission, Servitude, and Escape*. London: Zed Books.

Weller, Robert P. 1994. *Resistance, Chaos and Control in China: Taiping Rebels, Taiwanese Ghosts, and Tiananmen*. Seattle, WA: University of Washington Press.

White, Robert Orr. 1983. "The Evolution of the Chinese Environment." In David Keightley, editor. *The Origins of Chinese Civilization*. Berkeley, CA: University of California Press.

Winchester, Simon. 2004 (c. 1996). *The River at the Center of the World: A Journey Up the Yangtze and Back in Chinese Time*. Toronto: HarperCollins Publishers.

Winchester, Simon. 2008. *The Man Who Loved China: The Fantastic Story of the Eccentric Scientist Who Unlocked the Mysteries of the Middle Kingdom*. New York: HarperCollinsPublishers.

Winn, Michael. 2009. "Daoist Internal Alchemy in the West." In Kohn, Livia and Robin R. Wang, editors. 2009. *Internal Alchemy: Self, Society, and the Quest for Immortality*. Magdalena, NM: Three Pines Press.

Wolf, Marjory. 1970. "Child Training and the Chinese Family." In Maurice Freedman, editor. *Family and Kinship in Chinese Society*. Stanford, CA: Stanford University Press.

Wong, Eva. 1997. *The Shambhala Guide to Taoism*. Boston: Shambhala Publications.

Wong, Eva. 2007. *Tales of the Dancing Dragon: Stories of the Tao*. Boston: Shambhala Publications.

Wong, Jan. 1996. *Red China Blues: My Long March from Mao to Now*. Toronto: Doubleday/Anchor Books.

Wong, Jan. 1999. *Jan Wong's China*. Toronto: Doubleday Canada.

Wright, Arthur F. 1960. "Introduction," and "Sui Yang-ti: Personality and Stereotype" In Arthur F. Wright, editor. *The Confucian Persuasion*. Stanford, CA: Stanford University Press.

Wu, K.C. 1982. *The Chinese Heritage*, New York: Crown Publishers Inc.

Xia Xiaohong. 2004. "New Meanings in a Classic: Differing Interpretations of Ban Zhao and Her *Admonitions for Women* in the Late Qing Dynasty." In Tao Jie, Zheng Bijan, and Shirley Mow, editors. *Holding Up Half the Sky: Chinese Women Past, Present, and Future*. New York: The Feminist Press.

Xinran. 2002. *The Good Women of China: Hidden Voices.* Esther Tyldesley, translator. Toronto: Random House Canada.

Xinran. 2008. *China Witness: Voices from a Silent Generation.* London: Chatto & Windus.

Xu Xiaobin. 2009 (c.1998). *Feathered Serpent.* John Howard-Gibbon and Joanne Wang, translators. New York: Atria International.

Xun Liu. 2009. "Numinous Father and Holy Mother: Late Ming Duo-cultivation Practice." In Livia Kohn and Robin R. Wang, editors. *Internal Alchemy: Self, Society, and the Quest for Immortality.* Magdalena, NM: Three Pines Press.

Yang Lien-shang. 1992. "Female Rulers in Ancient China." In Li Yu-ning, editor. *Chinese Women Through Chinese Eyes.* Armonk, NY: M.E. Sharpe.

Zarrow, Peter. 2008. "Social and Political Developments: The Making of the Twentieth-Century Chinese State." In Kam Louie, editor. *The Cambridge Companion to Modern Chinese Culture.* Cambridge: Cambridge University Press.

Zhang, Lijia. 2008. *Socialism is Great! A Worker's Memoir of the New China.* New York: Atlas & Co. Publishers.

Zhang Qiang, Jiang Tong, Shi Yafeng, Lorenz King, and Liu Chunling. 2004. "Paleo-environmental Changes in the Yangtze Delta During the Past 8000 Years." In *Journal of Geographical Science.* 14, 1, 105–112.

Zhang Zhijiang. 1995. "Monograph II, Changes in Women's Status as Reflected in Ancient Chinese Law." In The Chinese Partnership Research Group, Min Jiayin, editor. *The Chalice & the Blade in Chinese Culture: Gender Relations and Social Models.* Beijing: China Social Sciences Publishing House.

Zhao Liming. 2004. "The Women's Script of Jianyong: An Invention of Chinese Women." In Tao Jie, Zheng Bijan, and Shirley Mow, editors. *Holding Up Half the Sky: Chinese Women Past, Present, and Future.* New York: The Feminist Press.

Zhao Shiyu. 1995. "Brightness and Darkness: Gender Relations in the Ming and Qing Dynasties." In The Chinese Partnership Research Group, Min Jiayin, editor. *The Chalice & the Blade in Chinese Culture: Gender Relations and Social Models.* Beijing: China Social Sciences Publishing House.

Zhao Zewei. 1995. "Goddesses Worshipped by the Chinese." In The Chinese Partnership Research Group, Min Jiayin, editor. *The Chalice & the Blade in Chinese Culture: Gender Relations and Social Models.* Beijing: China Social Sciences Publishing House.

Index

Cao Wenyi (Daoist female master), vii, 178, 198, 282

Celestial Masters sect of Daoism, 189, 192-194, 196

Chang'e (goddess of the moon), vii, 74-75, 131, 161, 282

Chang Rong (immortal wild woman), 38, 192, 282

Chang Xi, Empress, 30, 282

Cheng Wei (or Zheng Wei, Daoist female saint), vii, 178, 288

Chengziya site, Shandong, Longshan culture, iv, 85, 105

Chen Jinggu (or Lady Linshui), vii, 7, 11, 40, 178-182, 282

Chia, Mantak, 190, 278

Ch'in dynasty. See Qin dynasty

Ch'ing dynasty. See Qing dynasty

Chinese language, roots of, 90, 100

Chinese people, origins of, 31, 91, 100

Chokyidronme, vii, 207, 282

Chongzuo site, Guangxi, iv, 85, 86

Chou dynasty. See Zhou dynasty

Chou En-lai (or Zhou Enlai), 116, 169, 260

Christianity
contrasts with Chinese tradition, 9, 11-14, 16-17, 74-75, 154, 188
criticisms of Chinese tradition, 37, 78
influence on Chinese religions, 173, 269
influence on Chinese women, 16, 173, 212-213, 276-277, 281
parallels with Confucianism, 22-23, 128, 214-215, 253, 264-265
parallels with Daoism, 177, 194-195

Chuang Mu (goddess of the bedroom), 10, 283

Chuang-tzu (or Zhuangzi), 17, 31-32, 38, 90, 101

Chu Hsi. (or Zhu Xi), 10-11, 77-79

Cishan-Peiligang culture, Henan and Hebei, iv, 85, 98

civilizations of the goddess
in other lands, 6, 16-17, 100, 102
in prehistoric China, 16-21, 26, 31, 45-53, 80-105, 97, 99
notions of "matriarchy," 12-13, 21, 29, 46-53, 82, 233

clan mothers
as local leaders, 24, 46-47, 112, 137, 107-108, 155, 165
values of, 20, 107-108, 121, 127-128, 270

clan names, roots of, 46, 64, 112

Clarity and Tranquility (Qingjing Pai) branch of Daoism, 198, 286

climate shifts, 82-84, 85, 91-92, 97-98, 118

Communism
modern, 19, 52, 171, 173-175, 268-270
primitive, 16, 20-21, 80-81, 99, 101-102, 132

Communist Party policy
on economic justice, 171, 174-175, 269
on religion, 173-174, 182, 228, 264-273, 275-277
on women and families, 47-48, 246-247, 254-256, 259, 261-263, 265-266

Compassion Relief Merit Society (Ciji gongdehui), 275

Compassion Society, The, vii, 275

competition between religions, 176, 195, 201-202

Complete Perfection (Quanzhen) sect of Daoism, 186-187, 198, 282-284, 286

concubines
origins of, 231-233
problems of, 137, 139, 141, 192, 238-244, 254, 288

Confucius, 18, 106, 112, 117, 147-148, 214-219, 233

Confucianism
concerning rulership, 18, 106-121, 123-128, 147-148, 218-228

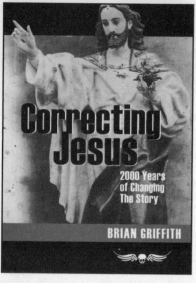

At EXTERMINATING ANGEL PRESS,
we're taking a new approach to our world.
A new way of looking at things.
New stories, new ways to live our lives.
We're dreaming how we want our lives and our world to be...

ALSO FROM
EXTERMINATING ANGEL PRESS

The Supergirls: *Fashion, Feminism, Fantasy,
and the History of Comic Book Heroines*
by Mike Madrid

Jam Today: *A Diary of Cooking With What You've Got*
by Tod Davies

3 Dead Princes: *An Anarchist Fairy Tale*
by Danbert Nobacon
with illustrations by Alex Cox

Dirk Quigby's Guide to the Afterlife
by E. E. King

Snotty Saves the Day: *The History of Arcadia*
by Tod Davies
with illustrations by Gary Zaboly

This Is US: *The New All-American Family*
by David Marin